EARLY CHILDHOOD EDUCATION

Prentice-Hall Viewpoints and Alternatives Series
Ronald T. Hyman,
Consulting Editor

APPROACHES IN CURRICULUM
    Ronald T. Hyman
EARLY CHILDHOOD EDUCATION
    Bernard Spodek

Written and Edited by
Bernard Spodek
Professor of Early Childhood Education
University of Illinois

EARLY
CHILDHOOD
EDUCATION

83095

Prentice-Hall, Inc., Englewood Cliffs, New Jersey

Library of Congress Cataloging in Publication Data

SPODEK, BERNARD, comp.
  Early childhood education.

  (Prentice-Hall viewpoints and alternative series)
  Includes bibliographies.
  CONTENTS: Part I. Introduction. The case for
early childhood education. Curriculum models in
early childhood education. Historical alternatives in early
childhood education. Contemporary models in early
childhood education. [etc.]
    1. Education, Preschool—1965—Addresses, essays,
lectures. I. Title.
LB1140.2.S73   372.21'08   72-10412
ISBN 0-13-222406-2
ISBN 0-13-222414-3 (pbk)

to PRUDENCE

© 1973 by Prentice-Hall, Inc., Englewood Cliffs, New Jersey

10 9 8 7 6 5 4 3 2 1

Printed in the United States of America

PRENTICE-HALL INTERNATIONAL, INC., London
PRENTICE-HALL OF AUSTRALIA, PTY. LTD., Sydney
PRENTICE-HALL OF CANADA, LTD., Toronto
PRENTICE-HALL OF INDIA PRIVATE LIMITED, New Delhi
PRENTICE-HALL OF JAPAN, INC., Tokyo

CONTENTS

PART II

PART I

INTRODUCTION

The past decade has seen an unprecedented growth in early childhood education in the United States. Enrollment in nursery school and kindergarten classes has increased significantly. Day care services for young children are becoming more readily available. Increased commitment by federal and local government agencies to provide opportunities for early childhood educational experiences to disadvantaged children and the involvement of private enterprise in developing services for children herald an increased interest in the field.

The changes in early childhood education in the United States are not limited to changes in the quantity of service alone. Besides the fact that there are *more* services for young children, the services that are being provided are *different* from the ones offered a decade or two back.

Weber, in her survey of contemporary early childhood education programs, has identified a number of trends. One trend is toward a decrease in the size of groups of children; another is the mixing of ages within groups. In addition, more programs are making an effort to reach the parents of young children and to involve them in the educative process. Little change was seen in the kindergarten, which Weber characterized as "the no-man's land of education." Many changes identified at the primary level were modifications of school organization, including multi-age grouping, team teaching, and other provisions for individual differences within classes of children. Changes also concerned new ways of teaching subject matter, including mathematics, reading, science, and social studies.[1] Most important, Weber identified changes in philosophic positions and values as well as in psychological beliefs relating to educational programs for young children.

Differences between contemporary programs and older programs lie both in the involvement of parents and community members in the determination of services being provided and in the proliferation of newer *models* of early childhood education. A decade or more ago the parents of children in an early childhood program were related to the teacher in a manner most characteristic of the client-professional relationship found in the medical profession. The professional (in this case the teacher) knew what was best for the child and told the parents and the child what the appropriate treatment (here, an educational program) ought to be. More and more programs, including those for the poor, now require that the professional meet with parents to identify the needs of the child through dialogue. Possible solutions to educational problems or program designs are presented for parents to approve, much as

---

[1] Evelyn Weber, *Early Childhood Education: Perspective on Change.* (Worthington, Ohio: Charles A. Jones Publishing Co., 1970), pp. 2–4.

an architect might present drawings and plans to a client for whom he is constructing a building.

This new relationship between parent and educator is the result of a number of factors. Such a relationship would not be possible, however, without the availability of different approaches to the education of young children. In the 1950's and earlier, the range of types of early childhood educational programs was slight. When differences in programs did exist they were the result of differences in the agencies that supported the programs (i.e., settlement houses might have supported day care centers whereas public schools tended to support half day kindergartens) as well as in the individual styles of teachers. Today programs exist that are designed specifically for different child populations, have different goals in mind, and are based upon different theoretical considerations.

The proliferation of these different early childhood programs suggested this book. In order for parents, teachers, school administrators and members of communities to make proper judgments about the kinds of programs they might wish to support, they need to know something about the nature of the programs themselves, as well as about the issues related to each program and to the field of early childhood education itself. The first chapter will deal with the identification of these issues. The justifications for, and purposes of, providing educational experiences for young children, and the social, psychological, and moral case presented in support of educational programs will be given. The concept of an *educational model* and a framework for the analysis of models for early childhood education that will be used later in the book is presented in the second chapter.

The third chapter is an analysis of four historical models of early childhood education. It is this author's contention that the range of programs available in early childhood education today is determined to no small degree by those previously available. Tradition has a great deal of influence in education, and some of the historical models are still in use today or provide the basis for contemporary programs. The fourth chapter will provide an analysis of contemporary models in early childhood education that represent two poles of a theoretical continuum.

The second section of this book is a set of essays, articles, and papers that present the many models of early childhood education as the practitioners or designers of these models themselves have represented them, as well as articles dealing with curriculum issues in early childhood education. It is hoped that the combination of original presentations and interpretive and analytic material will provide a balanced presentation of educational alternatives that could not be gained in a book of readings or in an interpretive work alone.

The period of early childhood is generally considered to encompass the ages three through eight. Programs at the nursery, kindergarten, and primary grade levels are therefore included in the definition of early childhood education. Since a number of current educational programs focus on children less than three years old, it might be useful to consider the period of infancy through early childhood as the legitimate scope of this book. Selection 19 in Part II discusses the possibilities in programing for these younger children. Such a definition of early childhood education has been used by Weber[2] and by the editors of the 71st Yearbook of the National Society for the Study of Education.[3]

---

[2] Weber, *Early Childhood Education: Perspective on Change*, p. 2.
[3] National Society for the Study of Education. 71st Yearbook. *Early Childhood Education*. (Chicago: University of Chicago Press, 1972).

1

THE CASE FOR EARLY CHILDHOOD EDUCATION

Traditionally, the formal education of children has begun at age six or seven in the United States. The primary grades and the beginning of reading instruction marked the entrance of the child into school, and schooling has been considered as synonymous with education. Even today compulsory attendance in school is not required in many states until the age of seven. When kindergarten began to be included in public education it was regarded as an appendage grafted onto the existing system. It was accepted only grudgingly, and nursery school or day care center attendance was considered a frill, and was sometimes even considered harmful to young children. Only recently has the schooling of younger and younger children begun to be accepted.

Early childhood educators have always viewed education as taking place both in and outside of the school. The home was not the least important of these contexts. Friedrich Froebel, the father of kindergarten education, viewed the home as the proper context of education, the parent as the proper teacher, and the earliest stages of childhood as the proper period for beginning education:

> The stage of infancy passes into that of childhood when the baby is able to use his physical and sensory activity to show his thoughts and feelings. Up to this stage his mind is merged into an undifferentiated whole of being. As speech develops, however, the child starts to express and organize the life of his mind and to distinguish its manifestations and purposes. It is a characteristic of this period that he strives to express his ideas in tangible shape and form.

> With this tendency the education of man properly begins, and there is now less attention to physical growth and more concern for mental development. This phase is the concern of his parents and family with whom he is still more closely associated. . . .[1]

> The aim and object of parental care in the home and family is to stimulate the child's entire powers and natural gifts and enable them to develop to the full. A mother does this naturally and spontaneously without any instruction or prompting, but this is not enough. It is also necessary that she should influence the child's growing awareness and consciously promote the continuity of this development, and that she should do this by establishing a positive and living relationship with him. So it is our concern to arouse intelligent parental love and show the modes in which childhood expresses itself.[2]

This belief in the importance of the instructional role of the

---

[1] Friedrich Froebel, "The Small Child, or the Importance of a Baby's Activity," in Irene Lilly, *Friedrich Froebel: A Selection from His Writing* (Cambridge, England: Cambridge University Press, 1967), p. 82.

[2] Froebel, "The Small Child, or the Importance of a Baby's Activity," pp. 84–85.

mother in the early years of life is still held. White, in a recent study of the conditions that tend to support development, has documented many of the conditions of the home that support learning for the infant and toddler. He has described many dimensions of the educational role of the mother, who often teaches her youngster "on the fly," interacting with them continually for short periods of time throughout the day.[3]

Early childhood education, therefore, is part of the child-rearing experiences provided naturally for all children. The issue presently being debated in the field is not whether early childhood educational opportunities ought to be provided, but rather how best these opportunities can be provided. A child's experiences in school are no less natural than his experience in other contemporary child rearing environments. Macdonald has stated:

> For years many of us have assumed that putting the child in school at an early age takes him out of his natural environment and puts him in a contrived setting. Only recently has our understanding of the ecology of human living and the nature of man's relationship to his technology clearly forced us to realize that the choice for educating young children is not between a contrived and a natural environment, but between a planned and a haphazard man-made one. This new understanding suggests that as a society we should deliberately intervene, as early and as often and for as long a time as possible, to provide the optimum man-made environment for our children.[4]

Macdonald has correctly characterized early childhood education (as indeed all education tends to be) as a form of deliberate social intervention. The provision of schools for children of all ages grows out of society's need to prepare children to fit into the existing order. School experience can either help children conform to an existing social order or help prepare them for a new social organization.

---

[3] Burton White, "An Analysis of Excellent Early Educational Practices: Preliminary Report," mimeographed, p. 51.

[4] James B. Macdonald, "A Proper Curriculum for Young Children," *Phi Delta Kappan* 50, No. 7 (March 1969): 406.

Education can be viewed as a socially positive activity, or it can be seen as socially dangerous. The Froebelian Kindergarten was banned by the Prussian government in 1851 as was Montessori education by the Germans in 1935 and by the Italians in 1936.[5] The inherently democratic philosophies of both Froebel and Montessori education were viewed as a threat by repressive regimes in each case.

The concept of early childhood education as a form of social intervention suggests that there is more involved in the provision of educational opportunities for young children than the intrinsic worth of the activities themselves, despite the fact that some early childhood educators have justified the existence of nursery schools as simply a "good place for children to be." The concept of *education* has embedded within it the concept of *change;* that children will somehow be different as a result of the program they have experienced. This suggests a deliberate program directed toward some intended end. Such a program can still consist of intrinsically worthy activities, but they are related to legitimate and fully achievable outward purposes.

At different times, the purposes for which early childhood education programs have been designed have varied. Even today programs for young children often have different stated purposes. Sometimes these purposes are determined by the identified needs of the children for whom the program is designed. At other times they result from social thought about all education. Early childhood education can be conceived as an extension of parental child rearing, or as a way of preparing children to fit into a social role.

EARLY CHILDHOOD EDUCATION AS CHILD REARING

Raising children requires a great deal of caring, but it also requires that the parents assume responsibility for what might be considered the most basic form of childhood education. Children not

---

[5] S. J. Curtis and M. E. A. Boultwood, *A Short History of Educational Ideas* (London: University Tutored Press, 1961), pp. 371–72, 499–500.

only learn to walk and talk during the early years, they also must learn self-caring skills, manners, values, and a host of other things.

Often the case has been made that the family (or the mother) alone does not have adequate resources to accomplish the complex task of rearing the child in a way that will provide him with the optimum conditions to develop and fit into the culture in which he will live. The statements by Froebel, cited above, provide an early example of this position. Froebel saw the child's education as encompassing a philosophically idealistic view of understanding the totality of the universe. From Froebel's point of view, although mothers intuitively knew how to care properly for their young, they could not, without either further training or the help of a *kindergarten* provide the experiences that would help children grasp the basic concepts of the universe, concepts that needed to be communicated symbolically to children at the earliest possible moment in their lives.)

The original nursery school developed by Rachel and Margaret McMillan was another form of social intervention into child-rearing practices. Appalled by the conditions under which working class children were being raised in England, the McMillan sisters began to seek ways to use schools as an extension of child rearing. Margaret McMillan had earlier fought to have the schools furnish baths, school dinners, medical examinations and treatments for children who needed them. She became aware that many of the problems observed in school-age children had their origins in their preschool years and could be prevented or more easily ameliorated with early care. The nursery school as it was developed became more than just an instructional unit. The concept of education was broadly conceived of as *nurturance*. Caring for children and providing them with the best conditions for growth became as important as providing them with an educational program.[6]

Because of social rather than philosophic circumstances, the family was considered by early nursery educators as unable to pro-

---

[6] Albert Mansbridge, *Margaret McMillan, Prophet and Pioneer* (London: J. M. Dent and Sons, 1932), pp. 21–111.

vide the best conditions for the development of the young child. Again an early childhood educational program was developed to provide the necessary requisites for growth not available within the family.

A number of contemporary programs for early childhood education that have been designed for disadvantaged populations are parallels of this first nursery school program. *Operation Head Start,* as originally conceived, provided much more than an instructional program. Medical, dental, and social services were included. Nutrition and hygiene were as much a part of the program as education.

As in the pioneer nursery school, the *Head Start Child Development Center* was created to provide the conditions for growth that were being denied to poor children. While the institution tried to alleviate some of the family conditions that were the result of social problems, no attempt was made to use the institution to correct the problems in the community. In each case, an early childhood program became an extension of the primary child-rearing institution, the family, which was no longer adequate to provide optimum child-rearing conditions.

Another institutional participant must be added to the home-school partnership for child rearing in contemporary American culture: the mass media. Young children spend large proportions of their waking hours each day in television viewing, often up to four hours per day for the preschool child. Much of the child's view of the culture comes to him through television where he can view sex roles, occupational roles, and cultural settings that might otherwise be ouside of his perceptual field. Television also provides the child with a set of models for behavior which he can emulate. Bronfenbrenner has brought together a number of studies that show the impact of these models on child behavior. Both positive and negative forms of behavior can be transmitted through this medium, which has become a powerful force in the child-rearing process.[7]

Stein has also concluded that television has a significant effect

[7] Urie Bronfenbrenner, *Two Worlds of Childhood: U.S. and U.S.S.R.* (New York: Russell Sage Foundation, 1970), pp. 109–15.

on young children's aggressiveness, morality, anxiety, social knowledge, cognitive functioning, and positive interpersonal behavior. Most television program content, however, reenforces immature aspects of children's thought and behavior because few programs developed for television capitalize on the true potentialities of the media.[8] Although the media offer opportunities for socialization that would extend their child-rearing function, they have yet to be used systematically to affect the child-rearing process.

This discussion takes on increased contemporary significance if one accepts Bronfenbrenner's analysis of the contemporary family in the United States. Bronfenbrenner sees the American family withdrawing from the traditional child-rearing function and identifies this withdrawal as a major factor threatening the breakdown of the socialization process in the United States. He recommends that some of the child-rearing functions be taken over by communities and institutions, including schools for young children, as well as those for older ones.[9] Whether one views this use of schools and day care institutions as a plausible or desirable agent of child rearing depends on one's social philosophy as well as one's view of the capabilities of social institutions.

EARLY CHILDHOOD AS A WAY
OF DEVELOPING A "NEW MAN"

Under a number of different circumstances early childhood education programs have included an emphasis on character development as well as physical and intellectual skills within a statement of their purposes.

Probably the most radical institution to concern itself with this form of education is the *Beth Hayeled* or *children's house* that is

---

[8] Aletha Huston Stein, "Mass Media and Young Children's Development," in *Early Childhood Education*, 71st Yearbook of the National Society for the Study of Education, Part II (Chicago: N.S.S.E., 1972), pp. 181–202.

[9] Urie Bronfenbrenner, *The Two Worlds of Childhood*, pp. 152–62.

a part of the Israeli kibbutz. The kibbutz has developed as a collective settlement based upon specific socialist precepts. These precepts may vary from kibbutz to kibbutz. The child-rearing unit in the kibbutz is the entire settlement rather than the nuclear family and the children are raised in separate facilities belonging to the settlement. Often the child is placed in the *children's house* during his first year, if not in his first few months of life.

In the early years, the education and rearing of children in a kibbutz are not separated. Children are cared for by a member of the kibbutz who is especially assigned and trained as a child rearer. The child rearer, or *metapelet,* has responsibility for a small group of children throughout the entire day except for the few hours each child spends with his parents. When the child enters the kindergarten, responsibility for the educational program is shared between the *metapelet* and the kindergarten teacher. Thus, in the kibbutz, a totally integrated education-child-rearing experience is provided for the child. The continued living and learning in the peer group provides the child with the basis of character training to enable him to live as an adult in a collective.[10]

Few educational systems are as all-encompassing as that of the kibbutz, for few societies are composed of such closely knit units with common agreements relating to social goals and purposes. Schools for young children in other societies also provide opportunities for character development, though. The Soviet preschool is a case in point. Bronfenbrenner identifies the importance of developing the Communist morality in these preschools, which also concern themselves with the development of collective consciousness in children. Self reliance is also emphasized. These elements of character development are considered to be important in the development of the Soviet Man.[11]

The stress on character education in early childhood education

[10] A. I. Rabin, *Growing Up in the Kibbutz* (New York: Springer Publishing Co., Inc., 1965), pp. 10–42.
[11] Urie Bronfenbrenner, "Introduction," in *Soviet Preschool Education, Volume I: Program of Instruction,* ed. Henry Chauncy (New York: Holt, Rinehart and Winston, 1969), pp. x–xv.

is not alien to American schools. In the late nineteenth and early twentieth century, kindergartens were established in settlement houses and in slum areas for children of the poor and of immigrant families. Weber has aptly described this phase in early childhood education:

> Coming upon the educational scene soon after Horace Mann had worked so effectively for a common school for all children as a means of alleviating the ills of mankind, the kindergarten became part of the vision of fostering the perfectability of man and society through education. The stress placed upon the moral goals of the kindergarten led many educators to believe it provided the very foundations of character. Industry, neatness, reverence, self-respect and cooperation were seen as results of the properly directed Froebelian kindergarten, and these moral benefits were linked to both individual and social advancement. The early exponents of the kindergarten had done their work convincingly as they attributed to it the power to start each child toward effective social living.[12]

Although the language has changed considerably over time, the use of early childhood education for the achievement of moral goals can be seen today in many contemporary programs of compensatory education. Through the experience in the preschool, the child is expected to gain what he needs to walk "hand-in-hand" with his middle class peers into the first grade and, after a successful school career, to take his place along with the members of the social majority in our society.

A community may be concerned with the development of character traits or of other attributes in its young. At different points in time, different aspects of child development have been singled out as worthy of support in early childhood programs. Sometimes the need has been felt for a more unified approach, with all aspects of development viewed as interrelated, and treated accordingly. The need to deal with the "whole child" characterized the "child devel-

---

[12] Evelyn Weber, *The Kindergarten: Its Encounter with Educational Thought in America* (New York: Teachers College Press, 1969), pp. 38–39.

opment point of view" in earlier decades. The 1960's saw a diminution in emphasis on development as personal integration and a corresponding emphasis on the extension of intellectual and academic traits. This emphasis was brought about, to some extent, by our concern for the needs of disadvantaged children.

The argument for the new emphasis on competence-oriented education for the disadvantaged suggested that an increasingly urban, technical society required people with higher levels of intellectual and language competence and schooling. As society changed, many roles requiring low levels of intellectual and symbolic competence, as well as little schooling, were eliminated. Newer roles were developing that had high educational qualifications. In addition, research suggested that a person's intelligence, language ability, and capacity for education varied as a function of his environment, and that early environmental manipulations could have a maximum impact in modifying development and increasing educability. Early childhood programs would provide the necessary compensation needed to increase later competencies, and the compensation needed could be determined by comparing advantaged and disadvantaged children. Whatever differences were identified, the argument went, might be labeled as "cultural deficiencies."

The compensatory approach to early childhood education, with its emphasis on academic and intellectual skills, also has its roots in the past. The Montessori school began in the early part of the twentieth century. The program was developed to teach particular skills to mentally retarded children. Success with retardates led to an expansion of this approach, first to children in a slum community in Rome, and later to "all children."

It is interesting to note how many early childhood programs have historically been rooted in concerns for the poor. The Free Kindergarten movement in the United States, the English Nursery School and the Montessori school all resulted from a concern to improve the childhood experiences of poor children. As each system of education was shown to have merit, however, its concerns were expanded to encompass more affluent children as well. Too often, because the programs were outside public educational systems they served affluent children only; poor children could not afford the cost of service.

It must also be noted that societal needs have sometimes led to the establishment of early childhood programs in which the needs of children proved to be only a secondary concern. During the depression of the 1930's, nursery schools were established first under the Federal Emergency Relief Agency (FERA) and later under the Works Progress Administration (WPA). Although many of these nursery schools provided excellent programs for young children, the primary purpose for their establishment was to provide jobs for unemployed teachers. Similarly the Lanham Act Day Care Centers were established during World War II to enable women who might have children of their own to work in war industries.

The Head Start program, which was established in the 1960's, was probably motivated as much by political considerations as by a genuine concern over the existence of poverty in our country. Poverty was with us a long time prior to the establishment of Head Start as part of the "War on Poverty" and it is doubtful that the existence of this early childhood program has done much to erase the cause of poverty, although it may have ameliorated the consequences of poverty for many of its clients. The civil rights movement and the rising pressure from minority groups, however, required the establishment of programs for the poor. The establishment of Head Start was one of the responses of the federal government to the political pressures of the civil rights group.

Other groups have asked for different kinds of early childhood programs in recent years and their establishment will depend as much on political and economic conditions as on their agreement with our knowledge of child growth and development. Women's liberation groups have demanded the establishment of day-care centers to allow women greater freedom of opportunity outside of the traditional child-rearing mold. Industrial groups and those concerned with the employment of women on welfare are also calling for the establishment of child-care facilities, although often for a more restricted clientele. Thus both the content and the structure of early childhood education programs are created in response to various social forces at different times and in different places.

THE PSYCHOLOGICAL CASE
FOR EARLY CHILDHOOD EDUCATION

The social framework of early childhood education provides a basis for determining the goals of programs. Whether these goals can be achieved by any particular program is quite another matter. We generally assume that all programs will have some effect: that any particular program will modify the young child's character or his intelligence or possibly his physical health.

But do a person's experiences affect his development and, if so, to what extent? Are there some experiences that can have a greater impact on a child's development than others? To some extent any answer to these questions is based upon faith, for few studies have been extensive enough or well enough controlled to test the long term effectiveness of educational experiences. More than faith is involved, however. To a greater extent answers to these questions are based upon a number of theoretical considerations.

One point of view in the study of human development suggests that it is a function of a process of "unfolding"; that what the child will become is determined genetically. The role of education and other child-rearing patterns is to support this development in some fashion and to see to it that the development of the human potential is not thwarted. Environmental conditions can help or hinder development, but they cannot create what is not there. Although the individual can never become more than he was destined to become, under adverse conditions it is possible that he may never achieve his true potential.

The early childhood pioneers Froebel and Montessori viewed development as a process of unfolding. They each saw the school and its activities as providing nurture for the child's development and support for this unfolding process. Although they were both committed to a concept of predetermined development, they each viewed education as vital to the achievement of that potential.

To Froebel, development was a philosophic concept; scientific child study had not yet been established. Only in the 1890's with the creation of the Child Study Movement did the study of childhood take on truly scientific dimensions. Through the development of reliable observation and testing techniques, an empirical approach to the study of children developed, and scientific theories could be expounded.

The work of the early child study specialists was primarily normative in nature. One of the prime tasks these scientists had before them was to develop a body of literature that described children as they were.

Typical of the work of this period was that done in the Yale Clinic under the leadership of Arnold Gesell. The concern of this group was the development of a description of children's behavior and development by age; norms that would provide guideposts for the typical development of children. Data was gathered from large groups of children about observable manifestations of development, both physical and behavioral. These observations were averaged for each age so that a composite picture of the two-year-old or the four-year-old or children of any age could be created. Such a composite set of norms was then presented to parents and teachers as the typical manifestations of an age.[13]

This normative study of childhood provided a wealth of information that had not been available before and was probably a necessary first step in the scientific study of childhood. The way these norms were presented and used in education, however, often led to narrow programs and limited expectations for children at various age levels.

The normative data was seen as a "natural map" of the process of human development. Unfortunately the averaging of large quantities of data masked the vast range of individual differences in the

---

[13] Arnold Gesell, *Infant and Child in the Culture of Today* (New York: Harper & Row, Publishers, 1943).

children observed. The normal child as presented by this picture was in no way like any individual child. The picture of the normal child was distorted by the very nature of the process used to create and project it.

Another problem with the norms developed by the Yale Clinic was that they did not truly represent the total population of children in America. The sample from which the observations were collected by the Yale Clinic were children from the academic community surrounding Yale University. The parents were well educated and generally from a higher than average socioeconomic stratum. Had the sample population included members of the lower socioeconomic groups and members of various ethnic and minority groups, the norms would have differed significantly from those developed. This sample selection procedure coupled with the way these norms were often used by educators put many, if not the majority of children at a disadvantage since they could easily be labeled "abnormal."

The criticisms of these normative studies of childhood cited above are technical in nature. A more fundamental criticism of the approach of this school of thought in child development is that it continued the belief that development was a natural unfolding of the individual based upon predetermined genetic factors that could not be modified to any great extent by environmental conditions. As in earlier theories of natural development, the environment was considered important in assisting or thwarting the achievement of potential, but not in creating potential.

Given the Gesellian approach, the role of early childhood education is to provide a congenial environment that would allow the young child to naturally reach his potential. Activities for each age level could be determined based upon a conception of readiness that was maturational in nature. What activities were good for a three-year-old or a five-year-old were chosen with reference to the norms of what it had been found they could do. If a child was not capable of achieving certain tasks, he was left to wait until he had sufficiently matured to master the task rather than be provided with prerequisite skills to ready him for this achievement. Placement at the proper grade level in school was considered important so that a child would not be frustrated or doomed to failure.

The proper curriculum for a group of children, it was felt, could be determined by reference to the norms for that age range. Kindergarten was considered a place for five-year-olds specifically designed for children of that age. Attempts to modify a program to meet the needs of a particular group of children were often met by teachers' fears that they were robbing children of the "chance to be five."

At the same time as the maturational approach to child development was being elaborated by developmental psychologists, other developmental theories were being expounded that also affected early childhood education. Psychoanalysis as a theory of development, as well as a method for the treatment of psychological problems, was being developed by Sigmund Freud and his followers. Their identification of the various stages in psychosexual behavior and in personality development greatly influenced early childhood educators from the 1920's to the 1940's. Unlike the maturational developmentalists described above, the psychoanalysts viewed the child's experiences in the early years of life as having a profound influence on the maturing individual. According to psychoanalytic literature, the stages of personality development are fixed, but all children do not go through these stages at the same pace. Furthermore, fixation, or arrested development at an early stage of development could thwart or distort development and create problems for the mature adult.

Early childhood educators caught up in the whirl of psychoanalytic theories developed programs of education that allowed for the child's expression of his inner feelings through behavior and language. In addition, great care was taken not to unnecessarily thwart a child or cause undue frustration. Unfortunately, not enough attention was given in many of these programs to providing some of the positive experiences children need in order to help them learn how to cope with life situations. Only later, with the development of ego psychology, did this become important.[14]

Another school of psychological thought that influenced early

---

[14] Lois B. Murphy, *The Widening World of Childhood* (New York: Basic Books, 1962).

childhood education was behaviorism. Thorndike's learning theory was a major influence on the development of the reform kindergarten movement in the 1920's and especially influenced the work of Patty Smith Hill and her colleagues at Teachers College, Columbia University.[15] The behaviorists did not accept the assumption that child behavior was a function of the unfolding of human potential through maturation. Rather, they felt that through an analysis of behavior and the uses of the process of conditioning, a wide range of behaviors could be elicited.

This early behaviorist theory led early childhood educators to develop programs designed to affect short-term change in children's behaviors. It was felt that schools should help children establish positive habits as early as possible and provide opportunities for children to practice these habits once they were established. Curriculum developers of the time concerned themselves with the identification of appropriate habits to be established in young children as well as with the creation of classroom activities that could be used as vehicles for habit training.

Behaviorist psychology remains an important influence in early childhood education, with the theories of Skinner supplanting the earlier ones of Thorndike as a basis for developing early childhood educational methodology. Skinner is concerned with the shaping of behavior through operant conditioning, which is designed to increase the rate at which certain normal responses will occur. This is done by reenforcing the responses with a minimum of delay. Responses that are strengthened by reenforcement can also be extinguished by a failure to be reenforced.[16] An eleboration of contemporary behaviorist theory and its impact on early childhood programs can be found in Chapter 4.

Other psychological points of view have had an impact on programs in early childhood education. A number of educational psychologists have rejected behaviorism as too mechanistic and too

[15] Patty Smith Hill, et al., *A Conduct Curriculum for Kindergarten and First Grade* (New York: Charles Scribner's Sons, 1923).

[16] B. R. Bugelski, *The Psychology of Learning Applied to Teaching* (Indianapolis: The Bobbs-Merrill Co., Inc., 1964), pp. 208–12.

simplistic to provide an adequate framework for understanding complex human processes, including learning, and also reject psychoanalytic theory as a framework for understanding. Members of this group have been called "third force" or phenomenological psychologists. How these psychologists differ in their view of man is illustrated in the material in Chapter 4.

Snygg and Combs, representative of these psychologists, suggest that a person's behavior is a function of his understanding of a situation. Learning, for both children and adults, is a process of change in the phenomenological field. The meanings of situations and of behavior become more important than their manifestations. Learning, therefore, requires the development of organized frameworks that give meaning to situations, a point of view not incompatible with Piagetian theory.[17]

From the point of view of the phenomenological psychologist, an early childhood program should concern itself with helping children change their phenomenological fields, rather than with directly changing their behavior. The starting point of the program would be the individual child's personal knowledge. Children could be provided with experiences that would increase the information they had or that would be different from their present ways of viewing and understanding the world. By providing the child with an environment that does not quite match his level of knowing, the teacher helps him reintegrate his knowledge in more mature ways. While this form of teaching might be done on an individual basis, the group process could also be used as the vehicle of learning to help children move from idiosyncratic modes of learning to more socially based modes.

Social learning theory has also affected early childhood education. According to social learning theorists, learning can take place by watching others. The process of modeling through which children acquire many of their response patterns is more than just imitation since children learn to manifest symbolic equivalents of the

[17] Donald Snygg and Arthur Combs, *Individual Behavior* (New York: Harper & Row, Publishers, 1949), pp. 204–24.

behaviors they observe.[18] Much of the character development that concerned early childhood educators in the past is probably learned through the modeling process rather than through the development of specific habits or behaviors.

Learning theories concern themselves with relatively short-term changes in behavior. Behavioral changes that might result from a response to specific stimuli, or a reassessment of the phenomenological field are short-term ones, and may not essentially relate to the long-range impact of early childhood education on a person at all. Newer approaches to psychodynamic theory, including those of the ego psychologists, have suggested long-term relationships between early experiences and personality development. Up until the 1960's, however, most early childhood educators held with the maturationists that whereas personality development may be related to early experience, intellectual development is not significantly affected by environmental changes. A book that was influential in changing this point of view was J. McVicker Hunt's *Intelligence and Experience*.

Hunt took issue with the assertion that intellectual development is genetically fixed and argued instead that an individual's encounters with his environment can determine to no small extent both the rate of development and the final level of intellectual achievement. In his analysis, Hunt used the model of the computer, comparing thinking to data processing. Although Hunt based his arguments chiefly upon the developmental theories of Jean Piaget, he integrated evidence from a wide range of sources. He suggested that the early years of development play a significant role in providing the generalized conceptual skills needed for later learning. Hunt postulated the major problem of education as "the problem of the match," that is, the need to provide encounters with the environment that correspond to the child's developing levels of intellectual maturity.[19]

---

[18] Urie Bronfenbrenner, *Two Worlds of Childhood*, pp. 120–51.

[19] J. McV. Hunt, *Intelligence and Experience* (New York: The Ronald Press Company, 1961).

Jean Piaget, whose work on the development of intellectual structures in children spans almost half a century, has significantly influenced the field of early childhood education in the United States during the past decade. The framework of intellectual development that Piaget has developed provides educators with insights into how the child's understanding of the world changes as he grows.

Knowledge, according to Piaget, grows out of *operations*, which are ways of acting upon objects. A child must classify, measure, count, or order objects, or act on them in some other fashion, to achieve a degree of knowledge about those objects. The ways in which children operate on their environment change as the child develops. Piaget has developed a theory of stages to characterize these changes. Four basic stages, each with substages, are postulated.

The first stage is a sensorimotor, preverbal stage that encompasses the first eighteen months of life. During this stage, the child gains practical knowledge that provides a basis for later development. This knowledge includes a concept of object permanency, sensorimotor space, and sensorimotor causality. In the second stage, the child develops preoperational representations. The beginning of language is important to the development of this preoperational thought. The third stage has been identified as the period of concrete operations in which the child can operate on objects, but not yet on verbally expressed hypotheses. The fourth stage is one in which the child reaches the level of formal operations, can operate on hypotheses as well as objects and construct the operations of propositional logic.

Piaget suggests that there are four main factors that explain the development of new intellectual structures in the child. These are *maturation, experience, social transmission,* and *equilibrium* or self-regulation. Given these factors the modifiability of development is no simple matter. Nor will education alone change a human being's intellectual ability. Maturation plays an important role, but it alone cannot account for the total development of the child. Experience alone will not suffice either, for a single experience will mean different things to a child at different levels of development. Social transmission or education is also an important factor but it must be geared to the level of the child's understanding. The fourth factor of equilibrium is a fundamental one to Piaget, for the child to some extent regulates his development by operating on his experience at his own particular level of development.[20]

Thus Piaget has provided not only a series of guidelines that can be used to assess children's levels of development and to select experiences that may be appropriate for children at a particular point in time, but he has also suggested possible limitations to the accomplishments of educators. In addition, Piaget has highlighted the role of the child as an active participant in the educative process. His work has led to the development of early childhood programs designed specifically to teach "Piagetian tasks" to young children. More appropriately, Piagetian theory has been used to analyze classroom practice in order to determine the potential influence of certain activities on children's intellectual development, as well as to help to identify certain levels of intellectual readiness in children. Piagetian theory has also been used to justify the inclusion or exclusion of curriculum elements as well as the use of certain instructional techniques in early childhood education programs.

Neither social nor psychological influences determine early childhood education practices, but they do affect them. An understanding of the underlying influences can help an individual to comprehend the nature of the field of early childhood education today and place these various influences in their proper perspective. Insight into the content of early childhood education programs might best be gained through an analysis of the various components of each program.

---

[20] Jean Piaget, "Development and Learning," in *Piaget Rediscovered*, ed. R. E. Ripple and V. E. Rockcastle (Ithaca, New York: Cornell University, 1964), pp. 8–14.

2

CURRICULUM MODELS IN EARLY CHILDHOOD EDUCATION

At different times, cultures have identified different purposes for the education of young children. In addition, the field of psychology has spawned a number of different conceptions of how children learn, how they develop, and what experiences might affect their development. Each of these must be taken into account, along with the *values* of a community that might emphasize one area of learning or development over others, when creating a program of education for young children. All of this leads to diversity in the area of early childhood education.

The history of early childhood education can be traced at least as far back as the first half of the nineteenth century, but its nature has changed drastically since that time. Although some of the change is a result of uses of newer educational technology, many of the changes relate to new views of the purposes of education, and the demands placed upon education by society. Changing conceptions of childhood, as well as of human learning and development (some of which were referred to earlier), have also had significant influence on programs. These earlier programs, while related in many ways to contemporary programs for young children, differed significantly from them.

There are presently a number of competing approaches to the education of young children. Evidence of this diversity can be found in the Planned Variations research project of the Head Start and Follow Through programs. In both cases, a wide variety of alternative models of early childhood education have been made available to program sponsors who must select from among them. The collection and comparison of data on the effectiveness of programs might ultimately lead to the development of authoritative statements about the usefulness of these different programs and their many effects on children.

There is a certain amount of overlap among the program models presented in Head Start and Follow Through. No one program is ever totally different from all the others in every respect, and thus it is difficult to truly compare programs. In addition, one must be aware that a program "model" is different from the program in actual operation, and is necessarily modified when implemented due to the contingencies of current local situations. In the Head Start and Follow Through models the distinctions among programs is lessened by the requirements set by the Federal government for *all* programs. All programs, for example, must involve parents.

Empirical data that are collected through the Planned Variations research project, in which different models are implemented and studied, can be used to assess these programs. Whether the model can truly be assessed using data based upon implementation will be determined by how strictly the implementers have adhered to the models.

The term "model" has been used in many ways in education.

A "program model," as used above, is an idealized form of a program that can be copied or emulated. The model is a referent. Those persons who wish to implement a program based upon the model may use it to determine the new program's important elements, as well as a standard by which to judge the degree to which the program as implemented approximates the ideal.

A model is a representation, an ideal construction. It identifies the essential elements in the program, both practical and theoretical, and may also identify the relationships and interactions between those elements. Models can be communicated as three dimensional forms or as two dimensional charts and graphs. They may also be narrative in form. Because of their representational nature, models are simplifications of reality. They highlight the essential elements in a program and eliminate the nonessential ones. They may also eliminate the situation-specific elements of a program, focusing instead on those elements that are generalizable and replicable.

Because they are ideals, program models cannot be assessed empirically. They can be analyzed internally, however. As a result of analysis, models can be compared and judgments can be made about idealized programs. A framework for analysis of program models helps to identify the significant elements of different program models, and to compare various models, since such a framework allows one to abstract the significant elements of each model for purposes of comparison.

Programs in early childhood education all contain similar elements. Seldom, however, are the programs presented in such a manner that these elements are clearly identified and, therefore, easily compared. In the next two chapters, the author's framework for analysis of early childhood education programs, presented below, will be followed.

A Framework for Analysis

Early childhood education programs can be analyzed and evaluated through the use of the following framework:

1.0   *Assumptions*—The basic "givens" of a program.

1.1 *Assumptions about the client.* How does the program conceive of the child and of childhood? Are parents considered clients as well?

1.2 *Assumptions about the educative process.* Are there specific theories of learning or of instruction underlying the program? Are they related?

1.3 *Assumptions about the school.* Is the school conceived of as a broad social agency or as narrowly concerned with limited learnings?

1.4 *Assumptions about the teacher.* Is the teacher considered as an instrument of the program or is she a major decision maker?

2.0   *Goals of the program*—The purposes of the program.

2.1 *Long-range goals.* What long-range objectives are to be achieved?

2.2 *Short-term objectives.* Are immediate objectives stated?

2.3 *Relationship between the two.* Are long- and short-range goals consistent?

2.4 *Degree of specificity of objectives.* Are objectives stated as observable behavior? Are objectives stated in other ways?

3.0   *Curriculum*—The content of the program.

3.1 *Range of content of the program.* Is the program broadly or narrowly conceived?

3.2 *Sequence of learnings or experiences.* Is a specific sequence prescribed?

4.0   *Method*—The teaching strategies used.

4.1 *Child-child transactions.* What is the nature of the child-and-child transaction behavior?

4.2 *Child-teacher transactions.* What is the nature of the child-and-teacher transaction behavior?

4.3 *Child-materials transactions.* What is the nature of the child-and-material transaction behavior?

4.4 *Explicitness of prescriptions.* How explicitly are these transactions prescribed?

5.0 *Style*—The degree of personalization allowed in teaching the program.

6.0 *Organization*—The way in which elements are put together.

6.1 *Scheduling.* How is time used?

6.2 *Spatial organization.* How are resources deployed?

6.3 *Grouping of children.* Are children grouped in some specific manner in the program?

6.4 *Use of staff.* What kinds of staffing patterns are suggested?

7.0 *Effectiveness.*

7.1 *Achievement of goals.* Is there information about the degree to which the program can achieve its goals?

7.2 *Comparisons with other programs.* How does the program compare with other available programs?

8.0 *Practicality.*

8.1 *Cost of program.* How much does the program cost to implement?

8.2 *Staff requirements.* How many staff members are needed? What sorts of qualifications are required?

8.3 *Space requirements.* How much space is needed?

8.4 *Materials requirements.* What kinds and quantities of materials must be used in the program?

8.5 *Availability of supportive resources.* Are the necessary materials available? Are resource materials and persons available to support the program?[1]

The *assumptions* upon which a program is built in many ways represent the philosophy of the program. They identify a conception of school or teacher and of child or parent that has led to the

---

[1] Bernard Spodek, *Teaching in the Early Years.* (Englewood Cliffs, N.J.: Prentice-Hall, Inc., 1972), pp. 317–18, reprinted by permission.

development of a specific curriculum and methods of instruction. Underlying each program are statements about education, learning and, possibly, the relationships of experience to development. The *goals* of the program are derived from the purposes ascribed to education by the developer. Often these are related to larger goals of a society or a segment of society. They are also the outgrowth of assumptions which, by determining what results are worthy, help to set goals.

The *curriculum* of a program relates to the range of encounters to which a child may be exposed and how these encounters might best be ordered. The *method* used in a program describes the relationships and the nature of transactions that take place within these encounters. These transactions might be between the child and other people, or between the child and objects. In all programs the acceptable range of transactions is prescribed either broadly or narrowly.

Styles of teaching may also be more or less specified for a program. The degree to which an individual teacher may vary his method may be a function of the way in which style is prescribed. All programs require that the various elements, physical and ideational, be put together somehow. Time, space, materials, and personnel may be allocated differently in various programs. This is identified as *organization*.

The final two elements in the above framework relate more to the implementation of programs than to the program models themselves. If an educator is judging programs and wishes to choose one for implementation, he would want to know something about how effective such a program has been when implemented before. Can it achieve its goals? Are these goals achieved as well by one program as by others? Unfortunately such information is not always available. As a matter of fact, there is no way of determining the effectiveness of a program until it has been implemented for a considerable period of time and, even then, judgments may result from the nature of the implementation rather than the model itself.

There are also practical considerations in deciding to implement a program. Can it be done? Are there support systems? Can properly trained staff be hired and equipment procured? Will the costs be reasonable? All these issues are important ones for anyone selecting a program but are outside of the range of this book.

Using the Framework for Analysis

The framework is a tool to be used in understanding and comparing programs. Developers of early childhood programs seldom present the elements of a program logically in the written material they offer. This lack is due to the fact that much of this material highlights only limited aspects of the program, those that, in the judgment of the author, will be considered most important by the audience. Also, a large part of the literature that includes program descriptions is designed to influence the readers to accept the program. The requirements of a persuasive argument are different from those of a presentation designed to inform others. In addition, many of the elements of a program identified in the framework are not presented explicitly by program developers. Often the assumptions of the program may be implicit in the other elements, but never articulated. These assumptions may have to be inferred by the analyst from the descriptive material.

The sources of program descriptions are varied, and include curriculum guides, manuals of instructions, books, and journal articles. Descriptions may also be found in the speeches and presentations made by program developers and practitioners, and in research reports and monographs.

In the application of the framework, gaps in knowledge will be uncovered, for not all of the items in the analysis can be accounted for in many program descriptions. Historical models seldom have any information about effectiveness available, for example. This might also be true of the newer models presently being proposed. Often information about the practicality of a model must be determined individually for each locality. Generally, however, information on *assumptions, goals, curriculum, method, style,* and *organization* can be collected about all program models in early childhood education.

A background has been presented in Chapter 2 against which programs in early childhood education can be scrutinized. A framework for the analysis of programs to help sharpen our view of early childhood education has also been given. Let us now look at a number of historical and contemporary models in early childhood education and analyze them according to the first six categories of this framework.

3

HISTORICAL ALTERNATIVES IN EARLY CHILDHOOD EDUCATION

[Early childhood education programs are inventions of the past one and a half centuries. Some of these inventions have involved highly original conceptions of education, whereas others have been variations on existing themes.] Often similar ideas about education were interwoven in the programs of many educational pioneers. Practitioners who have accepted innovations have usually modified them in their implementation. Few programs currently exist that represent historical models in their original form. Most of the historical models of early childhood education have long been supplanted by newer programs, some of which may be within the same tradition or may retain the historical name.

Any educational model is time-bound. It is limited by the knowledge—about children and about learning—that exists at the time it is proposed. It also is designed to serve a definite purpose that may have more cultural legitimacy at one point in history than at another.

Of the wide range of educational programs that have been developed for young children, four have had a profound influence on current practice. These are the *Kindergarten* of Friedrich Froebel, the *Infant School* of Robert Owen, the *Nursery School* of Rachel and Margaret McMillan and the *Casa Dei Bambini* or *Children's House* of Maria Montessori. These four models will be presented in this chapter.

THE FROEBELIAN KINDERGARTEN

Friedrich Froebel (1782–1852) opened his kindergarten in Blankenburg, Germany in 1837. His interest in education predates this and his educational philosophy was actually framed by 1826 when he published *The Education of Man.*[1]

Froebel's work is deeply religious. He has been characterized as a pantheist, espousing the doctrine that God is the transcendent reality of which the material universe and man are only manifestations. His educational philosophy was an extension of that point of view, representing Froebel's deep religious convictions, as well as the various philosophic theories of his time. Froebel's idealism is close to that of Kant and shows the influence of Fichte and Schelling, German philosophers who were his contemporaries. Froebel's conception of the mediation of opposites is reminiscent of the dialectics of Hegel as well. His work also shows the influence of earlier educational theorists including Rousseau and Pestallozzi. Froebel taught for a period of time in Pestallozzi's school.

---

[1] A brief biography of Froebel can be found in P. Woodham-Smith, "The Origin of the Kindergarten," in *Froebel and English Education,* ed. Evelyn Lawrence (New York: Schocken Books, 1969), pp. 15–33.

Froebel's conception of childhood education is an extension of his conception of the world, of man, of the nature of knowledge, and of his view of the role that childhood plays in the development of the human being.

Assumptions

Froebel viewed the world as the living work and manifestation of God. The world contained a universal order that is "all pervading, self cognizant and everlasting." Man's responsibility was to understand the world and his own role in it, and man's divine elements would be revealed by leading a fully effective life.[2] In accordance with this outlook, Froebel established his conception of universal unity: the unity of God, nature, and man.

An extension of this idea of unity was Froebel's concept of *Gleideganzes,* or member-whole relationships. By this Froebel means that "each member repeats, or mirrors in some sense, the whole to which he belongs."[3] Each man, for example, reflects the whole of his culture, just as each tree reflects the totality of nature.

Another aspect of Froebel's conception of unity is to be found in the significance he attributed to the reconciliation of opposites.[4] Froebel felt that one could understand things only as one understood their opposites. Good is understandable only in terms of bad and the concept of "not round" needs to be mastered in order to assimilate the concept of "round." The reconciliation of the shapes of the sphere and the cube in the shape of a cylinder, the objects that make up Froebel's second *gift,* is an example of how his conceptions became translated into educational activities. These gifts are educational materials designed by Froebel. They are further described on pages 40–41.

---

[2] Friedrich Froebel, *The Education of Man* (New York: D. Appleton and Co., 1896), pp. 2–5.

[3] William H. Kilpatrick, *Froebel's Kindergarten Principles Critically Examined* (New York: Macmillan, 1916), p. 39.

[4] Froebel, *The Education of Man,* p. 42.

Froebel viewed man as innately good, unlike the modern idea of man as having the capacity for good or evil, or earlier judgments of man as being inherently evil.[5] This view of the goodness of man led Froebel to believe that providing the child with the greatest degree of freedom will allow him to develop into a good adult. If one fears inherent evil in man, then one must control the child's development in order to exorcise this evil. If the child can become either good or evil, then one must take care to shape his development. Freedom can be accepted as the basis of development only when one does not fear its consequences.

Given this assumption, the role of education is viewed as fostering natural development, rather than attempting to modify the child to make him over into something he would not naturally become.

Froebel used the metaphor of the garden to characterize childhood education. Just as young plants and animals grow naturally according to their own laws if provided with the proper elements of nurture, so should the young child. Froebel admonishes parents and educators not to regard the human being as a piece of wax or a lump of clay that can be molded into any shape but to follow the nature of their children so that they might gain beauty in the fullness of their power.[6]

To this end, Froebel prescribes a permissive education. Education should follow development, guarding and protecting the child. It should not direct, determine, or interfere. Such an education should be based upon freedom and self-determination. It should grow out of the child's free will rather than be imposed from the outside.[7] (It is interesting to note that despite the assumptions of the need for freedom and self-determination in education, Froebel's kindergarten activities were highly prescriptive.)

---

[5] Kilpatrick, *Froebel's Kindergarten Principles Critically Examined*, pp. 82–84.

[6] Friedrich Froebel, *The Education of Man*, pp. 7–11.

[7] Ibid., p. 7.

In many ways Froebel's concepts of development were close to those developed by G. Stanley Hall, whom he predated by three-quarters of a century, just as he predated Darwin. Froebel viewed the individual as having to go through the same patterns of development as characterized earlier levels of human culture. This recapitulation of human experience was viewed as helping man to interpret the past, as well as the present, human condition.[8]

Froebel saw development as occurring in stages. Later development was dependent upon fulfillment of the requirements of the earlier levels.[9] Ideas could also be learned by children in stages and even complex ideas could be embedded in the child's consciousness at an early age. According to Froebel, during the early stages of development knowledge grew as a result of actions, an idea not unlike that of Piagetian theory. True education, according to Froebel, must originate in activity. Living, doing, and knowing were connected processes, and insight and knowledge developed hand in hand with the creative process.[10]

Play, according to Froebel, is one form of creative self-activity and an essential part of the educational process. Play was seen as both a creative act and a way of copying the natural life of man. It was considered a serious and deeply significant activity of childhood.[11]

Goals

The goals of the kindergarten were derived from the above assumptions. Simply stated, the kindergarten was to support the child's development and to help him achieve an understanding of the

---

[8] Friedrich Froebel, "The Education of Man," in *Friedrich Froebel, A Selection from His Writing,* ed. Irene Lilly (Cambridge, England: Cambridge University Press, 1967), p. 58.

[9] Friedrich Froebel, "The Education of Man," in Lilly, ed., *Friedrich Froebel: A Selection from His Writing,* p. 64.

[10] Ibid., p. 43.

[11] Friedrich Froebel, "The Young Child," in Lilly, ed., *Friedrich Froebel: A Selection from His Writing,* pp. 83–84.

undergirding concepts of the universe, especially that of unity. The early years were especially crucial since at that time the child achieves his first connection with his environment, makes his first intelligent interpretations of it, and attempts to grasp its real nature.[12]

Curriculum

Since Froebel viewed knowledge as being achieved through the grasp of symbols, the Froebelian curriculum consisted of activities and the use of materials that had the larger meanings Froebel considered so important symbolically embedded within them. The manipulation of a ball, for example, was not important because of the sensory impressions a child might gain from this manipulation, but rather because the ball symbolized the unity of man, God, and nature.

The basic elements of the kindergarten curriculum were the *gifts,* the *occupations,* games and songs, nature study, and work in language and arithmetic. The first three elements of the curriculum were considered highly innovative. It is these that characterize the Froebelian kindergarten and make it different from other educational programs.

Froebel's *gifts* consisted of ten sets of manipulative materials to be used by children in a prescribed manner. The first gift was a set of six colored worsted balls. The second gift contained a wooden ball, cube and cylinder. The third, fourth, fifth and sixth gifts were sets of small wooden blocks, each set made up of similar blocks of a different size and shape, each set creating a cube when put together. The seventh gift consisted of two sets of wooden tablets, one of squares, the other of equilateral triangles. The eighth gift included lines made of straight strips of wood, and circles of metal or paper. The ninth gift consisted of sets of seeds, pebbles, cardboard, and paper all representing points. The tenth gift, representing recon-

---

[12] Ibid., p. 82.

struction, consisted of soft peas or wax pellets and sharpened sticks or straws.[13]

Froebel's *occupations* also dealt with solids, surfaces, lines, points, and constructions. The activities provided included work with clay, wood, and cardboard as well as paper cutting, paper weaving, paper folding, and paper pricking. The stringing of beads and buttons, drawing pictures, embroidering, and weaving were also Froebelian occupations.[14]

The games and songs used in the Froebelian kindergarten included those taken from Froebel's *Mutter und Kose-Leider* despite the fact that many of these mothers' songs and games were seemingly developed for much younger children. Movement plays were also included.

Nature study in the kindergarten consisted of the observation of plants and animals and discussions about these observations. Fairy tales and fanciful stories were told to the children and pictures presented to the class were discussed. Poems about nature were memorized, lessons were given in arithmetic, writing, and grammar. Short walks and excursions rounded out the program. Throughout the nature study, Froebel attempted to arouse a strong religious feeling in the children.

As stated earlier, activities were selected for inclusion in the curriculum because they conveyed a deeper sense of the world to the child. This can be illustrated by the use of the first two gifts. The first gift (worsted balls), consists of objects having but a single outer surface. This symbolizes the concept of unity, the oneness of man, God, and nature. The second gift includes a ball, a cube, and a cylinder. The ball again symbolizes unity; the cube, unity within diversity (it has many sides); and the cylinder represents the mediation of the two opposite forms.

Although no specific sequence was prescribed for many of the Froebelian activities, the gifts were designed as a sequenced set and were to be offered to the children in the proper order.

---

[13] Friedrich Froebel, *The Education of Man,* pp. 285–86.
[14] Ibid., p. 287.

Method

Froebel's writings seemed to reverse the traditional roles of teacher and child, with the teacher acting less as an instructor and more as a follower of children's leads. In reality, however, the system that developed was a highly formal one, very much teacher-directed, with specific prescriptions provided for the use of the didactic materials. The literature suggests that although Froebel's activities might have been written as exemplary ones, they were used as prescriptions followed exactly by classroom practitioners.

ROBERT OWEN'S INFANT SCHOOLS

"He originated and founded Infant Schools," begins the inscription on Robert Owen's monument in a cemetery in London.[15] For, in addition to being a social philosopher and a founder of Utopian communities, Robert Owen originated the infant school, the institution of primary education in England, as a means of rational, popular education.

Robert Owen (1771–1858) began his career as an industrialist in Manchester, England. He moved to New Lanark, Scotland, where he took over the management of what had been his father-in-law's cotton mill. There he became concerned with the working conditions of children who were employed in the mill from the age of six. He also became concerned with the living conditions of the families of the workers in the New Lanark community.

Owen attempted to limit the employment of children in the mill, starting them at the age of ten rather than six. He also implemented a number of reforms in the community itself. These included the provision of improved housing for workers, the creation of a company store that sold merchandise at less than the prevailing prices, as well as measures to increase the cleanliness and sobriety of

---

[15] John F. C. Harrison, *Utopianism and Education: Robert Owen and the Owenites* (New York: Teachers College Press, 1968), p. 1.

the inhabitants of New Lanark and the establishment of a school to serve both the children and adult population of the community.

In his career as a social philosopher, Owen directed his attention first to the improvement of working and living conditions in New Lanark, then to educational reform with the establishment of the Institution for the Formation of Character, as his school in New Lanark was called. Finally Owen moved to the establishment of a communitarian form of society. This society grew out of Owen's creation of a general concept of a society fashioned to satisfy human needs. Property was held in common and all human needs were met by the society.

After the New Lanark experiments, Owen and his followers emigrated to the United States and established a community in New Harmony, Indiana, based upon their communitarian ideals. Owenism flourished in both Great Britain and the United States for a period of years in the early nineteenth century.[16]

Education played a central role in Owen's scheme of things, for he felt that individuals must be developed that could live in the yet uncreated ideal society. This development would be a result of rationally based educational experiences. As more people were rationally educated, Owen felt, they would want a more rational ("Owenite") form of community existence.

Assumptions

One of the assumptions that underlies Owen's concept of community, as well as his concept of education, is that man's fundamental motivation is the pursuit of happiness. Individual happiness, however, can be obtained only through the promotion of happiness for the entire community. Society and all of its institutions, therefore, should be concerned with the promotion of the maximum amount of happiness for the greatest number of individuals.

Another assumption relates to the importance of the rational

---

[16] Ibid., pp. 1–38.

processes of thought. Knowledge, according to Owen, is derived from the objects surrounding the individual. Truth is distinguished from error through reason, error being evident in the discoveries of inconsistencies. Owen defined truth as what is consistent with nature.

Similarly Owen thought that concepts of right and wrong could be derived from the natural consequences of behavior. Artificial rewards and punishments had no place in the education of children.

A third set of assumptions held by Owen relates to human development. Man's character, it was assumed, was developed for him, not by him. Any fault in the individual's character was the result of the teaching he had received and the conditions under which he lived. By changing the conditions under which he lives and the nature of the teaching he receives, one could change the character of an individual or an entire population.

Finally, Owen assumed the importance of the early years of life in the education of the child. The things learned even in the first year of life have serious consequences. Proper education in these early years can be most effective because the child does not have much to unlearn. Owen recognized individual differences in the faculties and inclinations of both adults and children. His educational program, however, did not provide for these differences.[17]

Goals

The goal of the New Lanark school was to train the students "in good practical habits." The most important of these for the student was "to endeavor to make his companions happy." In addition boys and girls were taught to read well, to understand what they have read, to write, and to understand the rules of arithmetic. The girls were also taught sewing, cooking, and housekeeping skills. Ultimately the children were to be able to make rational judgments on any subject.[18]

---

[17] Robert Owen, "Essays on the Formation of Character," in *The Life of Robert Owen, Written by Himself* (London: Effingham Wilson, 1857), Vol. I, pp. 287–307.
[18] Ibid., pp. 294–95.

Curriculum

The curriculum of the Institute for the Development of Character included reading, writing, arithmetic, sewing, geography, natural history, modern and ancient history, dance, and music. While play was viewed as a natural and valued aspect of child behavior and permitted in the school, the educational uses of play were not recognized. Owen felt that reading should not be taught to a child until after he has developed an adequate understanding of the world around him, so as to make the reading process meaningful. Because of parental demands, however, reading instruction began at an early age. Nevertheless, a principle was set that children should not be directed to read what they could not understand.

Writing was taught by methods similar to those used in other schools of the time, copying from books or from dictation. Arithmetic was taught by a method developed by Pestalozzi, with emphasis placed upon understanding the different arithmetic operations.

Children were also taught about the various aspects of the animal, vegetable, and mineral worlds, the shape of the earth and its general divisions. Different countries were compared with that of the children. These subjects were approached so as to show the connections between history, geography, and natural history. Although religious doctrine was not taught per se, a nondenominational approach to religion was presented by having the children achieve the greatest understanding of the world around them and by inculcating them with practical moral principles. In addition, children were taught to sing by ear as well as by note and to dance Scottish reels, country dances, and quadrilles.[19]

Method

Owen did not develop new educational methodologies, but rather made use of the humane ones already available. Reading was

---

[19] Robert Dale Owen, *Outline of the System of Education at New Lanark* (Glasgow: Wardlaw and Cunningham, 1824), pp. 35–74.

taught with existing materials, with one child reading to the whole class and the rest responding to questions. Writing lessons consisted of copying written and dictated material. History, geography, and natural history were taught primarily by lectures to groups of forty or fifty. Teachers used anecdotal materials to enliven their talks and were admonished to be careful to limit the length of the lecture according to the degree of attentiveness of the children.

Extensive use was made of audio-visual aids in these lectures. Pictures, maps, globes, and a time-line were used to make the lecture material more understandable to the children.[20]

The method of instruction used in New Lanark was based upon kindness. Children were not rewarded or punished for their actions, but rather shown each action's consequences. A child who misbehaved was more pitied than blamed. The relationships developed were to be based upon love and mutual concern for happiness.[21]

Organization

The school in New Lanark was organized into three levels. The first class included children ages three to six, the second class included children from six to ten. The third level included evening classes that were held for children from ten to twenty for study after work. The school was built to accommodate 300 daytime students and 300 evening students.

In the upper story of the building were two apartments, the larger of which was designed for education on the Lancasterian plan (using older children as monitors to teach the younger ones). It contained mainly desks and chairs. The smaller apartment contained geographic and zoological specimens and representations hung around the room, and a gallery for an orchestra. Singing and dancing were taught and lectures were given here. The lower story had three

[20] Ibid., pp. 35–74.
[21] Ibid., pp. 14–15.

apartments used for teaching the younger children. A paved play-ground was immediately outside the building.

The classes of older children consisted of from twenty to forty children with about five and one-half hours spent in classes that were divided into two or three sessions. The younger classes were larger and about half the amount of time was spent in lessons daily. When not in lessons the younger ones spent the time in free, super-vised, outdoor play. There was no regular timetable for activities, children being taught when they seemed ready and kept at a lesson as long as they seemed attentive.[22]

THE MONTESSORI METHOD

Maria Montessori (1870–1952) was known throughout her life as a physician, university professor, educator, and feminist. She was the first woman ever to be graduated from an Italian medical school. After her graduation she was appointed to the Psychiatric Clinic of the University of Rome where she came in contact with "idiot children." Through this work she became acquainted with the work of Jean Itard and Edouard Seguin, French doctors who had worked with mentally defective children and developed innovative approaches to their education. This led to her directorship of a school for mentally deficient children. Building upon the work of the French physicians named above, Montessori developed an educational system which had visible success.

Reasoning that such success as her method had with retarded children would be repeated with normal children, Montessori accepted an opportunity to develop an educational approach for young children. The Rome Association for Good Building had built a number of flats in a slum section of Rome. With large numbers of children unattended during the day, vandalism became a problem. The landlords set aside space in their building and invited Dr.

[22] Ibid., pp. 27–35.

Montessori to set up a program on their premises. This was to become the first *Casa Dei Bambini,* as Montessori schools were to be called.

Montessori hired a young woman, who had not had previous training as a teacher to help her. Through the observation of natural activities of children, Montessori elaborated her activities and materials, modifying the Seguin materials and approaches that were the basis for her education of defective children.

News of the successful innovative program for children brought visitors from all over Italy and ultimately from all over the world. Dr. Montessori extended her school and began to develop teacher training programs for "directresses" of these schools, as the Montessori teachers were called. Soon an international movement had developed, with Montessori schools established throughout the world and Montessori teacher-training programs being provided internationally, all supervised by an international Montessori association. Dr. Montessori herself continued to write, lecture and train teachers until her death in 1952.[23]

Assumptions

Much of the Montessori method can be understood only in relation to her conception of childhood. Montessori held the young child in reverence. The child has within him the capacity for his own development, which is a process of unfolding from within. Environment holds a definite, but secondary, role in this developmental pattern. Although environment can modify development by either helping or hindering it, it does not serve a creative function.

As the child develops he goes through a series of stages, each of which provides a predisposition for particular types of learning. These stages, or sensitive periods, determine the sequence of learning for the child. The teacher observes the child for the manifestation

---

[23] E. M. Standing, *Maria Montessori: Her Life and Work* (London: Hollis and Carter, 1957), pp. 3–68.

of each stage in order to provide the experiences that can support development. As a child reaches a stage, he will seek new experiences that are rewarding in themselves. Freedom of action allows the child to seek out situations from which he can learn.[24] Traditional schooling, Montessori felt, ran counter to the nature of the child. It forces the child to adapt to an adult oriented society, rather than providing an experience that is consistent with the child's nature. The new education was child-oriented, based upon the observation of the child in a free situation. The educational environment would allow the child to manifest his developing competencies without adult interference.

If a child is not ready for an experience, Montessori suggests that all the teacher can do is wait for the child's inner life to organize itself. The child must shape himself rather than be molded by the adult. The teacher is primarily an observer and a student of human development, rather than a lecturer and shaper of behavior.

The role of the school is to create an environment that will teach the child, with a minimum of adult intervention. The inner power of the child is utilized for his instruction. The child has great powers of observation even during infancy. The program of the school should build upon these powers of observation. Educational programs should begin with objects that appeal to the child's senses. More symbolic materials should be utilized later, after the child has gained some knowledge from original sensory impressions.[25]

Goals

The goals of the Montessori program are to support the general development of the child. While areas of development are not specified by Montessori, the areas of concern in the program include sensorimotor, intellectual, language, and moral development.

---

[24] Maria Montessori, *The Child in the Family* (New York: Avon Books, 1970), pp. 79–131.

[25] Ibid., pp. 61–76.

Curriculum

The curriculum of the Montessori school includes exercises in practical life, muscular education, education of the senses, intellectual education, language education, and the teaching of reading, writing, and numeration. Nature study and handicraft activities were also included in the original Montessori school.

The exercises in practical life included those activities that children needed in order to become relatively autonomous, and to prepare for the forms of social life, such as cleaning and caring for oneself and one's surroundings. Washing hands and face, and brushing teeth as well as cleaning and dusting the classrooms were included.

Education of the senses included attention to the visual, auditory, tactile, baric, and thermic senses and those of taste and smell. Children are taught visual perception of dimension, such as thickness, length, width, and height through the use of materials which manifest these attributes. Form and color perception are taught with materials that the children must first discriminate among, and then place into a series.

Sound discrimination is taught through boxes, containing different materials, that are shaken and emit different intensities of sound that may be matched or placed in a series. Sets of tone bells are also used. A silence game helps sensitize children to sound and its absence.

Exercises for the tactile sense include the use of smooth- and rough-surfaced material to be touched by children. Thermal sense is trained with bowls filled with water of different temperature, and the baric sense is trained through the use of wooden tablets of the same dimensions but different weights. Children were also blindfolded and asked to taste and smell different things.

Muscular education included helping children learn the movements necessary for the everyday activities involved in the exercises in practical life, as well as motor and respiratory gymnastics. Marching and some of the games developed by Froebel were included in initial Montessori programs.

Gardening and nature study were also part of the original Montessori programs, and Montessori herself suggested that all schools should have a readily accessible outdoor area that would include a garden. Gardening would help the children to understand cause-effect relationships when they saw the consequences of their work, and teach them to anticipate, but wait patiently for, consequences to occur. Clay modeling, pottery making, and building with bricks were also part of the early programs.

Intellectual education was evident in all of the children's work. Observation and manipulation of sensory materials led to their identification and labeling, as well as to the development of recall. Montessori adhered to the Seguin steps in sensory education in which the child first learns to associate a sensory perception with a name, then learns to recognize an object that corresponds to the name, and finally remembers the name of the object correctly.

Language was approached in a number of ways by Montessori. Sensory education was related to both language and the exercises in practical life. Teachers also named the materials with which they worked and children were asked to repeat the teacher's words. Emphasis was placed on teacher's correct pronunciation of words. Although the Montessori teacher speaks relatively little in the classroom, her utterances are important. Reading, writing, and graphic language are also approached sensorially at first, with writing preceding reading.

Many of the early activities prepared the child for writing, because in his use of manipulative materials the child is developing appropriate skills of motor coordination. Writing was taught by moving children from feeling the shapes of letters to making words with movable letters to writing letters. The sounds of letters were associated with the visual cues and words were created by putting letters together. Reading grew from the sounding out of words.

The child also learns to read words in the process of learning to construct and pronounce them. Cards or slips of paper with words written on them are provided for the children. In all cases, the writing of individual words, phrases, and sentences precedes their reading.

Mathematics also has its beginning in sensory activities. The child moves from comparing quantities to counting and associating written numbers with quantities. The decimal system and the basic number operations were also included in the early childhood program.[26]

Method

The Montessori method is one of auto-education. Children learn through interaction with materials. Many of the materials are self-correcting, allowing the children to determine immediately if their actions are correct (see pages 54–55 for examples). No group lessons are given and individual lessons are brief, simple, and objective. The teacher intrudes herself as little as possible into the lesson. Much use is made of demonstration and modeling with a minimum of speech, since too much verbal output may force the child to focus on the talk rather than the actions of the teacher.

Each area of curriculum has a series of prescribed activities and materials that go with it. In the Exercise of Practical Life, children use buttoning and lacing frames, as well as cleaning apparatus. Each activity has been carefully analyzed and children go through the steps of an activity in a prescribed sequence. Sensory education also takes place as a result of prescribed activities. The activities are arranged by gradation, as are the sequences in the activities.

The first step in writing is outlining geometric figures by tracing on insets (metal plates in various shapes). Two insets can be superimposed on one another and the outlines can be filled in as well. Filling in additional figures provides practice opportunities.

Soon the children are provided with letters cut out of sandpaper, which are mounted on smooth paper. The children trace these letters with their finger as the teacher pronounces the sounds of the letters. Groups of letters of similar composition are also presented to the children. With the availability of manipulable letters

---

[26] Maria Montessori, *The Montessori Method* (New York: Schocken Books, 1969), pp. 119–345.

of cardboard or wood, the children can begin to construct words that they can also pronounce. Actual writing follows.

The children, in using the sensorial materials, have already had an introduction to arithmetic, for many of the exercises are based upon comparisons of size or quantity. The introduction to numbers comes with the use of red and blue rods that are scaled to a decimal system based upon the unit of a decimeter. Children can learn to compare these in size and find multiples of the smaller ones. These units are then given the number names. The written names are presented in sandpaper much as the letters were, with children asked to say the name of the number as they trace it with their finger.

A number of exercises are presented with these rods and written numbers. The *Golden Beads* are also used for more elaborate mathematical operations. These beads are organized in units to ten, then in rows of tens, squares of a hundred, and cubes of a thousand. Children are allowed to work with materials as long as they wish and as long as they use them correctly. Lessons or requirements are not imposed upon the children. Rather, the teacher will observe children to determine their level of development, holding back the suggestion of involvement in particular activities until a child is ready for them. The right time is often suggested by the child's own selection of activities.

The method of instruction used is based upon a concept of child liberty. As children become experienced with the program they themselves make better use of their abilities and develop increased concentration. No system of rewards and punishments is used, since the competencies the children develop provide their own reward. Misbehavior would similarly not be punished, though children might be withdrawn from the group situation and isolated in a place where they could comfortably observe the other children in action. The freedom of the children is tempered by their natural love of order.[27]

---

[27] Maria Montessori, *Dr. Montessori's Own Handbook* (New York: Schocken Books, 1965), pp. 49–182.

Style

Although the behavior of teachers is not specified in Montessori's writings, a number of guidelines exist. The teacher is expected to be an observer of children, teaching much of the time by indirection, organizing the environment, and demonstrating activities. She works with individuals and small groups. Her lessons tend to be demonstrations of activities. When she speaks she is expected to use language with accuracy and clarity.[28]

Organization

Great stress is placed, in the Montessori method, on the prepared environment. The original Montessori school consisted of a number of rooms, a central one for intellectual activity, rooms for play and sleep, a dining room, a dressing room, and a room for games, as well as outdoor space that included a garden. The contents of the rooms were carefully determined. Furniture was to be light, attractive, and scaled to children's size, with tables for individual, as well as group, activity. Cabinets were provided for the proper storage of the didactic materials. Washstands and cleaning tools were available to the children. Everything was designed to be useful and appealing to the children.[29]

A large number of didactic materials characterize the Montessori school. These include the sensory materials, such as blocks in which sockets of various sizes are bored and into which cylinders of different sizes fit. The sets of cylinders differ only in size, with the dimensions of length, width, or both, varied in the set. The *Pink Towers, Brown Stairs,* the color tablets, as well as sets of metal inserts and different texture materials are also included. The mathematics materials include rods based upon the decimal system, the golden beads, and materials that show number symbols. Sandpaper

---

[28] Maria Montessori, *The Child in the Family,* pp. 133–60.
[29] Maria Montessori, *The Montessori Method,* pp. 80–83.

letters and other language materials, and the materials for use in the exercises in practical life are to be found as well. Many of the materials were designed to be self-correcting. Not only would the cylinder not fit into the improper hole, but pitchers that were carelessly handled might break. The environment was responsive to the children's actions.[30]

There is little structured time in the Montessori school. The day is divided into large blocks of time, including time for opening exercises, intellectual activities, gymnastics, lunch, manual work, and games. There are prescribed sequences of activities in relation to the different kinds of materials and activities. Although most Montessori schools are designed for preprimary children, the Montessori method extends through the entire elementary education sequence.[31]

THE NURSERY SCHOOL

The first nursery school was established in England by Rachel and Margaret McMillan in 1911. The nursery school was different from the day nurseries that had been available earlier. It was originally conceived as a separate institution for children, age two to seven, and was designed to supplement the child-rearing environment of the poor, giving the poor child the advantages in growing up provided by more affluent families. Grace Owen, another pioneer in the nursery school movement, conceived of the nursery school as an adjunct to the primary school, providing experiences for children age two to five.

Margaret and Rachel McMillan were both born in Westchester County, New York, just prior to the Civil War, and moved to Britain during their childhood. Rachel, the elder of the two by one year, died in 1917. Margaret carried on the work until her own death in 1931. Margaret McMillan was the speaker and writer, and

---

[30] Maria Montessori, *Dr. Montessori's Own Handbook,* pp. 49–182.
[31] Maria Montessori, *The Montessori Method,* pp. 121–22.

it is possible that the ideas underlying the nursery school were primarily hers.

Margaret McMillan studied music and acting during her formative years. She became involved in socialist causes and soon left her career as governess and companion to become a spokesman for the British Independent Labor Party. In 1894 she was elected to the school board of Bradford where she fought for the provision of medical inspection and treatment for school children, as well as for the provision of school baths and school dinners. Concerned with the health and welfare of children, she became convinced that many of the deficiencies she saw in school children could be corrected or prevented before their entrance into the primary grades.

Margaret left Bradford to join her sister in London in 1902. Soon afterward the two sisters opened their first medical clinic for children. Their work with children expanded and, in addition to the clinic, they were soon operating camps for boys and girls and a day-time nursery school. The nursery school and clinic were later moved to the Depthford section of London and, after a while, a training college to prepare nursery school personnel was established.[32] The Rachel McMillan Training College and the nursery school still exist in London.

Assumptions

The original conception of the nursery school was strongly influenced by the development of knowledge of human physiology and medicine in the latter nineteenth century. Rachel McMillan was concerned with the problems of poor children. She felt that they could not develop properly unless they were healthy during the early formative years. Good health required proper medical treatment, including the cure and prevention of disease. This required more than just having adequate medical attention provided. Adequate nutrition, cleanliness, fresh air, proper exercise, and living in a healthy

---

[32] Albert Mansbridge, *Margaret McMillan, Prophet and Pioneer* (London: J. M. Dent and Sons, 1932).

environment were all basic requirements for development and education, requirements that were not being met at that time for working class children in England, or elsewhere in the world.

The concept of supporting total development in the education of young children was given the label *nurture* by Margaret McMillan. She used the analogy of the garden to characterize development and education, much like Froebel, but without the mystical or idealist intent. The nursery school became the "human garden [that] may blossom in the slum." Education it was felt, could only operate in an environment that protected the health and welfare of the child. The physiological basis of development and education underlie the original conception of the nursery school.[33]

Margaret McMillan, like Maria Montessori, was influenced by Edouard Seguin. She felt that perceptual-motor development was an important basis for education. The training of the senses was as necessary a part of early education as the training of the various muscles of the body through exercise and movement.

Unlike Montessori, McMillan placed high value on the education of the imagination. She saw expressive activity, play, art, and movement as imitative in character but good preparation for tool-making later in human life.[34] Imagination is necessary for advancement in all spheres of life. It is as important for the workmen as for the scientist and artist. Although imagination might create a good deal of trouble, it is worth developing in school. Imagination grows naturally in children during the early years, and can be utilized to provide a framework for an "organic" form of education.[35]

Goals

The goal of the nursery school was to support the physical and mental development of young children. The nursery school would

---

[33] Margaret McMillan, *Education Through the Imagination* (New York: D. Appleton and Co., 1924), pp. 57–59.

[34] Margaret McMillan, *Labour and Childhood* (London: Swan, Sonnenschein and Co., 1907), p. 67.

[35] Margaret McMillan, *Education Through the Imagination*, pp. 9–15.

provide, in a collective form, the qualities of a child-rearing environment available in more affluent homes.[36]

Curriculum

The curriculum of the McMillan Nursery School, included a range of instructional activities. Central to the program were its *caring* aspects: eating, sleeping, and outdoor activities were the basis for the school life of the child.

Learning activities were specified and also differed by age levels. The younger children were provided with activities to teach them self-caring skills. Buttoning, lacing, and tying frames were provided for the children and analyses were made of the movements involved in specific self-caring activities such as washing, dressing, and hair brushing. This reflected the influence of Seguin. This influence is given further evidence in the perceptual-motor activities prescribed for children. McMillan provided younger children with form boards and older children with alphabet boards, colored wooden squares, and color wheels as a way of teaching form and color discrimination.

McMillan went beyond just perceptual-motor activities, providing children with many activities for self-expression. Handcrafts such as clay modeling, building with "bricks," and using other creative materials were very much a part of the program.

McMillan created a school setting where children would be close to nature, a rather difficult task considering the slum conditions surrounding the nursery school. Gardens were planted in the schools with trees, and beds of flowers and vegetables. Herbs were grown to provide sensory experiences of taste and smell, as well as vision. Animals were kept in the nursery school and children were given responsibility for the care and feeding of these pets.

Movement activities were developed for children. These in-

---

[36] Margaret McMillan, *The Nursery School* (London: J. M. Dent and Sons, 1919), pp. 21–31.

cluded movements to extend their physical ability, and movement as a way of studying music. In this area, McMillan's work shows the influence of Jacques Dalcroze.

As the children grew older they were also provided with lessons in the three R's. The children were introduced to reading, writing, and arithmetic in the nursery school by the age of five. Science was taught through nature study.[37]

The curriculum of the nursery school presented by Grace Owen is similar in most ways to the McMillans' with the exclusion of any formal lessons in academic areas. In the Owen program, however, the children received these lessons at about the same age as in the McMillan program, but in the infant (primary) school, rather than in the institution called a nursery school. Owen suggests the use of Montessori materials and of Froebel-type activities such as finger plays in the nursery school. She placed greater stress on dramatic play and the uses of toys by children than does McMillan.[38]

Method

McMillan viewed teaching in the nursery school as a role that combined the care and education of children. The practitioner was a "nurse-teacher." All aspects of care were considered educational. While informal teaching was considered the basic instructional method, formal lessons were provided especially in the academic areas.

Owen, on the other hand, viewed teaching as providing an environment to nourish the child's growing mind and body, and supporting the development of social relations. Formal instruction had no place in the nursery nor should tests of progress be used.[39]

---

[37] Ibid., pp. 83–153.
[38] Margaret E. Egger and Grace Owen, "Education of the Nursery School Child," in *Nursery School Education*, ed. Grace Owen (New York: E. P. Dutton, 1920), pp. 55–94.
[39] Grace Owen, "Aims and Functions of the Nursery School," in *Nursery School Education*, pp. 22–25.

Organization

The McMillan Nursery School was much like the modern day care center. Children were in attendance from early morning until five-thirty or later in the evening. The children were washed upon arrival and were sometimes provided with clean clothes. No time schedule was set for daily activities but specific periods were allocated for meals and sleeping. The physical facility included rooms in an open-air shed with direct access to play areas and gardens. The children spent much of the time outdoors and the entire space was considered to be educational space.

While Owen also supported the "Open Shed" nursery as a nursery facility, she suggested other alternatives, including use of cottages, houses, and gardens or additions to infant schools. She suggested a school day of five or six hours, with certain fixed times for meals and sleep and the rest of the time unstructured. Owen suggests beginning the day with a group meeting including a "service," routines, songs, and a discussion time. The last period of the day should be devoted to quiet games and a story.[40] Owen's suggestions for the time structured into large blocks of "activity periods" are very close to those practiced by many contemporary nursery schools.

These five educators, Friedrich Froebel, Robert Owen, Maria Montessori, and Margaret and Rachel McMillan, developed their educational schemes in different historical and geographic contexts. All have influenced current practice in early childhood education. For each, education developed out of what would today be called a humanist tradition, a concern for young children, for the support of their autonomy and development, and a belief in the importance of early experiences in the lives of people. Inconsistencies can be seen between the theory and the implementation. In the Froebelian program, for example, freedom was to be developed as a result of constrained activity. In Owen's school, reading was taught at an

---

[40] Margaret E. Egger and Grace Owen, "Education of the Nursery School Child."

early age because of the wishes of the parents even though this ran counter to the philosophy of the educational scheme.

There are significant differences between these programs as well. One set of differences is highlighted by the emphasis on symbolism in the work of Froebel, and on realism in the work of Owen. The hierarchically structured presentation of the Montessori school was different from the less structured presentation of activities in the McMillan school, even though both educators emphasized child freedom. Ultimately, the forms of education developed by each of the historical model makers was unique. Similar differences can be found in programs advocated for young children today.

These models are more than historical relics, for elements of each can be found in programs presently being used. The model of *open education* that will be analyzed in the following chapter has its antecedents in the four models presented here. The use of children's play as a vehicle for education, originally developed by Froebel, is still valued by most early childhood educators and is an integral part of the open education approach. The concern for the development of character, and the testing of the validity of ideas in existing reality, both parts of Owen's original infant school, are similarly a part of contemporary open education. The basis of education in nurturance, originally proposed by McMillan, is paralleled by the identification of goals in the total developmental structure of the child by open educators. The careful preparation of the environment and the emphasis on independent learning found in Montessori education is also to be found in open education.

There are other striking parallels between historical and contemporary theory and practice. Froebel's tenth gift of sticks and wax pellets is surprisingly similar to the materials provided by science educators today who wish to help children understand the nature of structures. In addition, many of Froebel's ideas about play and the nature of child learning as a result of interaction with the environment seem to be a surprising anticipation of the concepts being studied by Piaget and his followers.

In the following chapter we will bring our framework to bear on contemporary programs in early childhood education, analyzing ideal early childhood education models.

4

CONTEMPORARY MODELS IN EARLY CHILDHOOD EDUCATION

The educational models described in the last chapter were major forces that shaped the field of early childhood education over the last century. Although many models of early childhood education are presently being implemented, few seem to have the same power to influence the direction of education. This may be a function of historical foreshortening; we are so close to these contemporary programs that we cannot see their full impact or it may be that few of the current models are as distinct as the historical ones. Contemporary models of early childhood education seem to have much in common with each other, and overlap on a number of dimensions.

An analysis of contemporary programs in early childhood education may suggest that differences among alternate program models might actually be differences in style or degree of emphasis, rather than differences in goals, methods, content, or assumptions. Many of the models might best be understood by placing them on a philosophic continuum of the view of man upon which they are based. The goals, content, and method of the programs can be derived from these.

TWO VIEWS OF MAN

Contemporary psychology and education might best be understood in terms of the different ways that theorists and practitioners view the nature of man. For a number of years there has been a conflict in psychology between those who adhere to a *behaviorist* view of man and those who adhere to a *phenomenological* view. Although the conflict is clouded in education by a number of other issues, political as well as professional, the same conflict exists. Early childhood programs that view man from a behavioral point of view include the Behavior Analysis approach, the DARCEE early intervention program, and the Bereiter-Engelmann-Becker program, to name just a few. Adherents to the phenomenological point of view include the proponents of the English infant school, the Bank Street Model, the Tucson Early Education Model, and the Piagetian Ypsilanti model.

Hitt has characterized these two views of man as follows:

The behaviorist views man as a passive organism governed by external stimuli. Man can be manipulated through proper control of these stimuli. Moreover, the laws that govern man are essentially the same laws as the laws that govern all natural phenomena of the world; hence it is assumed that the scientific method used by the physical scientist is equally appropriate to the study of man.

The phenomenologist views man as the source of acts; he is free to choose in each situation. The essence of man is inside of man; he is

controlled by his own consciousness. The most appropriate methodology for the study of man is phenomenology, which begins in the
world of experience.[1]

Although this statement may essentially be an oversimplifica-
tion of the differences of the two schools of thought, the identification of these positions is useful in understanding the assumptions
under which different programs operate, and the essential differences between the methods used to justify the arguments between
these two classes of programs.

Hitt goes on to characterize the essential differences between
the two views of man. A summary of these differences has been organized here in parallel columns to aid in the making of comparisons.

Behavioral Model of Man	*Phenomenological Model of Man*
1. Man can be described meaningfully in terms of his behavior.	1. Man can be described meaningfully in terms of his consciousness.
2. Man is predictable.	2. Man is unpredictable.
3. Man is an information transmitter.	3. Man is an information generator.
4. Man lives in an objective world.	4. Man lives in a subjective world.
5. Man is a rational being.	5. Man is an arational being.
6. One man is like other men.	6. Each man is unique.
7. Man can be described meaningfully in absolute terms.	7. Man can be described meaningfully in relative terms.
8. Human characteristics can be investigated independently of one another.	8. Man must be studied as a whole.
9. Man is a reality.	9. Man is a potentiality.
10. Man is knowable in scientific terms.	10. Man is more than we can know about him.[2]

---

[1] William D. Hitt, "Two Models of Man," *American Psychologist*, 24, No.
7 (July 1969), pp. 651–658.
  [2] Ibid., p. 657.

Given the behaviorist view of man, the science of man must be the science of behavior. Observable behavior, and its relationships with other observable phenomena in the physical world become the objects of this science. The laws governing these relationships become the basis for psychological theory. The strategies of the theorist require that investigation take place primarily in laboratory settings where researchers can control the significant variables.

The phenomenologists, on the other hand, are concerned more with the meanings of behavior than with its visible attributes. The "self" plays an important role in determining these meanings. Although observation is a tool of phenomenological psychology, most observations must be made outside the laboratory, in field situations. The relationship between a person's behaviors and his environment is so complex, it is felt, that limiting the environment and controlling or eliminating variables creates a distorted view of this relationship. The model of the phenomenological investigator might more closely resemble that of an anthropologist or an ecological biologist than a laboratory physicist, the model used by the behaviorist psychologist.

Behaviorist psychology has developed a well conceived theory and a parallel set of strategies that can be used in investigating human behavior and development. A similar system of theory and strategies is not available for the phenomenologists. A review of the concepts used by behaviorists should help give an understanding to the educational programs they support.

Behaviorist Theory

The child, from a behaviorist point of view, might be conceived of as a system of interrelated responses interacting with stimuli. The child's behavior is made up of basically two kinds of responses: *respondents* and *operants*. Respondents are controlled by stimuli that precede them, whereas operants are controlled by stimuli that follow them. The environment is thought of as the events that act upon the child. Some of these events act as stimuli, but some are setting events, actually creating the settings in which behaviors occur. Respondent behavior is most like ordinary reflex behavior. These behaviors are not controlled by their consequences and hence cannot be trained, although it is possible to attach some respondent behavior to new stimuli. Operant behavior, because it is related to the consequences of the response, can be controlled, and hence trained.

Operants may produce positive reenforcers, in which case the consequence of the behavior is a valued stimulus, which in turn will strengthen the operant response. Another consequence of operant behavior might be negative reenforcement, or the removal of a negative stimulus. Other reenforcement situations include neutral stimuli that operate in neither a positive or negative way, and punishment, which is a negative consequence of behavior. By controlling the reenforcement an individual receives as a consequence of behavior, it is possible to increase the probability of this behavior recurring. This change in the behavior based upon the control of reenforcement is called *operant conditioning*. Since an operant is sensitive to its consequences, the time lapse between an operant behavior and its reenforcement is an important variable in the process of conditioning. The strongest reenforcers should be those that occur immediately after the response has occurred. Too long a lapse between the behavior and its reenforcement may lead to the reenforcing of the wrong behavior, as other behaviors might intervene.

Different procedures may be used to schedule reenforcement of behavior. Continuous reenforcement takes place when every operant behavior is reenforced. Intermittent reenforcement occurs when reenforcement is provided for every nth behavior or provided regularly over a period of time (interval schedule). Operant behaviors generally disappear when reenforcement ceases. They do, however, persist for longer periods of time after some form of intermittent reenforcement than after continuous reenforcement. An intermittent reenforcement schedule is not effective for initial learning. It is possible, however, to begin a program of training using continuous reenforcement, then later move to some form of intermittent reenforcement, and finally allowing the reenforcement to fade. Such a program would allow the conditioned behavior to persist after reenforcement ceases.

Any number of rewards can be used as positive reenforcement. Whatever works for an individual is considered a proper reenforcement. Rewards that have been used by psychologists and educators include food, toys, additional stimuli, or social stimuli. Tokens that can be traded for various rewards have also been used. The key to successful operant conditioning, however, is not in the kind of reenforcement used but rather in the consistency of the reenforcement schedule.

No new behavior is ever created through a program of operant conditioning. New organizations of previously existing behavior may be conditioned, however, which will lead to what might be considered novel behavior. Elaborate learning is often the consequence of the conditioning of a series of successive approximations beginning with some behaviors that the organism already has in his repertoire and moving through a series of continually more complicated reorganizations until the individual reaches the final, predetermined stage. Such a procedure is called *shaping*. In order to shape behavior, one must have a clear understanding of what the terminal behavior should be, and a sense of where the individual is at the present time. With this, a series of intervening steps for the individual to be taken through, under a carefully controlled environment, until the terminal behavior is achieved can be created. This is the process used in most programs of early childhood education using the behavioral analysis principles.[3]

Behaviorist theory grows out of an extensive body of research with animals and humans in laboratories. Although it focuses primarily on behavior, its technology has been used to teach a broad range of human activities, including emotional behavior, skill behavior, cognitive behavior, and discrimination and categorization, the basis for conceptualization.

With this background, let us analyze two models of educational

---

[3] Sidney W. Bijou and Donald M. Baer, *Child Development I: A Systematic and Empirical Theory* (New York: Appleton-Century-Crofts, 1961).

programs much as we have analyzed the historical models. For purposes of clarity as well as brevity we will present a combined model of the behaviorist approach, but use the framework of "open education" as the basis for our analysis of the phenomenological model.

BEHAVIORIST MODEL

Assumptions

Many of the assumptions regarding a behaviorist program of early childhood education can be inferred from the discussion above. A major assumption is that the behavior of a child is determined by external stimuli. Therefore, by controlling the stimuli in the environment, one can modify the child's behavior. In addition, by carefully specifying the goals of education in terms of observable behavior, and by specifying the criteria for successful learning, one can begin to design a program of education. One important aspect of such a model is the behavior shaping. An analysis is made of the steps needed to attain the goals of a program. The steps bring the child through a series of successive approximations to those goals, each step being small enough to insure success. Failure of any kind is to be avoided. Also, rewards are contingent upon the production of the correct behaviors.

The determination of the goals of instruction and the methods to be used to achieve these goals is outside the domain of the child and of the individual teacher. The role of the school is to create an environment where the production of appropriate behaviors can be supported and the accessibility of the child to stimuli can be controlled. The role of the teacher is to control the environment and the availability of rewards to the child.

Goals

No specific set of goals can be attributed to the behaviorist model. Although they are an important part of any behaviorist program, the goals are external to the system, which is more concerned with the method of achieving them, than with the goals themselves. The only condition is that goals must be stated in behavioral terms and that the means of assessing them must be stated as well.

In most of the programs of early childhood education, goals are stated in terms of the behaviors necessary for success in later schooling. These might be cognitive skills as in the DARCEE program, or academic skills as in the Bereiter-Engelmann-Becker program, or a combination of social skills necessary for the role of student and academic skills as in the Behavior Analysis program (see Part II of this book).

Curriculum

As with goals, no standard curriculum can be stated for behaviorist programs. The curriculum is determined by the goals of each individual program.

The DARCEE program, for example, is one that teaches sensory, abstracting and mediating, and response skills. The content of the program is organized into units.

The Bereiter-Engelmann-Becker program includes a series of separate distinct lessons in reading, language, and mathematics, with particular emphasis on language remediation. The Behavior Analysis program focuses on academic, as well as social skills.

Method

Behavioral programs are all characterized by similar methods of instruction. Learning is broken up into small discrete steps and is carefully sequenced. Heavy use is made of associative learning, with discrimination and categorization learned as a result of association. Each child is moved along a linear continuum at a rate that will insure success.

All behaviorist programs use some form of reenforcement. The reenforcement used, however, might change as the children continue in the program. At first tangible reenforcers such as raisins or M&M's might be used. Later in the program a token system might be implemented whereby the child is given a poker chip or other token as a reward. Although the chip in itself is not valuable, it may be traded for a valued reenforcer. The number of tokens needed for the reenforcer becomes the basis for the classroom economy. Often the reward used in a program is social reenforcement, including praise, or the showing of affection. In some programs the ability of the children to participate in valued activities may be made contingent upon performance in less valued activities. For example, children may be allowed to play or to use arts and crafts materials only upon successful completion of a task aimed at teaching academic skills.

Style

A general style of teaching is prescribed by this approach, although variations in style might be found. The teacher must be knowledgeable about the goals of the program and the steps along the way towards their achievement. She must be aware of the behaviors that children manifest at each level so that appropriate activities can be prescribed. She must be able to control and structure the environment so that each child is reached at his own level and achieves a high rate of success.

The teacher must also be sensitive to the actions of the child at all times and be ready to reward him for the proper behavior, but be able to ignore improper behavior so that it is not rewarded. Most of all the teacher must maintain a high degree of consistency in maintaining contingency schedules. All of this, by the way, can and should be done in a climate of support and warmth.

Organization

As with curriculum, each program has its own forms of organization. In general, however, certain threads can be found joining each program. The activities of the children are under the control of the teacher at all instructional times. Activities are sequenced and children must stay within the prescribed sequence. Often there is a high ratio of teachers and other adults to children to allow the staff to observe children closely enough to provide them with rewards at appropriate times.

Lessons must be organized on an individual basis or on a small group basis in the various programs. In addition use is often made of programmed materials as the children become capable of using them. The teacher uses programmed material as an extension of herself, freeing her for other activities. The child begins to manage his own contingencies with these materials, and the motivation for instruction may be in the recognition of competency inherent in the materials themselves rather than in the use of external motivational devices.

OPEN EDUCATION

The programs labeled here as "open education" include those of the English infant school, as well as the programs presented by Educational Development Center in Boston, Lillian Weber's programs in the New York City schools, and the Open Education Project at the University of Illinois.[4] Many other educators are also involved in developing and disseminating educational programs in an open education framework, along with untold numbers of individual teachers working alone in their classrooms. Many of the statements used here are abstracted from a study of the characteristics of open education developed by Walberg and Thomas.[5] The advantage of

---

[4] See Lillian Weber, *The English Infant School and Informal Education* (Englewood Cliffs, N.J.: Prentice-Hall, Inc., 1971); Eleanor E. Maccoby and Miriam Zellner, *Experiments in Primary Education: Aspects of Project Follow Through* (New York: Harcourt, Brace, Jovanovich, 1970); Joan Thachary, Juanita Chaudkry, and Dorothea Grive, *Open Door: New York City* (New York: Center for Urban Education, 1971); Minnie P. Berson, "Inside the Open Classroom," *American Education*, 7, No. 4 (May 1971), 11–15.

[5] Herbert J. Walberg and Susan C. Thomas, *Characteristics of Open Education: Toward an Operational Definition,* mimeographed (Newton, Massachusetts: TDR Associates, 1971).

this resource as the basis for this discussion is the agreement Walberg and Thomas have obtained from practitioners and experts in their method of validating statements regarding open education.

Assumptions

Open educators view the school as a place to help children learn how to learn, to extend their intellectual and emotional resources, and learn to use these resources in making decisions, organizing experiences, and utilizing knowledge. Schooling at all levels should be justifiable as an experience in its own right, not simply as preparation for later tasks.

The child is perceived in open education as having the right to make important decisions regarding his own educational experience. He is capable of making intelligent decisions about significant areas of learning, given a degree of adult support. The child's interests and curiosity provide the basis for learning in school.

Knowledge is viewed as a personal synthesis of one's own experience. Different children may create different kinds of knowledge as the result of the same school experience. Similarly goals may be arrived at in different ways by different children who learn in their own style and at their own rate. Because of the idiosyncratic approaches to learning that children have, short-term evaluation of learning is often misleading. More legitimate evaluation of development can be made over longer periods of time.

Education should take place in an environment that communicates trust, openness, and mutual relationships among children and adults. Such an accepting and warm environment supports learning. Each child in school has the right to be treated with kindness, courtesy, and respect.

Goals

The goals of an open education program include the development of literacy skills, the dissemination of knowledge, and concept acquisition. Affective learning and the development of physical skills and modes of expression are equally important. Perhaps the goals of open education can best be defined as the support of the total development of the child.

Curriculum

The curriculum of the open education program has within it many of the elements that are found in traditional early childhood programs. Play is given a special place and no distinction is made between "work" and "play" in the program. The content of the program is organized in some integrated fashion, and topics or projects might be used as integrating vehicles. Exactly what will be studied and how it will be studied is determined jointly by teacher and children. There is no concern to cover any specific amount of content, nor is every child necessarily involved in the same curriculum or expected to achieve the same goals to the same degree. This is because individualization of instruction in an open classroom includes dimensions other than pace.

Method

No one method of instruction is used in an open education approach. Rather, the teacher will suggest a range of methods based upon her knowledge of the children's abilities and interests. In general, an active mode of learning characterizes these classes and there is a high degree of support for what might be considered "discovery learning" rather than "telling," although lectures might be given on occasion. The children will be involved in inductive forms of learning during much of the time.

Even within a single curriculum area or project, different instructional methods might be used at various points in the study. Hawkins describes, for example, three phases of science study. The first he characterizes as "messing about," the free exploration by the children of materials available, allowing them to make their own discoveries in an unstructured environment. The second phase is one in which the child's study is externally guided, though still highly individualized. This is accomplished through the use of "multiply programmed" materials that are designed for the greatest variety and ordering of topics. There will be material available to help the child in almost any way that he can evolve on his own. In the third phase, the child moves from concrete perception to abstract conceptualization. Theory is built upon the child's experience and experimentation.[6]

Style

Many of the elements that set open education apart relate to teacher style. While no one particular approach to teaching is prescribed, there are certain characteristics about the teacher that are central to this approach to education. First the teacher herself is viewed as an active learner and experimenter with educational method and materials. She is knowledgeable enough about goals and different methods of achieving these goals that she can operate without a prescribed curriculum. She sees herself as a source of knowledge along with other sources in the classroom. She acts as a guide for the children's learning, never abrogating her responsibility for it, but allowing the children to assume responsibility for it as well. She demonstrates her trust of the children and her concern for them. She will allow her feelings, as well as the feelings of the children to be voiced in the classroom. She respects the children with whom she works, values their abilities and their products, and continually strives to create an air of warmth and support in the classroom.

The teacher evaluates the work of the children, setting standards based upon the individual child's abilities rather than on grade level norms. She develops activities that will appeal to the children with whom she works based upon her diagnosis of their needs. She will keep records of the children's work, often through both direct

---

[6] David Hawkins, "Messing About in Science," *Science and Children*, 2, No. 5 (February 1965), 5–9.

observation and recording of activities, and the collection of pupil product.

Organization

In order to support the activity orientation of the program and the involvement of the children in the decision-making process, the open education classroom is organized in a somewhat loose fashion. Often, rather than having discrete periods devoted to different subjects or activities, large blocks of time are provided in which many different activities will be going on simultaneously. Children will be able to select activities. They will also be able to determine how long they wish to be involved in an activity, whether to initiate new activities and when to terminate activities. Children may also be allowed to move in and out of the room at will and use the area of the school for learning activities, including corridors and outdoor play areas.

Because many activities will be going on simultaneously, the room may be divided into interest centers. Materials and equipment will be deployed to support activities in particular areas of the room and will be set up so that there will be a minimum of interference among activities and among children. Although individual desks and chairs may be eliminated, children will be provided with space to keep their things.

Books, materials, and equipment will be readily accessible to the children. They will not have to ask the teacher to provide them with materials nor ask permission to use those available. Materials in the class will include a wide range of books, as well as structured and unstructured manipulative materials to support the diverse range of activities. Along with commercial material, teacher-made and child-made materials will be part of the environment. Although teachers might demonstrate their uses, children will be free to use materials in many ways, including ways that the teacher might not have foreseen.

The organization of the room and the materials available will be determined by the needs of the activities. As activities change, room arrangements and organizational patterns may also change. Furniture will be moved, new material added and material that had been previously used by the children may be taken out of the environment.

Groups of children are generally heterogeneous in ability and, possibly, in background, as well as in age. The class is seen as a social group. Interactions among children are supported, as is collaboration on learning tasks. Much of the activity takes place on an individual or a small group basis, although the teacher may call the children together as a total class for particular purposes. Grouping may be voluntary in nature, but the teacher may group children for particular learning activities. Generally these groupings are temporary in nature.

ANALYZING PROGRAMS

Although our framework has necessarily helped us focus on the differences in these programs, there are certain similarities that should be mentioned. Both programs require an active mode of learning from the children, though the actions are different in each. Both also require the teacher to help the child begin at whatever stage of learning he has reached, rather than set arbitrary starting points based upon age or grade level. There is also a high degree of overlap in the content of the two programs.

Most of the programs in early childhood education that are represented in the selections to be found in Part II of this book, can be ranged in psychological theory on a continuum from the ideal behaviorist approach to the ideal phenomenological approach. Other considerations besides psychological theory, of course, have led to the particular way that each model has been developed.

The first four selections in the second part of this book should help to further clarify issues underlying programs for young children. These are: "What Are the Sources of Early Childhood Curriculum?," "The Open School: Curriculum Concepts," "Preschool Education: Enrichment or Instruction," and "Implicit Assumptions

Underlying Preschool Intervention Programs." The next two selections, "Britain's First Nursery-Infant Class," and "Are Kindergartens Obsolete?" present historical models. The final eight selections describe current educational alternatives. Included in this is "Reaching the Young Child Through Parent Education," which describes a program of education that takes place outside the school.

PART II

5

WHAT ARE THE SOURCES OF EARLY CHILDHOOD CURRICULUM?

BERNARD SPODEK

During the past half dozen years a large number of innovative programs have been proposed for the education of young children. Each purports to provide the *right* kind of educational experience for young children. Each supports its contention that the experiences provided within it are best for young children. While many of the programs were originally designed for special subpopulations of children, such as the "disadvantaged," the proponents of at least some of these programs have generalized the appropriateness of

Young Children, October 1970. Reprinted with permission. Copyright © 1970, National Association for the Education of Young Children.

their curriculum to all young children. While some programs described as "new" are primarily modifications of existing practice, the difference between a number of innovative programs and traditional nursery-kindergarten practice is great. Even greater than the difference in practice has been the difference in the sources of these curricula.

CHILDREN AS A SOURCE OF THE CURRICULUM

How does one derive a curriculum? Let me define curriculum as the organized experiences provided for children in a school setting. One of the earliest identified sources of an early childhood curriculum was children themselves. If you read the works of Friedrich Froebel or Maria Montessori, you will quickly note that both of these pioneers of early childhood education used their observations of children as the main source of their curriculum.

The kindergarten of Friedrich Froebel consisted of the ordered use of manipulative activities, or *occupations,* and the use of songs and finger plays, *his mother's plays and songs.* Froebel conceived of these activities as revealed to him by the children themselves (Froebel, 1967). Similarly, Dr. Montessori developed her educational approach by observing the uses children made of didactic materials provided, abstracting the essential elements for learning and ordering them into her famous *Montessori Method.* The observations of children were for Dr. Montessori the essence of scientific pedagogy (Montessori, 1964). Froebel's analysis of child behavior was more mystical than scientific.

Many supporters of traditional nursery school practice as well as modern English infant school educators support their curriculum by recourse to children's natural activities. Practitioners in both of these educational institutions may respond to questions about what they do with children by referring to the "natural" activity of children. Often when I asked the English infant school teachers I visited last year how they determine what to do with the children, I was told that they (the teachers) were simply following the leads of the children. (The slogan "I teach children, not subjects," a slogan reminiscent of the days of the Progressive school in the United States, uses the same recourse to natural childhood as a source of curriculum.)

The use of "natural" childhood as the source of curriculum smacks of romanticism. Such educational arguments can be traced as far back as Rousseau. The ideal of the unsocialized savage whose best instincts are destroyed by the surrounding culture is echoed as much in Goodman's *Compulsory Mis-education* as in *Emile*. Educators who use such arguments take comfort in the feeling that they are not violating the child in any way but are rather "doing what comes naturally."

Unfortunately the arguments using natural childhood as a source of the curriculum do not hold up well. There is nothing natural about any school, even a preschool. Nursery classes and kindergartens cannot be directly derived from the natural activity of children. The very nature of the educational process requires that if it is effective, the child ought to be different as a result of his experiences within it. The child should exit from the program in a less natural state than the one in which he entered. All schools, as a matter of fact, are cultural contrivances to *do* things *to* children; to change them.

Looking more closely at the curricula contrived from the natural observations of children, one becomes aware of the selectivity of the observations and the uses to which these observations have been put. When one observes an object, one must define certain attributes of the object as critical. This definition provides a focus for the observation and the descriptions that follow. Other attributes besides those observed may exist, but they are overlooked because they are considered uncritical. The purpose for which one is observing determines what one is looking at and what one will see. Thus, a young lady preparing for a date may consider the color and cut of a dress in her observations of that dress. The mother of the same young lady may observe the fabric and stitching with which the dress has been assembled. Ralph Nader might be more concerned with the flammability of the garment as well as its price, while a sociologist might be more concerned with the effects of the garment on the wearer and on outside observers. Who has seen the real garment?

In analyzing the arguments about the natural activity of childhood as a source of the curriculum, one becomes similarly aware that the purposes of the observer or educational theorist often determines what is seen and the products of such observations are far from natural.

For few contemporary educators can fail to see the contrived nature of either the Froebelian kindergarten or the Montessori school. If one were to understand the curriculum determined by a Montessori, a Froebel or by other educational developers, one must go beyond simple natural observation and identify the basis for selecting the observations and the conceptual framework used to give meaning to these observations in developing educational experiences for children.

DEVELOPMENTAL THEORY AS A SOURCE
OF THE CURRICULUM

A second curriculum source that has been used by early childhood educators has been child development theory. Generally two types of theory have been used. One has been Gesellian theory. This type of theory considers child development as primarily maturational. Children are studied to identify the process of the unfolding of childhood. As a result of Gesellian theory, children have been grouped by age in nursery-kindergarten classes and have been provided with experiences that are considered appropriate for their age level.

Arguments derived from Gesellian theory have been used to exclude inappropriate activities from the school life of children as well as to insure that appropriate experiences are provided. The argument that we must "protect the right of the child to be five" has often been heard when the suggestion has been made to include reading instruction in the kindergarten program. However, the nature of fiveness is difficult to determine for age norms do not adequately describe the range of heights, weights, skills, abilities or any other attributes of children at any age. Nor would these attributes remain constant at all times for all persons, in all cultures, if they could be identified. Average heights and weights of children have risen in the last 50 years and will vary from one geographic area to another, not necessarily the result of natural differences, but rather the result of environmental differences. Other attributes of childhood will also vary as a result of environment, cultural as well as physical. What a child is at any level of development is to some extent a result of what a culture says he ought to be.

More recently the recourse to child development theory has used the work of Piaget as a source of the curriculum.[1] Gesell is no longer as fashionable. A number of recent projects have aimed at enhancing intellectual development as the basis for creating specific curriculum for "disadvantaged" children. Lavatelli reports on a project she directed that aimed at developing a number of intellectual schema in children. These included one-to-one correspondence, classification, and seriation. Additional activities involved children in conservation of quantities (Lavatelli, 1968). Feigenbaum has also described activities that nursery school teachers can use to teach conservation (Feigenbaum, 1969). A Piaget-based curriculum that was developed in Ypsilanti, Mich., has been described by Sonquist and Kamii. Using a Piagetian scheme of analysis, activities are designed to move children through levels of representation from the index level, to the symbol level, to the sign level (Sonquist & Kamii, 1967).

Is child development theory, Piagetian or otherwise, a legitimate source of the educational curriculum of young children? The "child development point of view" has been a popular point of view

---

[1] While Piaget is primarily a developmental epistemologist, the theories of Piaget have been used as theories of developmental psychology by many American psychologists and educators.

in early childhood education for many years. However, I seriously question the appropriateness of child development theory as a source of the curriculum.

Child development is a descriptive science. At its best it can tell us what is. Education by its very nature deals not with what is, but with what ought to be. Choices and preferences are involved in creating educational experiences that cannot be rationalized by recourse to child development theory. If anything, child development theory can provide us with useful information, often of a negative kind about what we cannot do to children at a particular point in their development if we want them to learn, or information about readiness stages for learning.

LEARNING THEORY
AS A SOURCE OF THE CURRICULUM

Child development theory is only one form of psychological theory that has been identified by program developers as a source of curriculum; learning theories and theories of intelligence have also been used. Developmental theory deals with change in the human being over long periods of time. Learning theory attempts to account for short-term change. The recourse to learning theory as a source of curriculum of early childhood has been manifest in several different ways. One way is through the admonition to develop behavioral objectives. Actually there is nothing psychological about the use of behaviorial objectives, nor are objectives more profound because they are stated in behavioral terms. The translation of goals of the curriculum into behavioral objectives, however, allows for an easy and often misleading evaluation of achievement.

Psychological processes are not directly observable; they must be inferred. Behaviors are observable. Psychologists often forget that the meanings of these behaviors must still be inferred. A psychologist may identify as a legitimate goal of nursery or kindergarten education the ability to attend to auditory signals. This might be translated into the following criteria behavior: "The ability to sit still for

10 minutes and listen to a story as part of a group." Whether or not a child is actually gaining meaning from the auditory environment is not directly observable. The relationship between sitting still and listening (which is certainly not a 1:1 relationship) has led the psychologist to list as his goal a behavior which might better represent *conformity* than *attention*.

Psychological theory focusing on behavior and behavior modification has determined the structure of a number of curricula in early childhood education. While short-term change is easily observed and evaluated, there are seldom any attempts to study long-term effects of these curricula. In the final analysis such programs may be based as much on ultimate faith as are any of the more traditional programs. The description of a program in psychological terminology and the great emphasis on the evaluation of effectiveness without analyzing ultimate goals may, in the long run, obscure the ultimate consequences of these programs.

TEST ITEMS
AS A SOURCE OF THE CURRICULUM

One other facet of psychology that is often used as the source of the curriculum is psychological testing. This is more practice than theory. Many of the programs in early childhood education are justified as a way of increasing intelligence. One way of judging the intelligence of children is through the administration and scoring of an intelligence test. Such a test consists of items which purport to sample a broad range of intellectual behaviors in children. Each item achieves its validity from the fact that it represents many other kinds of behaviors that might have been elicited from the total population of intelligent behaviors.

Since programs can demonstrate their effectiveness by having the children enrolled in them achieve higher scores on intelligence tests, it is easy for tasks taken from intelligence tests or for related tasks to become the content of the program. Justification for this approach to curriculum development often takes the form of an argument that suggests that since these items are selected as samples of intelligent behavior, having children practice these behaviors is the same as having children practice behaving in an intelligent manner. Such logic is devastating. Rote learning of responses to particular stimuli cannot be called intelligent behavior. Such distortions of psychological testing and curriculum development are not limited to the area of intelligence testing. They may take place in the realm of language development or in any other area where samples of behavior are mistaken for the total population of behaviors they represent.

SCHOOL CONTENT
AS A SOURCE OF THE CURRICULUM

While the area of psychological theory represents one area used in justifying curriculum proposals, it is by no means the only source of justification used. Another source used popularly is the content of later schooling. "Reading readiness" is important because it prepares children for reading instruction. The readiness skills have no importance by themselves. Often certain kinds of organization are considered good for children because it prepares them for later school expectations. The pressures of later life and of later schooling is heaped upon the child in anticipation of what is to come.

A caricature of such a justification is to be found in the Bereiter-Engelmann Program. The content of the program (reading, language and mathematics) is important because it is required of children in primary grades. The organization also prepares the child for behaving appropriately for his school life ahead. The legitimacy of such a justification is questionable. Whether such preparation will offer a better chance to children later on is often unfounded.

One of the few long-range studies of the effects of education, the *Eight-Year Study of Progressive High Schools,* showed that children in open school situations did better than those from more restrictive school environments when they went to college. While extrapolation to a younger age level may not be appropriate, the study certainly raises questions about the desirability of providing children with rigid early schooling as preparation for rigid later schooling.

Unfortunately, such recourse to later learning also obscures the concern for the sources of curriculum. For later school learning is not a goal in and of itself but is again a means to a goal. Using such a justification only pushes decisions about curriculum content back further. As it is, too little concern is given to the proper sources of the curriculum.

WHAT IS THE PROPER SOURCE OF A CURRICULUM

If neither psychological theory, testing procedures, the content of later schooling nor children themselves can be considered an appropriate source of curriculum what is left? I would like to suggest that the proper source of a curriculum in early childhood is the set of goals which are the aims of education for children. This in essence is a value statement about what children ought to be.

From these goals curriculum experiences can be derived and using these goals the effectiveness of a curriculum can be judged. The areas of knowledge and human endeavor described earlier must be used as *resources* in the curriculum rather than as *sources*.

Dearden has suggested that the goal of education is "personal autonomy based upon reason." He describes this autonomy as follows:

There are two aspects to such an autonomy, the first of which is negative. This is independence of authorities, both of those who would dictate or prescribe what I am to believe and of those who would arbitrarily direct me in what I am to do. The complementary positive aspect is, first, that of testing the truth of things for myself, whether by experience or by a critical estimate of the testimony of others, and secondly, that of deliberating, forming intentions and choosing what I shall do according to a scale of values which I can myself appreciate. Both understanding and choice, or thought and action, are therefore to be independent of authority and based instead on reason. This is the ideal (Dearden, 1968).

The concept of autonomy is not alien for early childhood education. Erikson's framework for human development includes the stage of autonomy early in the scale, just after the development of *trust* (Erikson, 1950). The child's autonomy in these early years may not, however, be based upon reason. As the child's intelligence continues to develop the basis for personal autonomy becomes more rational.

If we accept the goal of "personal autonomy based upon reason" as legitimate for early childhood education then of what use is psychological theory to the educator? For one thing, psychological theory helps us determine ways of testing the effectiveness of a program in achieving the ideal. Secondly, knowledge of developmental processes can help us to order the activities we provide to children in terms of what can be of use to a child at a particular level of development and what activities might precede or follow others. Developmental theory becomes a tool for the analysis of curriculum, rather than a source of the curriculum, and the content of school programs must be recognized as products of the imagination of educators to be tested by psychological means, rather than as natural consequences of children's behavior, adult's thinking, or institutional organization.

REFERENCES

DEARDEN, R. F. *The Philosophy of Primary Education.* London: Routledge & Kegan Paul, 1968, p. 46

ERIKSON, ERIK H. *Childhood and Society.* New York: W. W. Norton & Co., Inc., 1950.

FEIGENBAUM, KENNETH. Activities to teach the concept of conservation. *Young Children,* 24, 3, 1969, pp. 151–153.

FROEBEL, FRIEDRICH. The young child. In Irene M. Lilley (ed.), *Friedrich Froebel: A Selection from his Writings.* Cambridge: Cambridge University Press, 1967, pp. 68–119.

LAVATELLI, CELIA S. A Piaget derived model for compensatory preschool education. In Joe L. Frost (ed.), *Early Childhood Education Rediscovered*. New York: Holt, Rinehart & Winston, 1968, pp. 530–544.

MONTESSORI, MARIA. *The Montessori Method*. Cambridge: Robert Bently, Inc., 1964, pp. 47–88.

SONQUIST, HANNE D. and KAMII, CONSTANCE K. Applying some Piagetian concepts in the classroom for the disadvantaged. *Young Children,* 22, 4, 1967, pp. 231–240.

6

THE OPEN SCHOOL:
Curriculum Concepts

JAMES MACDONALD

The concept of openness is presently one of the major organizing ideas in a number of disciplines. Biologists have been talking about open and closed systems for a number of years. Most biologists conceive of the human organism as an "open" system with energy input and behavioral output.

But the idea of openness is also useful at the personality level. Rokeach and others have talked a great deal about open and closed

Reprinted with permission from *Open Education: The Legacy of the Progressive Movement*. Copyright © 1970, National Association for the Education of Young Children, 1834 Connecticut Ave., N.W., Washington, D.C., 20009.

people. Maslow and his study of self-actualizing people is dealing with an open concept.

The concept of openness is also useful in looking at inter-personal relations. Carl Rogers has been especially concerned about this as noted in his book *Freedom to Learn*. As a matter of fact, Esther Zaret and I did "A Study of Openness in Classroom Inter-actions" (mimeograph, Zaret, Marquette University, Milwaukee, Wisc.) which turned out to be a useful way of looking at classrooms.

Organizational structures can also be seen in terms of opening and closing potentialities of communication systems, status and role relationships.

So the open school concept is in good company when we are talking about human beings, whether at the biological, personal, interpersonal or institutional levels.

The open school is a concept which is easily related to Pro-gressive Education. It may not have originated there, since Come-nius, Rousseau, Pestalozzi, Froebel and others preceded the formal American Progressive Education era; but it was given a special meaning by John Dewey and others.

Progressive Education, then or now, was and is a fundamen-tally ethical movement. As John Childs said, "Those educators who have combined the psychological principles of child growth with the moral principles of democracy and have developed the concep-tion that the supreme aim of education should be the nurture of an individual who can take responsibility for his own continued growth have made an ethical contribution of lasting worth" (Childs, 1950, p. 15).

The crucial philosophical concept embodied in Progressive Education and subsequently in the idea of an open school is the concept of transaction. An open school is a school organized to facilitate transactions. A closed school, in contrast, is developed to play roles.

The concept of an open school as the bridge for then and now, is essentially a moral statement. That is to say, it is unlikely that one would arrive at this concept without overriding ethical concerns as one attempts to construct social situations and technical conditions.

Moral concerns are grounded in a form of personalism. In what came to be a Progressive Education "cliché," the open school has no rationale for existence unless one sees another as a whole person (or a whole child). If there is no article of faith in the worth, dignity, integrity and uniqueness of each person there is no need for open schools.

In this sense, even the concern for the individual can be misleading. Our child development heritage is connected with the general growth of behavioralistic psychology in many ways. When people speak of the individual and his differences, they have often violated the concept of "the one," "the unity," and segmented him. By psychological concepts and tools we have become adept at objectifying the inner substance of individuals and selecting out traits or characteristics to utilize for the manipulation of the person.

One does not need an open school if one can describe the inner qualities of individuals, can relate these qualities to specifiable tasks, and can manipulate individuals through these tasks efficiently and effectively. In fact, were we able to do this, we would have a completely individualized and prescribed curriculum. What would look "open" on the surface would be completely closed for the individual.

Thus, the open school not only must be committed to whole persons, but must be functionally open in the perceptions and actions of participants, not simply in the eyes of an observer.

The entry point for the concept of a transaction lies in the experiences youngsters are having in the school. An experience is a transaction in time and space. It is a name for the various elements which result in an action which integrates past and future, and the inner subjective space of the person with outer objective cultural space.

Role-oriented programs, in contrast, are focused upon objectives. Objectives are not the same as purposes, at least not in the meanings of the progressive educator. Purposes arise out of the transaction of the subjective and objective conditions of experience. Objectives, in contrast, are projected into situations and used as bases for shaping the roles of individuals in relation to things, ideas and other people.

A purpose which arises out of a transaction could come to resemble what may be called an objective, though not necessarily so. An objective is exactly what it says. It stands out from the subject and has no necessary relationship to any subject in a specific situation. Purposes arise *from* the subject whom, it is implied, intentionally seeks some end. Purposes by this definition cannot arise outside the situation, whereas objectives may be predetermined and used to shape situations prior to the transaction.

Open schools are transaction-oriented to the extent that programs and curricula are flexible enough to allow for personal responses to the reality of the ongoing experiences. Closed schools are role-oriented to the degree that experiences are monitored by plans, ideas, rules, etc., that are projected into the situation but do not arise out of the situation.

It should be made clear that the concept of an open school is in no way related to an unplanned curriculum. To my knowledge, no progressive educator—past or present—has ever been naive, or perhaps better, stupid enough, to suggest that schooling places each individual in a vacuum. The very concept of transaction means action arising through the relationship of inner subjective qualities of persons with outer cultural realities within some social context that has a past history and a future orientation.

The curriculum, as Dewey once remarked, is a contrived environment. It is an environment that should be the result of a plan that emerges from the consideration of the selection and organization of subject matter, methodology, discipline, material, facilities and the social organization of the school; all of these factors to be seen in relation to both the inner subjective and outer objective potentialities of situations.

Planning in the open school is planning in light of the potentialities of the children and the environment. It is the structuring of a living situation with a wide range of educative alternatives. The transactions that take place within this structure cannot be planned in the same manner. They are more in the nature of "planned accidents" and have somewhat of the quality of a "happening" to them.

CURRICULUM CONCEPTS

Let us examine in more detail some of the curriculum concepts that are fundamental to an open school. The concept of an open school as a moral stance existed prior to the American Progressive Education period, and it has continued on with the demise of the leaders of progressivism. Progressive Education might best be thought of as the most extensively developed historical position which is relevant to open schooling. There are, however, advocates of open schools who disagree with some of the fundamental tenets of the progressives, and specifically with the philosophy of Dewey.

I shall try to focus primarily on the question of subject matter in the curriculum at this point, and taking a cue from Joseph Schwab (1964), I shall use the analytical concepts of structure, syntax and organization of subject matter as stepping off points.

What this means is that I shall focus upon:

The manner in which we classify and group subject matters in relation to each other (organization).

The sequence of encountering an isolatable aspect of subject matter (structure).

The modes of inquiry or rules of discovery (syntax).

This decision is directly in line with Dewey's warning (1938) that "It is a ground for legitimate criticism, however, when the ongoing movement of progressive education fails to recognize that the problem of selection and organization of subject-matter for study and learning is fundamental."

Organization

The problem of organization is in many ways a question of how are we to "package" the environment. This is not as commercial or crass as it sounds at first hearing because as was noted earlier, the environment will be there anyway and the real question is, in what manner will social conditions and agents intervene to shape this environment.

The traditional approach has been to begin with an analysis of the knowledge and skills necessary for persons to function adequately, then break these down into manageable time units and adjust the specifics to the general capabilities of youngsters at various age levels in our culture. The subject matter is pre-formed in terms of adult-organized bodies of knowledge, and skills are seen as necessities for learning within these disciplines. It is precisely this which structures a closed school, and it was precisely this which progressive educators fought against.

As Kilpatrick (1936) said, "The new curriculum must put first things first. The child must for us come before subject matter as such. This is everlasting and final condemnation of the old curriculum." Subject matter would be learned as it was useful for children as they engaged in the concrete experiences of social living in the classrooms.

This led Kilpatrick and others to the development of such concepts as projects and units, the concepts of interdisciplinary studies and interest centers as bases for organizing subject matter in a meaningful manner.

The extreme position, never proposed by Dewey or other major progressive educators, but still prevalent in the statements of some advocates of "open schooling" is the concept of an incidental curriculum. A. S. Neill's "Summerhill" and the Green Valley School in Orangeville, Fla., reflect this view. The primary goal in both of these cases is a healthy psychological and social climate, and only incidentally an intellectual education.

Most advocates of the incidental curriculum do not bother to change its traditional subject matter structure. The subject matter is simply there in its traditional form with teachers and children interacting with little or no compulsion.

Structure

The structure, or sequence which flows from the structure, presents a dramatic contrast between traditional and progressive curricula. For the progressive educator, the structure of a discipline is an end point of educational experience. For the traditionalist, it is the beginning point.

Thus, Bruner's (1960) statement to the effect that anything worth teaching can be taught in some intellectually honest way at any level implies that the structure of what is taught is pre-formed by adults and unknowable by children. However, Dewey might well argue that beginning with concrete experiences which arise out of social living is indeed an intellectually honest way of beginning with young children.

A classic discussion of sequence by Leonard (1950, pp. 70–79) identified five bases for deciding the sequencing of school experiences. They were (1) chronological order, (2) logical order, (3) order of difficulty, (4) geographical expansion and (5) unfolding of the child. Three of these sequence rationales call for subject matter priority or the definition of educational objectives without any special concern for an individual child. Thus, chronological order in time (or its reverse, from present to past) is used in history; logical order of primacy is often used in science and mathematics; and difficulty (from simple to complex) is often used in language activities such as reading, spelling, vocabulary and arithmetic.

The open school and/or progressive school would reject these bases for sequencing experiences. Rather, they might opt for the child's expanding social world as a source of sequence. Thus, very young children would deal with home and school, slightly older ones expand into the community, and so forth.

However, it is impossible to see how any advocate of open schooling would deny the primacy (whether in the context of expanding social experiences or not) of the individual's development as the source of determining the sequence for acquiring knowledge and skill in terms of his maturing personality.

Syntax

There is perhaps one aspect of curriculum where modern traditional practices and Progressive Education begin to blur somewhat into a common commitment. This relates to the syntax of the disciplines, or their emphasis upon inquiry.

Dewey, Kilpatrick and others believed that problem solving was the basis of intellectual activity in relation to subject matter. Dewey's reflective thinking in *How We Think* is essentially a general model for "scientific" methodology. Scientific methodology in this context held its older 19th century meaning of systematic thinking about phenomena, rather than a highly specific set of principles unique to only the experimental sciences.

Problem solving, as a process, was the activity that integrated the child and subject matter. Today, the modes of enquiry tend to be much more specific processes or rules for relating to the subject matter under concern. Still, enquiry begins with a problem, a discrepancy or a curiosity that is pursued in order to solve the problem, integrate the discrepancy into a new perspective or satisfy one's curiosity. For the progressive educator, "modes of enquiry" are a step in the right direction provided they do not become pre-set goals which have to be learned in skill-like fashion prior to engaging in inquiry.

A third position (and perhaps still others) is available on this matter. Some of the many English schools I visited reflected this third orientation. It might be called "fooling around" or "mucking about." The emphasis here is upon freely experiencing the subject matter in a playful, self-expressive way. It reflects what George von Hilscheimer (1966) meant when he said: "Progressives as a whole cannot stand idly by and watch a child dally in a puddle of water. It must be turned into a learning experience, which is to say, the teacher must interpose her abstract structures between the child and the reality he is experiencing and learning."

There is some merit in talking about this third position in terms of personalized instruction. This term, which has occurred in our literature from time to time, is often confused with individualized instruction.

Dewey, I have come to think, was essentially a proponent of individualized instruction. In some ways he "wanted to have his cake and eat it too," for he wanted people to arrive at a closed culture through an open process. It is not at all clear that one can do this.

*   *   ■

Be that as it may, the interesting question is whether the open process, so ably described as crucial to developing intellectual capacities, will in any way interfere with the learning processes so central to mastering specific subject matter. Dewey thought not, I personally suspect that you have to give something to get something in this case, and that personalized instruction means setting your priorities with the whole person, rather than individual traits he may possess.

AN ILLUSTRATION OF A NONPROGRESSIVE SCHOOL

It would seem appropriate at this point to present one variation of an open school in some detail. For this purpose, I have selected a fairly full description by von Hilscheimer of the Green Valley Elementary School in Orangeville, Fla. The Green Valley school is run on a "commonwealth" principle, and includes children of all ages. Here is what von Hilscheimer (op. cit.) says about what he calls an open but nonprogressive elementary program.

> There is somewhat more structure in our elementary education. The elementary classroom always has at least two teachers, often as many as 10. The number of students is always under 30. The room is large and has an easily accessible half-second-story for reading and solitary, quiet study or sloth. The main room is organized with messy corners, book corners and display corners, and it leads into a small shed with a shop and very messy things. The two core teachers establish themselves as active and emotional "poles" in the room.

Without directing the children to either teacher, each teacher moves into his own activity as the day begins. One is active, outgoing, paying loud attention to painting, clay modeling, building and rambling outside. The other is quieter and more passive—the reader, the writer and composer of songs and other scholastic activities. It is important that these divisions are not made in a merely mechanistic fashion and that either teacher may perform any task in the school room. Every effort is made to associate books, schooling, reading with relaxed purposiveness.

The children move freely between the teachers or take up their own activity. Reading, writing on paper or on the board, drawing, painting, making things, or simply crooning to the floor go on all the time. Some children seldom, if ever, cross from one teacher pole to the other; most oscillate without self-consciousness or concern. All elementary and kindergarten ages are present.

Reading periods are about the same time each morning. They are sometimes skipped entirely as the teacher senses the tone of the children—or they tell her, "None of that stuff today." Sometimes reading classes consume all day. The smallest children are asked what words they would like. They are printed on a card and given to them, or they are written on the board and the teacher builds a sentence suggested by others, sometimes grammatically and developmentally, sometimes working the sentence out from the middle or ungrammatically. This kind of linguistic analysis goes on from the earliest classes.

Writing is developed in much the same way. Children write what interests them, and they read the writing with others. Tape recordings or transcripts of their own little stories or nonsense or refusals are made, typed or mimeographed, and reading proceeds apace. There is no "Up, up, up, John" at Green Valley. Illustrations of words made by the children, collages of words and illustrations, "dada" stories made up by pasting word cards and other techniques well known to all good teachers are part of our regular armament.

Rather than bringing bits and pieces of the world into the classroom, we make every effort to take children out into the world. Children are not interested in seedlings in eggshells when they have eggs in eggshells and seedlings in the ground. Nature corners are redundant when an important part of the day is given to rambles with teacher to point, question, prod and leave alone. The city, no less than the countryside, is a vital classroom and this does not mean guided museum tours. Quite young children can see the dramatic change of neighborhood lines, the abrupt economic change at a state line, the significant flow of foot traffic, the flow of vehicular traffic seen from the street and a high building, the difference in taste of commercial bread and home-baked bread or salad dressings. They can ask and answer penetrating questions about reasons for such phenomena.

And above all, we try never to forget that for adolescents and elementary school children alike the role of the teacher is to point, prod, to prick, to question and always, to draw back from and to look and learn from what the children are seeing and asking. A cultured teacher, living in a community of cultured persons, cannot avoid communicating that culture to children when she is actively involved with the children. The only textbooks she needs are the ones which she uses herself.

Whether this is Progressive Education or not is, at this point, superfluous. We live in the present and are recipients of a noble heritage to which Progressive Education is one of the main sources of inspiration. What the curriculum is can be summed up nicely by von Hilscheimer's (op. cit.) comment: "Essentially, once a child has learned to read and to compose and to put some distance between criticism of his effort and his personality needs, there is little a teacher can do except to enjoy the growth and cultivation of another unique and precious individual."

The Counter Culture in Education

The trend in theory and philosophy of education relevant to open schools is moving beyond the progressive era. The locus of morality is shifting from the social conditions of living to concern for the person. A counter culture, as in Theodore Roszak's *The Making of a Counter Culture,* is stirring mixed with elements of Zen Buddhism, Western Existentialism and personal experiencing.

In some ways, Dewey now sounds as old-fashioned as Marx, for the counter culture is an attempt to renew the aesthetic wellsprings of humanity. It is a rejection of the rational and cognitive as the dominant mode of relating to the world.

Dewey, in the end, was an empiricist and the "new" man is a phenomenologist. Both accept the inner and outer reality, but progressive educators essentially looked *in from the outside,* while the "new" man looks *out from the inside.*

What this means to me is a rather dramatic change in orientation. The spirit of the new progressivism (if we can use that word) is caught in the rather trite phrase "doing your own thing." The progressive had no faith that the person could transcend the social conditions of his existence. The new radical has faith that men can make their selves through individual choosing.

It is a religious spirit without the trappings of the traditional Christian church. Where it will lead us is not at all clear. How it will be reflected in curriculum proposals of the future would be pure conjecture. Yet it is asking of us that such phenomena as joy, wonder, awe, justice, beauty, service and vitality be foundations for human experiences in schooling. Thus, in this sense, Progressive Education has been transcended.

REFLECTIONS ON SOME OF THE NEW CURRICULA FOR YOUNG CHILDREN

Before finishing this statement, I would like to look briefly at two illustrative examples of new curricula for young children. They have been selected because I knew something about them and I believe they are fairly representative of new curricula in this area. I would like to reflect upon them in light of my previous remarks. I have drawn heavily from a recently published book by Evelyn Weber of Wheelock College for the description of these programs.

Weber's work is the outgrowth of her experience on a year's leave for travel, study and visitation of early childhood education programs in the United States and abroad. Her point of orientation was upon new program developments. She summarizes the general trends she found as follows:

The pervading concern is for the intellectual growth of the very young child.

Special concern is predominant in new programs for the economically disadvantaged young child.

Reduction in child-adult ratios is prevalent.

Attempts to involve parents more directly are common.

The reorganization of programs in terms of such things as multi-age grouping is extensive.

The upgrading (or downgrading?) of disciplined content in terms of new subject matter programs is extensive.

The two curricula I have chosen to discuss represent what I believe to be an exciting open model and a highly closed model.

Bereiter-Engelmann

The closed model, as you might guess, has come to be known as the Bereiter-Engelmann program which originated at the University of Illinois. This program, developed in light of behavior modification techniques and originally focusing upon compensatory education for culturally deprived youngsters, is now in the process of being generalized to noncompensatory programs in a number of places.

In all fairness and with a great deal of respect, I must admit that this program has the great advantage of being grounded in a clearly definable set of goals and operating principles which are neither hidden nor disavowed by the proponents. The conviction, candor and enthusiasm of many persons involved in these programs is surely meritorious.

According to Bereiter, Engelmann, Osborn and Reidford (1964), the two basic principles of the program are:

To select specific and significant objectives and teach them directly.

To train in the formal, structural aspects of language.

Three content areas were chosen: basic language training, reading and arithmetic. The school ran (at that time) two hours a day, five days a week and was run in a highly task-oriented, nononsense manner. Full participation of all children in the learning tasks was required; emphasis was placed upon effort, attention and mastery, but not on competition.

In essence, the approach resembles in many ways a converted teaching of a secondary school foreign language program. Arithmetic was also conceptualized as a new language as a basis for devising instructional strategies.

The results reported appear to show fairly dramatic gains, and variations of this general approach are growing in use, at least in many American central city schools.

As an ethical position, it is untenable. We have no need for a concept of ethics if our curricula are justifiable morally on the basis of adjusting the child to a broader social pattern. The only important concern on this level is power, and the power to do this makes it right when the outcome can be predicted to satisfy the general stance of the broader society. On this basis, one can justify anything without resorting to ethics or morality.

There is no quarrel with good intentions here. But the philosophy involved is strictly political and technical. The teachers are good technicians and what works is good as long as it fits the child into the system.

It should be clear from the above that the organization, structure and syntax are deliberately selected out of the subject matter. It should also be clear that there is almost no connection between this approach and Progressive Education, other than a vaguely connected experimental attitude. It is a structured venture, a rather good example of a modern preschool program which is essentially closed.

The World of Inquiry

In comparison to this, we may look at the World of Inquiry School located in Rochester, N.Y.

In the World of Inquiry School, children are based in multi-age "family rooms" where instruction in reading and social studies forms a core of experience on an essentially individualized basis.

Centers have been developed throughout the school where children can pursue projects and materials in areas such as science, mathematics and the creative arts. Individual inquiry is promoted and encouraged in (and out of) these centers with considerable free choice of activity and center participation on the part of the children. Self-pacing within inquiry and with movement between centers is fostered as much as possible.

Inner *and* outer city children mingle together in this integrated school. Children represent a cross section of the economic and racial makeup of the city of Rochester.

The curriculum offers opportunity for growth in all the traditional areas and the teachers are well prepared to help children inquire and encounter substantive material.

The Rochester World of Inquiry School is well within the tenets of Progressive Education. The high degree of freedom and choice indicates a basic ethical commitment reflecting the worth, dignity and integrity of each child. The focus upon inquiry reflects a modern problem (type) solving approach and the flexibility, freedom and choice of children provide an organizational format that can accommodate the inner subjective aspects of children to the outer objective realities of culture. The structure of the centers allows for flexibility, but is still essentially subject centered.

Compare this with the closed and the "nonprogressive" examples previously described. To me, the aesthetic and moral flavor, the attitude toward relationships and the meaning of the rhetoric of Progressive Education are apparent.

CONCLUSION

Open schools are just that: a pluralistic concept of differing forms grounded in a fundamentally ethical and moral position. We owe much to Progressive Education for furthering our rationale and desire for open schools, yet we are beyond the progressive era and entering a new cultural thrust. Wherever this may lead us, I hope all of us here will be part of helping to open up more of the potential of each human being through our work which touches the lives of children in our school.

REFERENCES

BEREITER, CARL S., ENGELMANN, SEIGFRIED, OSBORN, JEAN, REIDFORD, PHILIP A. An academically oriented preschool for culturally deprived children. In Fred Hechinger (ed.), *Preschool Education Today*. New York: Doubleday, 1964, 105–135.

BRUNER, JEROME. *The Process of Education*. Washington: Howard University Press, 1960.

CHILDS, JOHN. *Education and Morals*. New York: Appleton-Century-Crofts, Inc., 1950.

DEWEY, JOHN. *Democracy and Education*. New York: The Macmillan Co., 1916.

——. *Experience and Education*. New York: The Macmillan Co., 1938.

KILPATRICK, WILLIAM H. *Remaking the Curriculum*. New York: Newson & Co., 1936.

LEONARD, J. P. Some reflections on the meaning of sequence. In V. L. Herrick & Ralph Tyler (eds.), *Toward Improved Curriculum Theory*. University of Chicago Press, 1950.

SCHWAB, JOSEPH. Structure of the disciplines: Meaning and significance. In G. W. Ford & Lawrence Pugno (eds.), *The Structure of Knowledge and the Curriculum*. New York: Rand McNally & Co., 1964, 1–30.

VON HILSCHEIMER, GEORGE. Children, schools and utopias. In *This Is All About Schools*. Vol. 1–2. Toronto, Canada: Aug. 1966.

WEBER, EVELYN. *Early Childhood Education: Perspectives on Change*. Worthington, Ohio: Charles A. Jones, 1970.

7

PRESCHOOL EDUCATION
Enrichment or Instruction?

DAVID ELKIND

I want to deal with two rather different orientations to preschool education, which for lack of more precise terms can be called
enrichment and *instruction* respectively. In general, these two orientations correspond to the two approaches to education that Dewey
(revised 1962) described as centering upon "development from
within" and "enforcement from without." Although in the past these

Reprinted by permission of the author and the Association for Childhood Education International, 3615 Wisconsin Ave., N.W. Washington, D.C. Copyright ©
1969 by the Association.

two approaches to education have existed peaceably side by side, they are currently in open conflict and the nursery school is the battleground. I shall briefly sketch the history of the conflict, note some of the issues and then suggest some needed precautions on both sides.

HISTORY

After a score of years, during which interest in preschool education was practically dead, there has been in the last decade a resurgence of interest in early childhood. Head Start, the burgeoning Montessori School movement, and the many programs for disadvantaged preschoolers at universities around the country are only some of the evidences that attest to the stature of preschool education today.

Reasons for this new interest in the nursery school child, as is usually the case for most educational upheavals, were eminently practical needs. One need grew out of the attack upon the American educational system that began in the early fifties and was participated in by educators (such as Robert Hutchins) and noneducators (such as Admiral Rickover) alike. Critics berated the educational system for not adequately preparing children for the scientific age. The Russian Sputnik, launched in 1957, years after many of the critics had already published their arguments, seemed to give validity to their attacks. Preschool education did not rest immune from criticism. Instead of getting children moving up the academic ladder, the traditional nursery school, it was said, was permitting children to mark time while they enjoyed fun and games. Writers such as Fowler (1962) and Berlyne (1965) pointed out that the preschool child's potential for profiting from instruction was being left dormant because of some misguided notions carried over from progressive education to the effect that "pressure is bad."

The other major cause for rebirth of interest in the preschool child has come from the "War on Poverty" and the new concern with disadvantaged children. As the tragedy of slum schools was gradually revealed in books and articles, schools responded in their own defense. The children, they said, were not prepared for school, "or at least the kind of school we have to offer." They were deficient in the linguistic, cognitive, perceptual and personal-social skills so routinely found in the middle-class child that they almost appear to develop entirely from within. If disadvantaged children were to profit from what the schools had to offer, it was argued, then they needed a "Head Start" in order to catch up with middle-class children.

When those interested in accelerating middle-class children or helping disadvantaged children catch up looked to the traditional nursery school for guidance, they found little of use to them. They turned instead to Montessori, Piaget, and their own ingenuity for methods of training advantaged and disadvantaged preschoolers in language, cognition, attention and social skills. Among the most notable programs are those of Fowler (1968) and Moore (1965) with advantaged children and of Deutsch (1963) and Bereiter and Engelmann (1966) with disadvantaged children.

The point of this brief and sketchy recent history of the preschool instruction movement is that it is bound to influence preschool education as a whole. That is to say, there will be increasing pressure for more instruction at the preschool level not only by the middle-class parents who send their children to private nursery schools (Maya Pines's 1967 book, for example, may well get many middle-class parents to agitate for more instruction in the preschool) but also by local and state governments that may move as they have in New York, California and Massachusetts to incorporate preschool education within the educational system. What is shaping up then is a battle between the traditional middle-class nursery school teachers who see preschool education as development from within and the new breed of preschool workers who see education as enforcement from without. Let us look at the two positions with respect to some of the issues on which they differ: readiness, pressure, and self-expression and creativity.

THE ISSUES

Before sketching some of the contrasting arguments of the enrichment-instruction conflict, it is necessary to make clear which positions are *not* in conflict. It must be stressed that the conflict is *not* between those who advocate enrichment for the middle-class child and those who advocate instruction for disadvantaged children. As far as I can determine, those concerned with disadvantaged children, such as Martin Deutsch (1964) and Bereiter and Engelmann (1966), are trying to compensate the disadvantaged child for not having received the kinds of instruction that most middle-class children ordinarily receive from parents and which Strodtbeck (1967) has called the "hidden curriculum of the middle-class home."

There is no conflict between those who advocate enrichment for middle-class children and those who propose instruction for lower-class children. It is not a question of *either/or* but rather of *who* does *what*. Middle-class children usually get heavy doses of instruction at home for which the enrichment of the nursery school provides a necessary antidote. Lower-class children, however, who experience the lack of pressure and instruction at home, need to find it in nursery school if they are to acquire the skills and motivations necessary for successful achievement in schools dominated by middle-class values.

The conflict we are concerned with now has to do with the *preschool education of the middle-class child*. I do not want, here, to recapitulate the evidence for enrichment and against instruction or vice versa, since this has been marshaled repeatedly elsewhere. (For a number of the arguments against instruction see LeShan, 1967, and Rasmussen, 1966; for arguments on the other side see Bruner, 1962, and Fowler, 1968.) On the contrary, I would like to convey the flavor of the arguments on both sides so as to suggest the rather different value systems implicit in each position. This can best be done by reviewing the enrichment and instruction positions with respect to three major issues: readiness, pressure, and self-expression and creativity.

Readiness

Within the traditional nursery school, readiness is a pervasive concept and presupposes a general maturational, motivational and social disposition that must be present if a child is to master any particular activity or skill effectively and efficiently. Implicit in this notion of readiness is that individual children are "ready" for particular activities at different times. The following remark by Keliher expresses this view of readiness:

> We know that a few are ready to read at five but that the great majority are not. Research has consistently shown that a mental age of six and one-half or over is necessary for reading with understanding. We are told, again and again, to expect a four-year range of ability when children enter first grade. Oculists warn us that most children's eyes are not mature enough even at six for close application to print and figures. (Keliher, 1960, p. 109)

In general the enrichment orientation supposes that the child has had a reasonably optimal environment and that any retardation in readiness does not arise from a lack in his experiental background but rather from his individual growth pattern.

According to this view, four- and five-year-old children are on the whole not yet ready for formal instruction and stubbornly resist it. As Butler puts it:

> Under the circumstances [the knowledge explosion] it is natural to ask why children should not be taught the fundamental skills in kindergarten so they can begin to master some of this vast knowledge. In the interest of children it is also natural to ask who feels the need of these skills? The parent, the teacher or the child? Much too often comes the reply that the child should be put through these paces whether he likes it or not. Most five-year-olds show unlimited curiosity for knowledge, but their interest in formal learning is fleeting. . . . Pushing the child to learn skills before he is ready rejects his right to grow in his own way, to take the time he needs. (Butler, 1962, p. 11)

In short, implicit in the enrichment conception of readiness is the belief that the child has grown up in an optimal environment and that his growth is as advanced as can be expected considering his own abilities and talents. The child's own needs to grow, to play and to express himself are regarded as being as important to his later growth as any formal instruction because they encourage attitudes of independence and self-confidence essential for later academic work.

In contrast to this view of readiness, which is seen as development from within, the instruction orientation sees it as a matter of environmental preparation. Readiness is not a fixed attribute of the child but rather is always relative to our ingenuity in constructing materials appropriate to the child's level of development. This position was given elegant expression in Bruner's now famous phrase:

> We begin with the hypothesis that any subject can be taught effectively in some intellectually honest form to any child at any stage of development. (Bruner, 1962, p. 33)

One of the most vocal and research-oriented spokesmen of the instruction position for the preschooler is Fowler (1968). In Fowler's view, and he has data to support his contentions, early intellectual stimulation results in superior achievement that is maintained throughout the elementary school years without negative personality or social effects. Fowler has been particularly involved in attempts at early reading instruction, as has another prominent advocate of early instruction, O. K. Moore (1961). For these writers, readiness is a term that merely expresses our ignorance regarding the methods of effectively programing instruction, and once the appropriate programs are available children, it will be discovered, are "ready" to read and write before the first grade.

The issue then is whether "readiness" is an absolute phenomenon determined by the child's own rate of development and interest or whether "readiness" is a matter of being clever enough to devise techniques to capitalize upon whatever abilities the child has at the moment. In a sense, one could almost say that the instructional approach accepts the traditional readiness concept but not the implication that it cannot be by-passed by choosing the appropriate materials. We turn now to a second issue about which discussion has been considerably more heated, the notion of pressure.

Pressure

The enrichment position is very clear with respect to its stance on pressure. The child will be exposed to pressures soon enough and early exposure could well be harmful. Pressured children develop learning blocks and evade learning. The preschool child's major task is to grow; he will have time later to master academic skills. He needs all the time he has now to grow in his own way and in his own directions. As Jenkins wrote:

> Wherever we go in the world, we hear talk about pressures that grownups are under. At the very time we bemoan pressures which bedevil us, we do not seem to be fully aware of the pressures which we are pushing on boys and girls: pressures to behave in a socialized way; to be popular—to belong to the group; to achieve in school and get to college; to hold their own in a competitive world; to take advantage of all the advantages; to live in a world which even grownups cannot say is safe and secure. As if these pressures were not enough for our children to face, many adults are adding to pressures in the name of education. . . . Their motivation is right, their realization for the need of intelligent and productive manpower is right, but their knowledge of children and how they grow and develop is inadequate. (Jenkins, 1960, p. 53)

The position on the instructional side seems to run something like this. By and large, it is claimed we have underestimated the abilities of our children and they can go much faster than we have them going now. In effect we do the child an injustice by coddling him rather than challenging him intellectually. Besides, if we choose our materials appropriately we will not have to push children at all; they will go ahead of their own accord because of spontaneous interest and motivation. Berlyne said it this way:

The period during which North American education was dominated by Dewey's influence was one marked generally by a fear of hastening the educational process and of over-straining the child's intellectual capacities. Recent psychological research concurs with the experience of educators around the world in suggesting that the rate at which the average child, let alone the gifted child, can advance has been grossly underestimated, with unfortunate consequences. . . . Above all, there was a grave underestimation of the extent to which the ordinary child can find intellectual substance appetizing and intellectual effort satisfying, provided they are introduced at the right time and in the right way. (Berlyne, 1965, pp. 75–76)

The issue then is joined but is not entirely clear cut. The enrichment position is that academic pressure adds further burdensome pressures upon the child; whereas the instructional position holds that we are underestimating the child's ability to learn and are placing a negative value on academic learning, which can be as enjoyable as play activities provided that—and here lies the difficulty —it is introduced "at the right time and in the right way." Closely tied to this issue is another, that of self-expression and creativity.

Self-Expression and Creativity

One of the prime aims of the traditional nursery school is to foster self-expression and creativity. The materials of the nursery school speak for themselves. One finds finger paints, tempera paints and easels, modeling clay, carpentry tools, and clothing and props that can be used in dramatic play. Through these materials it is hoped the child can learn to further define himself by finding out what he can do. Through dramatic play he can work out emotional problems and prepare himself for adult roles. Most of all, he can express the feelings and energies inherent in being a three- or four- or five-year-old. Here is Hymes's vivid description of this position:

They are only four and five, in the early springtime of their lives. But this is the time—more than any time they will ever again know

—when they are reaching out, peeking and curious, thirsty for the new . . . They are popping to use their bodies: to test their strength, to climb new heights, to achieve a tingly fitness. They are thirsty for new ideas, for new words and new sounds and new sights, for new skills and accomplishments and achievements. And they are full of ideas of their own. Ideas to say, if someone will listen. Ideas to paint out and act out. Ideas to build with, if they have the tools, materials, time and space. (Hymes, 1962, p. 6)

Those who favor the instructional position do not deny the preschool child's press toward creativity and self-expression in word and deed. What they suggest is that the child's creative as well as intellectual energies be channelled more appropriately. If children are interested in music, let us teach them to sing on key and begin them on musical instruments. If they are going to draw and paint, let us give them some instruction in these endeavors so that they can realize their abilities more fully and be better at what they are doing. This point of view has been argued most forcibly by Fowler:

Accordingly, the role of early stimulation emerges as more than of fleeting interest. In no instance (where documentation exists) have I found an individual of high ability who did not experience intensive early stimulation as a central component of his development. It is, therefore, essential not to write off the studies of "giftedness" as of no relevance to early education because it is biased evidence. The unvarying coincidence of extensive early stimulation with cognitive precosity and subsequent superior competence in adulthood suggests that stimulation is a necessary if not sufficient condition for the development of his abilities. (Fowler, 1968, p. 17)

PRECAUTIONS

It is obvious from the foregoing resumé of the two conflicting positions that we are dealing here with more than a question of educational policy. On the contrary, what we see expressed are two quite different value systems that resemble in miniature the humanitarian versus the scientific value systems described in C. P. Snow's *Two Cultures* (1963). Therein, in fact, lies the danger. When underlying value systems are at stake, it is difficult to be objective and it is easy to ignore or misinterpret the relevant evidence. In this section I want to suggest how these value systems have shortsighted the vision of both sides of the controversy. But before doing that it might be well to sketch briefly the major components of the two value systems.

With respect to the enrichment position, it is clearly *child* oriented, being concerned with the child's individuality, his personal needs and his personal limitations. It is also *present* oriented in the sense that it sees the important role of education as that of allowing the child to live his immediate life to the full without too much consideration for how his present activities will affect his future success in society. From this point of view, it is believed that the interests of the child are best served by the teacher's setting limits rather than providing instruction. Basic to this position is an implicit faith in the soundness of the child's own inner needs and compulsions toward activity.

The instruction position, on the other hand, is quite clearly *goal oriented* in that it is concerned with the child's adaptation to the kind of society in which he will live and work. It is *future* oriented in that it sees the role of education as starting the child as early as possible in the conviction that the earlier the child begins developing his abilities and attaining his skills the further he will go with them. From this point of view, it is believed that the interests of the child are best served by the teachers providing explicit direction not only in academic subjects but also in the child's artistic and athletic endeavors. Basic to this position is an implicit faith in the soundness of the adult's judgment as to how the child should be trained and instructed.

Now let us look at these two positions more closely. First, with respect to the enrichment position, it is one of the characteristics of an accepted and well-established point of view that it tends to be regarded as an unalterable reality. This is as true of political and scientific positions as it is of an educational orientation, but this should not blind us to its possible limitations and defects. A certain openness is required, indeed is dictated, if we are truly concerned with what is best for children. A case in point is the "readiness" concept, which in view of our knowledge of the disadvantaged child has become a much more relative and less absolute conception. It may well be that the highly verbal, self-motivated, creative child we know in middle-class nursery schools already expresses not only spontaneous growth tendencies but more important the particular influences of his home environment. *We must be aware of mistaking the product of middle-class upbringing for normative patterns of growth.*

With respect to the instructional emphasis, the opposite danger is present. There is a tendency to be overzealous for change and to be overconfident about the benefits of intervention. One aspect of this overzealousness is the tendency to be rather selective and short-sighted in marshaling evidence. Let me cite a case in point; namely, the widely quoted research of Harold Skeels.

As you will recall, Skeels noted that two scrawny underdeveloped girls from an orphanage, after having been placed in a home for the mentally retarded, made a remarkable physical and intellectual recovery. The cause was their adoption by mentally retarded girls of mental age five to nine, who loved and cared for them. On the basis of this observation, Skeels arranged for eleven other children from the orphanage to be transferred to the home for the retarded.

A follow-up study of these children and of a matched contrast group twenty years later revealed remarkable differences between the experimental and contrast groups. The differences were striking.

Eleven of the 13 children in the experimental group were married; 9 of the 11 had a total of 28 children, an average of three per family. On intelligence tests, those second-generation children had IQ's ranging from 86 to 125 with a mean of 104. In no instance was there any indication of mental retardation or demonstrable abnormality.

In the contrast group, four were in institutions and only two of the subjects had married. One had one child and subsequently was di-

vorced. Psychological examination of the child revealed marked
mental retardation with indications of probable brain damage. Another male subject had a nice home and children of average intelligence. Educational and vocational level of the contrast group was
markedly lower than that of the experimental subjects. (Skeels, p.
55)

I cite this research only because it is often used to illustrate
the importance of early *intellectual* stimulation upon mental growth.
What strikes me as odd about this interpretation, particularly in
view of Skeels' own stress upon the loving care the children received,
is that the surrogate mothers were *mentally retarded.* It seems odd
to argue for the *intellectual stimulation* of such care. An alternative
interpretation would be that the love and care given these children
provided the emotional bases which are the necessary prerequisites
for spontaneous intellectual growth. The importance of the one-to-
one affectional ties is acknowledged as important in many of the
preschool programs for the disadvantaged. We need to be careful
then not to bias the selection of evidence so as to favor a particular
position.

One other point is made in this connection. Although the
retardation of the disadvantaged child is frequently stressed, his
prematurity in other respects must not be overlooked. In many
ways these children take responsibility very early for their younger
siblings and they learn the realities of life at a much earlier age.
Many are shrewd and cunning beyond their years at least in the
ways of human interaction. One consequence of this premature
development was elegantly illustrated by Freud's remark when he
was asked what became of the clever shoeshine boys who abounded
in the streets. Freud's reply was, "They become cobblers." Piaget
made a similar remark when he pointed out that kittens take three
months to attain object conservation, whereas it takes a human
infant nine months: "The child takes longer but he goes further
so the nine months were not for nothing." The point is, early
instruction if it brings maturity too soon may, or at least could,
lower the limits of the child's ultimate achievement. I am not

suggesting that this is a real possibility for middle-class children, but I am saying that one could find evidence to support the position if one so desired. And the possible negative consequences of acceleration should not be ignored. Schools, for example, are not prepared for children who read and write when they enter kindergarten.

I must confess I have no answer to the question, instruction or enrichment in the middle-class preschool education. We do not have the longitudinal evidence yet on which to make that decision. Until the evidence is in, we can only urge that those who favor enrichment will keep open minds while those who favor instruction will not let their zeal influence their judgment. Preschool education is too important to be ruled entirely by rigid tradition or by innovative but unproven ideas.

REFERENCES

BEREITER, CARL, and ENGELMANN, SIEGFRIED. *Teaching Disadvantaged Children in the Preschool.* Englewood Cliffs, N.J.: Prentice-Hall, 1966.

BERLYNE, D. E. Curiosity and Education. In J. D. Krumboltz (ed.), *Learning and the Educational Process.* Chicago: Rand McNally, 1965. Pp. 67–89.

BRUNER, J. *The Process of Education.* Cambridge, Mass.: Harvard University Press, 1962.

BUTLER, ANNIE L. Hurry! Hurry! Hurry! *Childhood Education* (1962), 39, pp. 10–13.

DEUTSCH, M. "Facilitating Development in the Preschool Child: Social and Psychological Perspectives," *Merrill-Palmer Quarterly* (1964), 10, 249–63.

———. "The Disadvantaged Child and the Learning Process." In H. A. Passow (Ed.), *Education in Depressed Areas.* New York: Teachers College Press, 1963. Pp. 163–79.

DEWEY, J., & DEWEY, EVELYN. *Schools of Tomorrow.* New York: Dutton, 1962 (originally published 1915).

FOWLER, W. "Cognitive Learning in Infancy and Early Childhood," *Psychological Bulletin* (1962), 59, 116–52.

————. "The Effect of Early Stimulation in the Emergence of Cognitive Processes." Reprinted from Robert D. Hess and Roberta Meyer Bear (Eds.), *Early Education,* pp. 9–36. Chicago: Aldine Publishing Co., 1968; copyright 1968 by Robert D. Hess and Roberta Meyer Bear.

HYMES, JAMES L. "The Importance of Pre-primary Education," *Childhood Education* (1962), 39, pp. 5–9.

JENKINS, GLADYS G. "What Price Pressures?" *Childhood Education* (1960), 37, pp. 53–60.

KELIHER, ALICE V. "Do We Push Children?" *Childhood Education* (1960), 37, pp. 108–112.

LeSHAN, EDA J. *The Conspiracy Against Childhood.* New York: Atheneum, 1967.

MOORE, O. K. "Orthographic Symbols and the Preschool Child—A New Approach." In E. P. Torrance (ed.), *Creativity: 1960 Proceedings of the 3rd Conference on Gifted Children.* Minneapolis: University of Minnesota, Center for Continuation Studies, 1961.

————. "From Tools to Interactional Machines." In *New Approaches to Individualizing Instruction.* Princeton: Educational Testing Service, 1965.

PINES, MAYA. *Revolution in Learning: The Years from Birth to Six.* New York: Harper & Row, 1967.

RASMUSSEN, MARGARET (ed.). *Readings from Childhood Education.* Washington: Association for Childhood Education International, 1966.

SKEELS, H. M. "Adult Status of Children with Contrasting Early Life Experiences," *Monographs of the Society for Research in Child Development* (1966), 31, Ser. No. 105.

SNOW, C. P. *The Two Cultures: And a Second Look.* New York: Mentor, 1963.

STRODTBECK, FRED I. "The Hidden Curriculum of the Middle-Class Home." In H. Passow, Miriam Goldberg and A. J. Tannenbaum (eds.), *Education of the Disadvantaged.* New York: Holt, Rinehart & Winston, 1967, pp. 91–112.

8

IMPLICIT ASSUMPTIONS UNDERLYING PRESCHOOL INTERVENTION PROGRAMS

MARION BLANK

The question of preschool intervention, like all problems of applied research, places unusual demands on the basic sciences from which it must draw. Requisite to well-designed intervention programs is knowledge in some of the most central issues in psychology —How does learning occur? What is the role of language in thinking? What is the effect of early environment on later development? Are there critical periods in human learning?—to enumerate just a few. Yet it is just because these issues are so basic and complex that

Journal of Social Issues. Spring 1970. Abridged and reprinted with the permission of the author and the Society for the Psychological Study of Social Issues.

we have no well-defined answers to any of them. Nevertheless, because of the atmosphere of urgency and the attendant publicity with which the issue of intervention arose, psychology and education had to use the limited information they possessed to establish some guidelines for action.

This has meant that influences from such diverse frameworks as behaviorism, Freudian psychoanalysis, Piagetian epistemological psychology, and Chomsky's transformational grammar, have formed an eclectic or, perhaps more correctly, a mosaic backdrop for deciding how to proceed in this area. In many cases, these theories are of questionable validity and relevance with reference to the functioning of the disadvantaged child. Nonetheless, they have played a major role in the establishment of intervention programs.

RATIONALE FOR PRESCHOOL INTERVENTION

The fact that preschool programs were established at all reflects the influence of several basic assumptions in our thinking. First, it mirrors our optimism about the almost endless modifiability and flexibility of human behavior (Hunt, 1964; Feuerstein, 1968). This view has been reinforced by the strong behaviorist influence in America where it is held that all aspects of learning and performance can be changed to a desired end through the proper manipulation of environmental events (Skinner, 1953). Our faith in the importance of environmental factors seems well justified by a substantial body of literature from both animals and humans (Hilgard & Marquis, 1961; Ulrich, Stachnik, & Mabry, 1966). There are, however, in almost all theories limitations to the degree of modifiability that can take place. In general, the major correlate for this limitation is age; that is, the older the organism, the less the change. The interpretations for this may vary. Thus, in a behaviorist model, slower learning in the adult may be seen as reflecting the need to unlearn previously established responses before new responses may be learned. In an ethological orientation, the change may be limited by what has been termed critical periods

(Lorenz, 1937). In this view, stages exist, particularly in early development, which allow rapid learning of certain skills. These skills *may* be learned at other ages—but only with much greater time and effort.

Thus, the hope for any modifiability rests strongly on the idea of early intervention. The problem remains as to what behavior is to be modified; this, in turn, rests on what is deemed to be the deficit in functioning. Our views here have been strongly affected by the developmental approach to behavior. Any developmental view has built-in expectations of increasing achievement with chronological growth. These expectations are clearly reflected in the institutions with which the child has contact. Thus, in the school situation we expect the average six or seven year old to be able to read, write, and perform other symbolic operations. In this situation, disadvantaged children show poor progress (see Wilkerson, 1967). Many other deficits may well exist—personality disorders, nutritional inadequacies, poor health, etc. But the school situation, with its emphasis on scholastic achievement, has inevitably meant that learning disorders would appear most prominent.

Arguments, of course, can be and have been raised against this view. Learning in the school situation refers mainly to skills of literacy and it does not necessarily include all higher learning. Thus, it is suggested that perhaps the disadvantaged child may not be deficient in other cognitive skills. Evidence suggests, however (Feuerstein, 1968), that the deficits may not be restricted to academic work but rather "characterize an entire approach and attitude towards life" involving such features as "inefficient problem solving, a chaotic outlook about world events marked by a lack of need for logical evidence, an episodic grasp of reality (p. 16)."

There is perhaps another reason for the stress on learning. Man sees himself, in comparison with all other animals, as unique in his mental development and, in particular, in his capacity for achieving high levels of symbolic activity. Thus the learning disorders of disadvantaged children are seen as representing a weakness in man's greatest strength.

Once one accepts the validity of a learning deficit, it inevitably follows that close attention be paid to all aspects of education. However, the influence of developmental theories as far apart as Piaget and Freud has meant that preschool intervention would perhaps receive the greatest attention. Despite their differing orientations, both these philosophies see early behaviors as laying the foundation for all subsequent growth. As a result, weaknesses in this initial structure leave the child not simply with a lag in development, but with an increasing disadvantage relative to his chronological age. This reasoning receives support in the finding of a "cumulative deficit" in which the discrepancy in IQ and achievement between middle class and lower class children increases with age (Deutsch & Brown, 1964).

FACTORS UNDERLYING THE LEARNING DEFICIT

Even with agreement as to the nature of the deficit, the problem remains of defining the course of remediation. Learning, even when limited to the academic situation, covers such a host of skills that it is essential to establish priorities of importance. In an effort to obtain a first approximation of some of the critical factors, comparisons were made of the environments of children who did well in school and those who did not. Frequently, this meant comparing the home variables of lower class and middle class families since so much early learning occurs in the home (Freeburg & Payne, 1967). Because of the myriad factors involved, attention was narrowed to those factors which armchair analysis indicated were logically related to poor school functioning. This method has been used at all levels of sophistication, from simple correlations (e.g., few books in the home associated with poor reading achievement) to much more involved analyses. For example, there have now been some studies documenting in specifics the kind of verbal interchange that occurs between mothers and children from different socio-economic groups (Hess & Shipman, 1965; Bernstein

& Henderson, 1968). For the most part, this selection of factors has been on a correlational basis and therefore no cause and effect could be demonstrated.

PROGRAMS OF OVERALL ENRICHMENT

The pressure for immediate action, however, meant that correlation would have to serve the role that should have been filled by causal relation. Thus the correlational approach formed the basis for what is probably the most common type of intervention program—namely, that of "overall enrichment." The general philosophy of such programs has been to select those environmental features which seem most central for cognition and offer these, in varying doses, to the disadvantaged child. The premise of these programs is that one enriches or supplements the child's background by offering trips, equipment, stories, conversation, audio tapes, and any other presumably beneficial experience.

The value of this approach is questionable on many grounds. First, it involves major intervention in many aspects of the child's life and thus requires costly, extensive educational facilities. Second, even if gains in performance are obtained, it is not possible to determine which aspects of the program are responsible since so many areas of the child's life are affected. Third, perhaps the most serious concern is that even with this massive intervention, the cognitive gains are equivocal (Weikart, 1967; Karnes, 1968). This conclusion is, if anything, understated since negative results are rarely reported. This does not mean, however, that we were overly optimistic in our goals since some programs have achieved gains in learning rates and skills (Bereiter & Engelmann, 1966a; Blank & Solomon, 1968; Weikart & Wiegerink, 1968). Rather, the limited success of overall enrichment may well rest in the inappropriateness of its philosophy which, like the materials offered, represents a melange of viewpoints. One is the developmental orientation, mentioned earlier, which stresses the continual emergence of new skills. A corollary to this approach, not previously noted, is that these skills will emerge in a uniform sequence in all children as they mature. The emphasis placed upon this uniformity has meant that the environment be viewed as a force that can only affect the rate but in no way alter the sequence. Thus the same techniques and materials can be offered to all children in the belief that they will foster the developmental sequence. As a result, aside from considering differences in the level of development reached, other individual differences are largely ignored. The basic idea seems to be that the presentation of enriched stimulation appropriate to a given level is bound to affect the behavior and learning.

This reasoning is reinforced by the successful experimental work of the behaviorists in manipulating learning independent of any individual differences. The Zeitgeist of this approach is so pervasive in our thinking that we are often unaware of its influence and we may even label it by some other term. Thus, a nursery school teacher may not recognize that she is not simply offering warmth and love but is also exerting control over her pupils with such verbal reinforcements as "that's a good job," "you're a big boy," "come on, try again." However, unlike the teacher, the laboratory experimenter has much greater control over his subject in terms of time, stimuli, rewards, sequencing, etc. He can even control such highly motivating physiological states as hunger and thirst. Thus, the laboratory experimenter does not simply present appropriate stimuli; he has immense power to control the organism's response to the stimuli with the result that his procedures can guarantee a high degree of success. It goes without saying that teachers of children do not have such power and would hesitate to use it if they could. As a result, well-designed and potentially useful learning material may be presented by the teacher but be ignored by the child with the result that it fails to serve as an effective stimulus.

In addition, the control that is available to the teacher is further limited by the permissive, activity-oriented nursery school tradition focused on self-expression, social behavior, and emotional adjustment. Many of these aims represent the attempt to bring psychoanalytic principles to early childhood training. These programs may be successful with the well-functioning middle-class child who has already developed strong internal controls in the cognitive sphere. However, the literature on the disadvantaged is replete with descriptions of their failure to have developed such internal skills (Mattick, 1965; Spaulding, 1966), with the result that they frequently withdraw from cognitive demands. In such a situation, the tendency of most permissive orientations would be to leave the material and wait until the child is "ready" to deal with it. As a result, the organization of traditional nursery schools may not be appropriate for the disadvantaged child since it does not afford the control necessary for "shaping" the child's learning.

THE VIEWPOINT OF PERCEPTUAL DYSFUNCTIONING

Some investigators have taken a different approach from that of overall enrichment in that they have attempted to delineate specific factors that may be responsible for the learning disorder. One of the most important viewpoints relies heavily on the genetic approach of Piaget (1952) in which it is hypothesized that sensory-motor schema must be fully developed before higher level concepts can be achieved. In this view, the IQ and achievement deficits at school age are seen as the result of earlier and perhaps even undiagnosed sensory-motor difficulties in early childhood (Hunt, 1964; Kohlberg, 1966). Surprisingly, although this view of hierarchical deficiencies is directed towards understanding weaknesses in man's unique language and cognitive abilities, support for this view has come mainly from research on animals. This research has shown that severe perceptual and sensory-motor deprivation in very young animals results in later distorted development. Thus, the lamb who is raised without its mother will turn out to be an isolate from other sheep, will prove to be an inaedquate mother to its own young, and so on. Studies on institutionalized human infants strongly reinforces this view of the damaging effects of a restricted early environment (Spitz, 1945; Goldfarb, 1945; Dennis, 1960).

Although this concept may be valid for particular groups of

infants, the question nevertheless arises as to its usefulness in understanding the disadvantaged. This view is relevant to the disadvantaged child only if it can be demonstrated that he, in fact, is deprived of early basic opportunities for sensory-motor experience. Speculations have been raised as to whether different levels of stimulation exist in lower and middle class homes. The key question, however, concerns the significance of any such differences in the development of sensory-motor skills. Unfortunately there are almost no systematic data on this issue. In addition, in contrast to the studies on institutionalized children, the data that are available suggest that disadvantaged children do not achieve lower developmental scores than middle class children under two years of age (Dreger & Miller, 1968; Bayley, 1965). In many ways it is premature to raise this issue since, for the most part, we have not defined what are the essential stimuli for normal development in the human. As a result, except for extreme cases like severe isolation, we cannot even say with any certainty that a child has experienced perceptual restrictions.

In spite of the lack of evidence in support of a perceptual deficit, this approach has aroused a great interest and a variety of studies have been conducted to demonstrate perceptual dysfunctioning in older disadvantaged children. Research in our unit, however, has indicated the need for much more careful controls before one can state either that perceptual deficiencies do indeed exist in disadvantaged children or, if they do, what role, if any, they play in later school failure. For example, research on children with learning disorders had indicated difficulties in auditory perception (Olsen, 1966; Deutsch, 1964; Katz & Deutsch, 1967). A test widely used in this research consists of pairs of highly similar words (e.g., cat-cap) which the subject is asked to judge as the same or different (Wepman, 1960). The finding that retarded readers did poorly on this task was of obvious interest since audition is the modality by which spoken language is learned. These results are intriguing since they raise the possibility that failure to learn written language (i.e., reading) is associated with some kind of failure in discriminating spoken language. In a study replicating and extending this work (Blank, in press), I found that the correlation between the auditory discrimination task and reading performance does not appear to reflect auditory deficiencies per se but rather reflects the deficiencies retarded readers experience in the seemingly simple cognitive demands imposed by this task (i.e., the ability to listen to a sequence, retain the sequence so as to judge one stimulus against the other, and then make a judgment as to their similarity or difference).

Another area of perceptual functioning which has aroused considerable interest is that of cross-modal integration (Birch & Belmont, 1964; Beery, 1967; Sterritt & Rudnick, 1966). One of the tasks in this area requires the child to select a visual spatial dot pattern (. . . . .) as representing a sequence of auditory signals (tap, tap, tap—long pause—tap, tap.) The uniformly poor performance of retarded readers on this task has naturally attracted interest since the need to make equivalences between auditory (e.g., spoken words) and visual stimuli (e.g., written words) is vital to the reading process. Research that I had done on cross-modal transfer (Blank & Bridger, 1964, 1966), however, indicated that this task, which is seemingly of a perceptual nature, actually requires a high level of abstract (verbal) conceptualization. The auditory stimuli used in all this research were, of necessity, temporally presented. We found that temporal stimuli, whether visual or auditory, could not be utilized unless coded in a number system. Since the retarded readers had significantly more difficulty in achieving this coding, they were unable to select the dot patterns representing these sequences. What appeared to be a cross-modal deficiency was in fact a failure to code accurately the temporally presented components of the task. These conclusions were reinforced by our findings (Blank & Bridger, 1967; Blank, Weider, & Bridger, 1968) that no differences existed between retarded and normal readers when the tasks were confined to non-abstract, perceptual components (e.g., repeating temporal rhythms without having to convert them into another modality).

These results also indicated the need to differentiate among levels of verbal skills. For example, the retarded readers were not deficient in applying verbal labels in certain situations, such as labeling spatially presented visual patterns. The difficulty they experienced was in using words to represent abstract concepts, such as temporal duration. These results suggested that a key deficiency in children with learning disorders was not simply a failure in language per se but rather in more abstract symbolic mediation. For brevity's sake, the deficiency might be called a limitation in the "abstract attitude." As indicated in the work of theorists in this area (Goldstein, 1959; Vygotsky, 1962), language is intimately linked with higher level abstract thinking, but language itself is not to be equated with such thinking.

Even though the evidence for perceptual dysfunctioning is ambiguous, many programs, particularly those that are Montessori-based, have been established to compensate for this hypothesized deficit. As discussed by Hunt (1964), this type of program has several potential advantages. The materials are well designed and lend themselves to meeting individual differences (i.e., the children can work on their own, at their own rate, and with the material they select). The basic assumption of the program, however, remains open to question; namely, do the materials actually lead the child to develop the concepts for which they were designed? Although the research on this issue is meager, evidence suggests that disadvantaged children do not necessarily assimilate the information provided by self-didactic material (Gotkin et al., 1968). This concern receives support from the fact that contrary to the original philosophy many Montessori programs have been altered to include more language training (Kohlberg, 1966). As a result, these programs may differ little from those of overall enrichment.

THE CENTRAL ROLE OF LANGUAGE IN LEARNING DEFICIENCIES

It should be noted that in all enrichment programs, regardless of orientation, language has emerged as a common denominator of the learning deficit. This had led many investigators to the belief that while other handicaps may exist, language is at the core of the difficulty for the disadvantaged child. The work of Bernstein (1960, 1961) on restricted and elaborated codes has been a major impetus to this approach. "In his definition, *restricted* codes are stereotyped, limited, and condensed, lacking in specificity and the exactness needed for precise conceptualization and differentiation. Sentences are short, simple, often unfinished; there is little use of subordinate clauses for elaborating the content of the sentence; it is a language of implicit meaning, easily understood and commonly shared. The basic quality of this mode is to limit the range and detail of concept and information involved (Hess & Shipman, 1966, p. 94)."

Even if these conclusions are valid, the problem remains of determining which of the extremely broad range of language skills needs most to be fostered. Unfortunately here again we lack the necessary empirical foundation on which to build our teaching. The most logical source for such information would seem to be the psychological laboratory. However, much of the experimental research in psychology conducted in the United States has been influenced by the behaviorist tradition in which one deals only with external behaviors; internal mental processes are seen as either unknown or unknowable (Skinner, 1953). This has meant that research on language has inevitably focused on those aspects of verbalization that can readily be observed and measured in the laboratory setting. As a result emphasis has been placed on simple verbal labels as in discrimination learning (e.g., red, large, man, chair, etc.) and in paired associate learning (e.g., man–coat, window–bread, picture–happy) (Kendler, Kendler, & Wells, 1959; Spiker & Norcross, 1962).

Research, however, has suggested that disadvantaged children, while often lacking certain labels, are nevertheless not seriously deficient in this aspect of verbalization (John, 1963; Blank & Bridger, 1964, 1966, 1967). Their difficulty seems to be in the use of more complex verbal structures (as in causal thinking, conditional statements, achieving deductions, retrieving past events, etc.). The aforementioned abilities involve internal mental processes and therefore they have received scant attention from the behavioral psychologists.

The limited view of language espoused by the behaviorists has been strongly criticized by linguists who use the transformational grammar model (Chomsky, 1957). This view emphasizes the fact that meaningful language involves not simply the learning of discrete words, but rather the rules by which these words are organized. Thus, the words "boy," "girl," "ran," "small," "the," "to," "a," tell us relatively little. These same words when organized into the form "A small boy ran to the girl" tell us a definite message. In recent years, work by psycholinguists using the transformational grammar model has led to considerable advance in our knowledge of the syntax (structure) of language and the way syntactic structures are mastered by the young child (Brown & Bellugi, 1964; Ervin & Miller, 1963).

This work has been largely responsible for one of the currently popular views about the language of the disadvantaged; namely, their language may not be the same as "standard" (middle class) dialect, but that does not mean that it is a poorer language (Baratz, 1968; Cazden, 1966; Labov, Cohen, & Robbins, 1965). This view is extremely relevant to the many attempts in public education directed at altering any dialects simply because they differ from "standard middle class." It should be noted, however, that much of the educational concern is not focused on dialect but on "the use of language for learning and communicating ideas (Cazden, 1966, p. 138)." This distinction was well illustrated in a study which found that lower class Negro children utilized the verbal descriptions of middle class white children more effectively than they utilized the verbal descriptions of their peers (Heider, Cazden, & Brown, 1968). Thus, familiarity of dialect need not insure adequate use of language.

These results also suggest that the organizational principles governing the structure of a language may be quite distinct from the function that the language serves in thinking and problem solving. Thus, the question is not simply one of determining their similarities and differences in the structural components of various dialect systems but rather how effectively the child is using the language he already possesses. The work of Richelle and Feuerstein (1957) seems particularly relevant here since it was initially motivated by a desire to determine the differences in thinking among lower class Israeli children from different cultural backgrounds. Contrary to expectations, they found few differences among children from various lower class communities since they tended to have simple, undifferentiated concepts in which language was used in a primitive way. On the basis of these results it appeared that differences in thinking existed only when people possessed complex, well-developed mental skills. In the case of lower class children, the necessary skills have not developed, resulting in a relative paucity of such differentiation. Thus while attempts to preserve the structural language of the disadvantaged may well be valid, concentration on this aspect may cause us to overlook functional components of language. As a result attention may unfortunately be drawn away from efforts to correct possible functional limitations.

INTERVENTION PROGRAMS FOCUSED ON LANGUAGE

The critical distinction between the form and function of language has been pointed out by many noted theorists including Piaget (1952), Sapir (1921), and Vygotsky (1962). Nevertheless, the work of the psycholinguists has concentrated almost solely on the structural and phonological rules of language (e.g., does the child have the negative form, does he have a means for indicating plurals, does he use compound sentences). Almost no headway has been made towards defining the functions that language may serve (for poetry, for description, for propagandizing, for problem solving, for psycho-dynamic defenses, etc.).

Thus, psycholinguistics, like behaviorism, provides an extremely limited empirical basis from which to derive guidelines for teaching language skills to children, whether disadvantaged or otherwise. The result has been that in the teaching of verbal abilities there has been an orientation similar to that in overall enrichment; namely, try to offer every possible language skill that *may* be important. This ranges across such things as verbal labels, verbal descriptions of objects, rote repetition of sentences, listening to stories, facilitating dialogue, etc. Weikart and Wiegerink's description

(1968) of "verbal bombardment" seems the most apt term for this approach. Although questions might be raised about the expense and redundancy of such a wide range of stimulation, the most serious questions concern the child's incorporation of the material. There is rarely adequate assurance that the child will partake of the verbalization or make it a meaningful part of his experience. At most, the child might be asked to respond to a specific item such as "Say what I say," "What do you see in the picture?", and so on. Most teaching, however, is done in a group situation with the result that any overt response that is required is asked of only one child. It is assumed that in any dialogue that occurs, the other children will attend and comprehend even though they are not required to answer overtly. If the attention and comprehension are lacking, however, the children cannot follow the dialogue and the teaching, no matter how well organized, is lost.

The recognition of these difficulties has led to programs geared to requiring more active participation by the children. One of the first attempts to offer a program of more focused and directed language skills was that of Bereiter and Engelmann (1966a, 1966b). Not only did they limit the type of verbalization to which the children were exposed, but they radically changed the behavior required of the child. For example, verbal responses were demanded of the children regardless of their interest in the material. In so doing, this program discarded the permissive orientation characteristic of nursery schools and adopted a more fully consistent behaviorist position.

Consistency does not necessarily yield success. However, in the case of the Bereiter-Engelmann program, the consistent behaviorist approach was ideally suited to the deficiencies of the disadvantaged child. Unlike so many other attempts at enrichment, the program demanded some level of response from the children. The material and teachers could not be ignored and thus the program refused to allow the children their well-documented mechanism of avoidance (Deutsch, 1966; Mattick, 1965).

Questions nevertheless remain as to the effectiveness of the material that the child is given to inject, particularly since Bereiter and Engelmann have given scant attention to several key areas.

First, their approach analyzes only the material to be taught; it ignores the cognitive processes in the child that may influence the way the material is incorporated. The hope is that with sufficient exposure to the minute components of any process the child eventually is bound to learn. This philosophy is largely responsible for their almost total reliance on rote drill. Second, although they are interested in developing higher-level thinking, they feel that the most fruitful path is the development of language structures (e.g., prepositions, adverbs, full sentences). Research is needed to determine whether the rote repetition of language eventually will lead to developing the underlying cognitive structures that Bereiter and Engelmann wish to foster. Third, this program, like many others, ignores individual differences in functioning. By this, I do not mean simply rate of learning, but such factors as style of learning, personality factors, motivation (Kagan, Moss, & Sigel, 1963; Witkin, Dyk, Faterson, Goodenough, & Karp, 1962).

It should be noted that almost no program in the sphere of public education grapples effectively with these issues. For example, we give lip service to the words "individual differences," but almost total reliance is placed on group teaching. At most, "individual teaching" means smaller groups or some degree of personalized attention in the group setting. This approach is then rationalized as representing egalitarian ideals since it is based on the assumption that all normal children are capable of achieving the same learning through the same techniques. As a result one-to-one teaching becomes tinged with either anti-democratice overtones or, worse still, the connotation of illness (e.g., psychotherapy) since it must be used only for children who do not fit the norm. These assumptions may be applicable to older children who already have a large body of consensually validated information, language, and attitudes. However, even here the large number of learning disorders makes group teaching a questionable method for many children. How much more questionable this method must be for introducing the precursors of abstract thinking to the young child who is distractable, egocentric, and limited in verbal skill. Another of the biases against individual teaching rests on the implicit assumption that individual teaching would or should occupy most of the teaching day. Little consideration has been given to the possible effectiveness of short periods of daily individual instruction, even though such instruction is widely and effectively used in the initial teaching of cognition to other language deficient groups, e.g., deaf children (Blank, 1965). In addition, the limited attention spans of young children suggest that relatively brief sessions involving frequent reinforcement of new (cognitive) skills would theoretically be the most effective means of teaching.

Difficulties in teaching higher-level cognition in the group setting may not matter to the middle-class child who has numerous opportunities at home for a rich one-to-one verbal interchange. The latter may even allow the child to partake more fully of the group learning situation since he is developing the necessary fund of skills for this activity. This often is not the case with the disadvantaged child who has limited access to such individual attention. He can only rely on the group setting where adult attention is diluted and sporadic. As a result, serious questions exist as to whether the group setting can provide the necessary opportunities for higher-level learning.

REFERENCES

BARATZ, J. The assessment of language and cognitive abilities of the Negro. Paper presented at the meeting of the American Psychological Association, San Francisco, September 1968.

BAYLEY, N. Comparison of mental and motor test scores for ages one–15 months by sex, birth order, race, geographical location, and education of parents. *Child Development*, 1965, *36*, 379–411.

BEERY, J. Matching of auditory and visual stimuli by average and retarded readers. *Child Development*, 1967, *38*, 828–833.

BEREITER, C., & ENGELMANN, S. *Teaching disadvantaged children in the preschool*. Englewood Cliffs: Prentice-Hall, 1966. (a)

BEREITER, C., & ENGELMANN, S. An academically oriented preschool for disadvantaged children: Results from the initial experimental group.

Paper presented at OISE Conference on Preschool Education. In Ontario Inst. Studies in Education Monograph Series #4, 1966. (b)

BERNSTEIN, B. Language and social class. *British Journal of Sociology*, 1960, *11*, 271–276.

BERNSTEIN, B. Social class and linguistic development: A theory of social learning. In A. H. Halsey, J. Flond, & C. A. Anderson (Eds.), *Education, economy and society*. New York: Free Press, 1961.

BERNSTEIN, B., & HENDERSON, D. Social class differences in the relevance of language to socialization. Report of the Sociological Research Unit. University of London Institute of Education, 1968.

BIRCH, H., & BELMONT, L. Auditory-visual integration in normal and retarded readers. *American Journal of Orthopsychiatry*, 1964, *34*, 852–861.

BLANK, M. Use of the deaf in language studies: A reply to Furth. *Psychological Bulletin*, 1965, *63*, 412–444.

BLANK, M. A methodology for fostering abstract thinking in deprived children. Paper presented at Ontario Institute Studies in Education Conference. Toronto, March 1968.

BLANK, M. Cognitive processes in auditory discrimination in normal and retarded readers. *Child Development*, 1968, *39*, 1091–1101.

BLANK, M., & BRIDGER, W. H. Cross-modal transfer in nursery school children. *Journal of Comparative and Physiological Psychology*, 1964, *58*, 277–282.

BLANK, M., & BRIDGER, W. H. Deficiencies in verbal labeling in retarded readers. *American Journal of Orthopsychiatry*, 1966, *38*, 840–847.

BLANK, M., & BRIDGER, W. H. Perceptual abilities and conceptual deficiencies in retarded readers. In J. Zubin (Ed.), *Psychopathology of intelligence*. New York: Grune & Stratton, 1967.

BLANK, M., & SOLOMON, F. A tutorial language program to develop abstract thinking in socially disadvantaged preschool children. *Child Development*, 1968, *39*, 379–389.

BLANK, M., & SOLOMON, F. How shall the disadvantaged child be taught? *Child Development*, 1969, *40*, 47–61.

BLANK, M., WEIDER, S., & BRIDGER, W. H. Verbal deficiencies in abstract thinking in early reading retardation. *American Journal of Orthopsychiatry*, 1968, *38*, 823–834.

BROWN, R., & BELLUGI, V. Three processes in the child's acquisition of syntax. *Harvard Educational Review*, 1964, *34*, 133–151.

CAZDEN, C. B. Some implications of research on language development for pre-school education. In R. D. Hess & R. M. Bear (Eds.), *Early Education*. Chicago: Aldine, 1966.

CHOMSKY, N. *Syntactic structures*. The Hague: Mouton, 1957.

DENNIS, W. Causes of retardation among institutional children. *Iranian Journal of Genetic Psychology*, 1960, *96*, 47–60.

DEUTSCH, C. P. Auditory discrimination and learning: Social factors. *Merrill-Palmer Quarterly*, 1964, *10*, 277–296.

DEUTSCH, C. P. Learning in the disadvantaged. In W. Harris (Ed.), *Analyses of Concept Learning*. New York: Academic Press, 1966.

DEUTSCH, M. Facilitating development in the preschool child: Social and psychological perspectives. *Merrill-Palmer Quarterly*, 1964, *10*, 249–263.

DEUTSCH, M., & BROWN, B. Social influences in Negro-white intelligence differences. *Journal of Social Issues*, 1964, *20* (2), 24–35.

DREGER, R. M., & MILLER, K. S. Comparative psychological studies of Negroes and whites in the United States 1959–1965. *Psychological Bulletin Monograph Supplement*, 1968, *70*, No. 3, Part 2.

ERVIN, S. M., & MILLER, W. R. Language development. *Yearbook National Social Studies Education*, 1963, *62*, Part 1.

FEUERSTEIN, R. The learning potential assessment device: A new method for assessing modifiability of the cognitive functioning of socioculturally disadvantaged adolescents. Paper presented to Israel Foundations Trustees, Jerusalem, January 1968.

FREEBURG, N. E., & PAYNE, D. T. Parental influence on cognitive development in early childhood: A review. *Child Development*, 1967, *38*, 65–87.

GOLDFARB, W. Effects of psychological deprivation in infancy and subsequent stimulation. *American Journal of Psychiatry*, 1945, *102*, 18–33.

GOLDSTEIN, K. Functional disturbances in brain damage. In S. Arieti (Ed.), *American Handbook of Psychiatry*, Vol. 1. New York: Basic Books, 1959.

GOTKIN, L. S., CAUDLE, F., CANS, H., SAGGESSE, V., & SCHOENFELD, L. Effects of two types of feedback on training and posttest performance in a visual discrimination task. Unpublished manuscript from Institute for Developmental Studies, New York, 1968.

HEIDER, E. R., CAZDEN, C. B., & BROWN, R. Social class differences in the effectiveness and style of children's coding ability. Report for Project Literacy Reports, 1968.

HESS, R. D., & SHIPMAN, V. C. Early experience and the socialization of cognitive modes in children. *Child Development,* 1965, *36,* 869–886.

HESS, R. D., & SHIPMAN, V. C. Maternal influences upon early learning: The cognitive environments of urban pre-school children. In R. D. Hess & R. M. Bear (Eds.), *Early Education.* Chicago: Aldine, 1966.

HILGARD, E. R., & MARQUIS, D. G. *Conditioning and learning.* New York: Appleton Century Crofts, 1961.

HUNT, J. McV. The psychological basis for using preschool enrichment as an antidote for cultural deprivation. *Merrill-Palmer Quarterly,* 1964, *10,* 309–348.

JOHN, V. P. The intellectual development of slum children. Some preliminary findings. *American Journal of Orthopsychiatry,* 1963, *33,* 813–822.

KAGAN, J., MOSS, H. A., & SIGEL, T. E. Psychological significance of styles of conceptualization. In J. C. Wright & J. Kagan (Eds.), *Basic cognitive processes in children,* Monogr. Soc. Res. Child Development, 1963, *28,* No. 2 (Whole No. 30).

KARNES, M. B. The research program for the preschool disadvantaged at the University of Illinois. Paper presented at the American Educational Research Association, Chicago, February 1968.

KATZ, P. A., & DEUTSCH, M. The relationship of auditory and visual functioning to reading achievement in disadvantaged children. Paper presented at Soc. Research Child Development, New York, March 1967.

KENDLER, T. S., KENDLER, H. H., & WELLS, D. Reversal and nonreversal shifts in nursery school children. *Journal of Experimental Psychology,* 1959, *58,* 55–60.

KOHLBERG, L. Montessori with the culturally disadvantaged: A cognitive-developmental interpretation and some research findings. In R. D. Hess & R. M. Bear (Eds.), *Early Education.* Chicago: Aldine, 1966.

LABOV, W., COHEN, P., & ROBBINS, C. A preliminary study of the structure of English used by Negro and Puerto Rican speakers in New York

City. Final Report, Cooperative Research Project No. 3091, Office of Education, 1965.

LENROW, P. B. Preschool socialization and the development of competence. Project Evaluation Report, Institute of Human Development, University of California, Berkeley, March 1968.

LORENZ, K. E. Imprinting. *The Auk*, 1937, *54*, 245–273.

MATTICK, I. Adaptation of nursery school techniques to deprived children: Some notes on the experiences of teaching children of multi-problem families in a therapeutically oriented nursery school. *Journal of the American Academy of Child Psychiatry*, 1965, *4*, 670–700.

OLSEN, A. V. Relation of achievement test scores and specific reading abilities to the Frostig developmental test of visual perception. *Perceptual and Motor Skills*, 1966, *22*, 179–184.

PALKES, H., STEWART, M., & KAHANS, B. Porteus maze performance of hyperactive boys after training in self-directed verbal commands. *Child Development*, 1968, *39*, 817–826.

PIAGET, J. *The origins of intelligence in children.* New York: International University Press, 1952.

PIAGET, J. Quantification, conservation and nativism. *Science*, 1968, *162*, 976–979.

RICHELLE, M., & FEUERSTEIN, R. Enfants Juife Nord Africaine: Essai psycho-pedagogique a l'intention des educateurs. Aliyah des Jeunes de l'Agenne Juive, Tel Aviv, 1957.

SAPIR, E. *Language: An introduction to the study of speech.* New York: Harcourt Brace, 1921.

SKINNER, B. F. *Science and human behavior.* New York: Free Press, 1953.

SPAULDING, R. L. The Durham education improvement program. Paper presented at OISE Conference on Preschool Education. In Ontario Inst. Studies in Education. Monogr. Series #4, 1966.

SPIKER, C., & NORCROSS, K. Effects of previously acquired stimulus names on discrimination performance, *Child Development*, 1962, *33*, 859–864.

SPITZ, R. A. Hospitalism: An inquiry into the genesis of psychiatric conditions in early childhood. *Psychoanalytic Study of Child*, 1945, *1*, 53–74.

STERRITT, O., & RUDNICK, M. Auditory and visual perception in relation to reading ability in fourth grade boys. *Perceptual and Motor Skills,* 1966, *22,* 859–864.

ULRICH, R., STACHNIK, T., & MABRY, J. *Control of human behavior.* Glenview, Ill.: Scott, Foresman, 1966.

VYGOTSKY, L. S. *Thought and language* (Trans. Eds. E. Kaufmann & C. Valtar). New York: Wiley, 1962.

WEIKART, D. P. Preschool programs: Preliminary findings. *Journal of Special Education,* 1967, *1,* 163–181.

WEIKART, D. P., & WIEGERINK, R. Initial results of a comparative preschool curriculum project. Paper presented at the meeting of the American Psychological Association, San Francisco, September 1968.

WEPMAN, J. M. Auditory discrimination, speech, and reading. *Elementary School Journal,* 1960, *60,* 325–333.

WILKERSON, D. A. Selected readings on the disadvantaged. In J. Hellmuth (Ed.), *Disadvantaged child,* Vol. 1. Seattle: Special Child Publications, 1967.

WITKIN, H. A., DYK, R. B., FATERSON, H. F., GOODENOUGH, D. R., & KARP, S. A. *Psychological differentiation.* New York: Wiley, 1962.

9

ARE KINDERGARTENS
OBSOLETE?

BERNARD SPODEK AND HELEN F. ROBISON

The kindergarten developed in the nineteenth century to foster the child's intellectual growth. But there is growing doubt that the kindergartens of the twentieth century are equipped for this task.

Friedrich Froebel, the German educator, pioneered in the kindergarten movement. The aims of the Froebelian kindergarten, like those of the modern kindergarten, encompassed the harmonious

Elementary School Journal, March 1965. Copyright © University of Chicago. Reprinted with permission.

development of the child. The modern school, however, taking its cue from the increasing complexity of contemporary society, requires attainments quite unlike those required in the past.

THE FROEBELIAN KINDERGARTEN

Froebelian education was symbolic in intent. The child was to be taught to understand the internal meanings of objects rather than their external manifestations.

In the Froebelian school, concrete manipulable materials called *gifts* were offered to the child. Each gift manifested a principle that might help the child unify the diverse elements in the universe. The "gifts" were offered in a specific sequence; first, colored balls of wool yarn; then, wooden spheres, cubes, and cylinders; and then, other objects.

Through this procedure, it was thought, the relationships within the cosmos would slowly and systematically be revealed to the child. The "gifts" were not available for free manipulative play but only for the purpose of understanding the physical environment; and that understanding was seen as a step toward achieving the inner spirituality that was basic to Froebel's philosophy.

In Froebelian education, intellectual understanding was closely linked with the spiritual. It was hoped that the kindergarten would help children understand the relationship between man and God, as well as relationships between man and man. Education dealt with reality only as it allowed the child to grasp the mystical essence of that reality.

The "occupations," of the Froebelian kindergarten included such activities as paper-weaving. They were designed to develop the spirit as well as the mind and the body. The "mother-plays," the songs that mothers and teachers sang and the games they played with children, were designed to contribute to the child's achievement of the stated aim of education: an understanding of the harmony of opposites and an understanding of the unity of the cosmos (1).

THE REFORM MOVEMENT

In the second half of the nineteenth century, the Froebelian kindergarten was transplanted from Germany, its native country, to the United States. Here the kindergarten developed as a separate, non-public school institution. Froebelian philosophy was not generally in harmony with prevailing school thinking in the United States. At that time, school thought here was primarily Herbartian.

Still, kindergartens gradually found their way into the public school systems. Their educational value was frequently questioned and minimized. Even today only a bare majority of American children enter public schools in kindergarten.

As American experience with the kindergarten grew, practitioners began to question the validity of its formal and symbolic aspects. With the growing impact of the child study movement at the turn of the century and the development of and interest in John Dewey's philosophy, a re-evaluation of the aims and the methods of the kindergarten was inevitable.

This reappraisal led to a reform movement in the first and second decades of the twentieth century. The movement eventually succeeded in thoroughly transforming the aims, methods, and materials of the kindergarten.

PATTY SMITH HILL

The original intent of the reform movement was to modify the practices of kindergarten but not its philosophy, which was Froebelian. Childhood experiences and development were seen as less universal than Froebel had assumed. Much of the original kindergarten program in the United States had grown out of an abstraction of the experiences of German children. Some practices that developed were alien to the American child. There was also a growing concern that the young child deal more with the manifest world than with its underlying symbolism.

The emerging philosophy of the reform movement was stated by Patty Smith Hill in 1913 in a report to the International Kindergarten Union (2). According to this point of view, which was influenced largely by Dewey, the curriculum of the kindergarten should grow out of the subject matter of the school and the nature of the child's mind as well as the relationship of these factors to the civilization of the past and of the future.

Subject matter, a reflection of human achievement, originates in and grows out of social life, Patty Hill said. The school curriculum is a reflection of social life, which is a unified whole. School subjects are aspects of the total social experience that are separated out for purposes of study. Kindergarten education, Hill felt, should help the child acquire the knowledge that has been accumulated in civilizations past and the knowledge that will be accumulated in the future. Only through social experience could this knowledge become meaningful to the child.

To help the child acquire this knowledge, he was to be given kindergarten experiences that grew out of his personal experience. These personally meaningful experiences would help the child gain the insights needed to reconstruct the experience of the past.

Several ideas were thus introduced into kindergarten education. There was the idea that knowledge grows out of the social lives of human beings and has meaning only in a social context; and there was the idea that the personal experiences of the young child are vital in helping him achieve understandings about civilizations past, present, and future.

Froebel counted on mystical experience to transcend the child's understanding and illuminate ideas. Hill proposed concrete, child-oriented experience. Under the influence of the reform movement, kindergarten education took a new direction.

While many Froebelian elements remained, including the emphasis on self-activity and art and music, the break with orthodox tradition permitted experimentation with new ideas and new materials. Some of Montessori's ideas were adopted, though her ideas, like Froebel's, were modified and integrated into the new curriculum.

The Froebelian kindergarten had offered tiny blocks. Now large pieces of equipment were provided, and they opened new possibilities for dramatic play and construction. In nature study, plants and animals were made available, not to help children learn to appreciate the beauty of nature, but to help them learn about the basic processes of life. The American contributions to the kindergarten included block and doll play.

Patty Smith Hill was among the more articulate and the more influential innovators in kindergarten education, but other experimenters were also at work.

PRATT AND MITCHELL

Caroline Pratt established the City and Country School in New York City to experiment with a new curriculum for the elementary school. Lucy Sprague Mitchell was one of the key supporters of the school. She developed the "Here and Now" concept in the education of young children. The idea flowed from her experiments in using the immediate environment as a laboratory where children could explore concepts and relationships to derive significant understandings.

Mitchell reasoned that children can understand best those concepts and relationships that are imbedded in familiar things. The neighborhood, she said, is an excellent center for study; in it children can discover many of the important concepts of the social sciences.

Mitchell was well aware of increasing urbanization and the growing distance between the child and elemental life processes. She protested approaches that confused children by directing their attention to unreality before they learned to know reality. She objected to procedures that substituted excitement for legitimate interests and failed to take into account children's need to see new relationships in familiar things (3).

To Mitchell the "Here and Now" basis for selecting experiences was a way in which children could make progress toward attaining significant knowledge. To her, the approach was not a way of denying children intellectual challenge.

She developed a geography program that extended from nursery school through the junior high school. At each level she offered experiences that built on previous learnings. In her plan, the learnings of the kindergarten child made a significant contribution to the program (4).

Caroline Pratt refused to write a curriculum guide based on the exciting developments in her experimental school. She feared the stultification and the petrification that could result from prescribed programs.

In her school she featured play, not as an end in itself, but as a stimulus to intellectual activity. To her, play was a manifestation and a codification of intellectual activity for the young child to whom the written word was not yet accessible: "Play, or as the children call it 'work,' with these materials [blocks] is an organizing experience. . . . what the information does to play is to keep it going and help it to organize as a whole, to raise new inquiries, and above all to offer opportunities for new [intellectual] relationships" (5).

In the decades that followed, other insights into child development and psychosocial development were to have their impact on the kindergarten.

EMPHASIS ON MENTAL HEALTH

Psychology pointed to the urgent need to look at the effect that school practices have on mental health, especially of young children. Psychiatrists stressed the fact that many emotional problems of adults have their roots in early childhood experience. Educators, therefore, began to concern themselves with children's feelings.

It became important to provide children with outlets for releasing feelings, whether of love or aggression. A new emphasis on creativity and on children's need for free expression further buttressed the move toward permissiveness and greater freedom for children.

As the significance of the child's inner life became more apparent, school practices that were more conducive to mental health were developed in kindergarten. There was less authoritarian discipline. Teachers became interested in studying the meaning of behavior in addition to its manifestations.

The climate of the kindergarten became more democratic and child centered, and in the 1940's and 1950's the "child development point of view" became the watchword of the kindergartens. Unfortunately, in too many schools the better the social climate of the kindergarten became, the more sterile its intellectual content and climate became.

During these years some kindergarten teachers misunderstood and misapplied the new child development point of view. Afraid of frustrating the child, teachers refrained from offering challenge. Afraid of repressing the child, teachers removed all restrictions. Afraid of inhibiting the child, teachers withheld their help or guidance in the development of needed skills.

Some teachers became confused about the role of play. Was it only an avenue for expressing feelings? If so, the chief value of kindergarten lay in helping the young child act out his feelings and problems.

Some teachers saw the kindergarten as a setting where the child could be helped to adjust to school. To them, the teacher's responsibility was to guide children to sit quietly for increasingly longer periods, to follow directions, and to fit into patterns that permitted the teaching of reading in first grade.

Kindergarten practices, as Caroline Pratt feared, became codified in teachers' manuals and prescribed courses of study. Individuality, variety, and flexibility disappeared. During the population boom after World War II, many "double" kindergarten classes were formed. Often these classes had fifty or more children in one room. Crowding at this level was regarded as less deleterious to learning than at any other. The large classes helped open the way to highly regimented procedures and greatly diluted and greatly simplified programs. The prime aim was to inculcate discipline and keep children from being troublesome.

Thus, the kindergarten programs made progress in some directions but moved further from the objective of fostering children's intellectual growth. The resulting dissatisfaction has brought demands for the return of challenging content in kindergarten.

The demands often lead to increased emphasis on "reading readiness" programs or even on reading instruction. In some communities, Montessori schools have been organized to teach children skills that are not being taught in kindergartens.

SYMBOLIC EDUCATION TODAY

The early teaching of reading does not seem to provide the final solution to the major problems of kindergarten education. Researchers have yet to report convincing evidence that early instruction makes a difference in later reading competency. Children's learning does not have to come from books. Indeed, do we know just how much young children are able to learn from books?

Dewey's vision still has some relevance to today's problem of educating the young child. He saw the problem as one of discovering "the steps that intervene between the child's present experience and their richer maturity" (6). These intervening steps must be different from children's changing experiences, and the quality must be different from that of their preschool lives.

The idea has been proposed that the structure of knowledge could be the basis for the kindergarten program, as well as for programs in all subsequent grades. The idea is being developed and tested in some promising new programs today. Bruner's popular statement of the proposal has sparked considerable research and innovation (7).

Significant programs can be offered in kindergarten, programs that build on meaningful experiences and include considerable free, manipulative, and dramatic forms of play. Through such programs the value of kindergarten in the educational hierarchy would become more apparent.

Perhaps reading readiness could be supplanted by symbol readiness. Concept development and language skill are prime requisites for modern education. Today's children need readiness for reading, but they also need readiness for mathematics, for map and globe concepts, and for a variety of symbols and signs used in abstract thinking. Kindergarten programs must offer activities that support learning in each of these areas.

Kindergarten education must also provide for the many differences found among children. A variety of "steps that intervene" must be developed if the school is to meet and provide for the great differences in the five-year-olds who are ready for school today.

If the modern kindergarten is to survive, it must contribute a greater share to the child's total learning experience. The mechanics of reading may or may not be important for some five-year-olds, but the development of basic concepts and verbal and symbolic skills are a necessity for all children.

The task of the kindergarten is to support the child's intellectual growth as part of his total development. The structure of knowledge can provide guidelines from which essential kindergarten goals can be derived.

REFERENCES

1. FRIEDRICH FROEBEL. "Fundamental Principles of Education," *Education by Development*, translated by Josephine Jarvis, pp. 161–214. New York: D. Appleton and Company, 1899.

2. PATTY SMITH HILL. "Second Report," *The Kindergarten*. Boston: Houghton Mifflin Company, 1913.

3. LUCY SPRAGUE MITCHELL. *Here and Now Storybook*, p. 6. New York: E. P. Dutton Company, 1921.

4. LUCY SPRAGUE MITCHELL. *Young Geographers*. New York: John Day Company, 1934.

5. CAROLINE PRATT. *Experimental Practice in City and Country Schools,* pp. 3–4. New York: E. P. Dutton Company, 1924.

6. JOHN DEWEY. *The Child and the Curriculum,* pp. 15–16. Chicago: University of Chicago Press, 1902.

7. JEROME S. BRUNER. *The Process of Education.* Cambridge, Massachusetts: Harvard University Press, 1960.

10

BRITAIN'S FIRST NURSERY-INFANT SCHOOL

ELIZABETH BRADBURN

Robert Owen, a Welshman from Newtown, founded Britain's first nursery-infant school in New Lanark in 1816, twenty-one years before Froebel opened his first kindergarten in Germany, forty-four years before Peabody established her own kindergarten in America. As 1966 marks the hundred and fiftieth anniversary of the school's inception, this may be an opportune moment for a fresh assessment of Owen's educational theory and practice.

Why did Owen, a wealthy cotton-mill owner, open a school

Elementary School Journal, November 1966. Copyright © University of Chicago. Reprinted by permission.

for young children? Did he think that by providing a nursery he could persuade more women to become cotton operatives? Did he think that, in school, children were out of harm's way? Did he wish to protect them from falling into the water that he used to drive the machinery in his factory? Was he just another philanthropist? Answers to these questions could never give a full explanation of Owen's reasons for providing the school. To understand his motives, it is necessary to consider his ideology.

Owen was a revolutionary who wanted to reform society. The dominant passion of his life was to create communities of people who lived by the principle of mutual consideration, not by self-interest. So gripped was he by this revolutionary purpose that he spent his life and a large fortune trying to rebuild society according to his pattern.

Although an idealist, Owen was enough of a realist to see that there could be no new society without new men. Having little faith in the power of legalism to create new men, he turned toward rationalism, atheism, and environmentalism to help him change human nature.

Owen believed that man was fundamentally good and degenerated only because he was "the creature of circumstances" (1: 281). He maintained that character was "formed for, and not by, the individual" (1: 110); and that man did not possess "the smallest control over the formation of any of his own faculties" (1: 280). The view that "infants, children, and men, are agents governed by a will formed by themselves and fashioned after their own choice" was quite unacceptable to Owen (1: 280). Consequently he struggled to remove the adverse circumstances that he believed created bad character and tried to promote the training of good character. Speaking at a public meeting in Glasgow in 1812, he made his aims clear. He said: "The object is no less than to remove gross ignorance and extreme poverty, with their attendant misery, from your population; and to make it rational, well-disposed, and well-behaved" (2: 250).

Believing that education and environment could entirely transform the nature of men and society, Owen was anxious that young and old, rich and poor, should have the privilege of being educated.

He maintained that the only way to make good citizens was to educate adults and children. Schools, he thought, should give training in right habits and provide an environment where children's better natures could grow. When able to establish his own school, he aptly called it an *Institution for the Formation of Character*. There he hoped that man's character would be developed and his ability to live in harmony with others fostered.

Owen was enlightened enough to advocate and provide schooling for the poor at a time when it was fashionable to scoff at the idea of educating the "lower orders." In a class-conscious society where mobility between the classes was neither envisioned nor encouraged, he said that, given the right education, "infants of any one class in the world may be readily formed into men of any other class" (2: 315).

Owen's thinking was well ahead of legislation on child labor. During his day it was not uncommon for children of six years of age to be working in factories for fourteen hours a day. No wonder Elizabeth Barrett Browning could write in her poem "The Cry of the Children":

> The young lambs are bleating in the meadow,
> The young birds are chirping in the nest,
> The young fawns are playing with shadows,
> The young flowers are blowing toward the west—
> But the young, young children, O my brothers,
> They are weeping bitterly!
> They are weeping in the playtime of the others
> In the country of the free.
> They look up with their pale and sunken faces
> And their looks are sad to see
> For the man's hoary anguish draws and presses
> Down the cheeks of infancy.

Owen, ever sensitive to human suffering, struggled to change opinion on the employment of young children. Two of his letters, the first to the Earl of Liverpool (1: 130) and the second to the Master Manufacturers (1: 140), show how earnestly he struggled to stop exploitation. Although the first effective Factory Act prohibiting children under nine years of age from working in cotton mills was not passed until 1833, in 1816 Owen refused to employ children under ten; for he believed that, prior to that age, children should be in school.

Owen held advanced views on educational practice. Speaking of him, Rusk said: "He anticipated by a century the present-day Nursery School movement" (3: 134). Undoubtedly much of what Owen did is only being recommended now by research workers.

While he would not have been familiar with modern terminology, the findings of recent investigations would not have seemed strange to him. He seemed to know intuitively much of what has now been established by tests and measurements.

Many aspects of Owen's building would have gained the approval of present-day school architects. It had amenities denied to many twentieth-century teachers. For example, his nursery was housed in ground-floor rooms that were surrounded by a garden and a large paved area. Yet, because even today many nursery and infant schools still lack these outdoor features, recent books on building requirements are at pains to stress their importance. One publication goes so far as to say, "A nursery without a garden is a contradiction in terms; it is no nursery school" (4: 5). Another says: "All great educationalists of the past have stressed the importance of play, yet few of the playgrounds in schools to-day have been planned to cater for the needs of the child's outdoor play" (5: 5).

Owen's conception was that of an open-air nursery, the school acting as a shelter from inclement weather—an idea popularized almost a century later by Margaret McMillan (6: 76). Showing his school building to the inhabitants of New Lanark, Owen said: "In this (room) their chief occupation will be to play and amuse themselves in severe weather; at other times they will be permitted to occupy the enclosed area before the building: for, to give children a vigorous constitution, they ought to be kept as much as possible in the open air" (1: 98).

On the floor above Owen's school were two large lecture halls where adults could be taught in the evenings. Here the parents of school children could obtain instruction. The need to educate parents, through parent-teacher associations, evening classes, and further education establishments, is only slowly gaining recognition in many parts of the world even today.

Owen's method of choosing his staff is worthy of note. He selected teachers primarily because of their qualities of character: good temper, patience, and a strong love of children were his first considerations. He wanted children educated in an atmosphere where kindness rather than corporal punishment predominated. In fact, he went so far as to inform his teachers that children were neither to hear an angry word nor see a threatening countenance. Today we are becoming increasingly aware of the beneficial effect of a warm, friendly classroom climate on children's performance, but Owen said over a century ago that there should be "increasing kindness in tone, look, word, and action, to all the children without exception, by every teacher employed, so as to create a real affection and full confidence between the teachers and the taught" (7: 319). The more recent researches of Moreno, Lewin, Anderson, Brewer, and others have shown the potent effect of friendly relationships on learning and group living (8: 112).

A FRIENDLY PLACE

Owen anticipated much of what social psychologists are now saying about the effect of individuals on groups and groups on individuals. It is clear from the questionnaire which William Rathbone sent to Owen after visiting New Lanark that the teachers' kindness to their children was reflected in the children's behavior to their teachers and to each other (9: 100). This spirit of friendliness invariably made a deep impression on visitors to the school.

After the school had been open for six months, Owen gave an account of the number of children he had admitted. It appears that he had sixty three-year-olds, forty-six four-year-olds, fifty-nine five-year-olds, and forty-eight six-year-olds. These children were organized into groups, each of which contained children of mixed ages.

To use the current phrase, Owen used vertical rather than horizontal classification. Understanding that education is a continuous process that should be organized in progressive stages, Owen did not organize children in strict chronological age-groupings.

The same principle was applied to the transfer of children from one school to another. He promoted children not so much on the basis of age as on the bases of ability and maturity, and made organization his servant, not his master. He said children remained in school "two or three years according to their bodily strength and mental capacity; when they have attained as much strength and instruction as to enable them to unite, without creating confusion, with the youngest classes in the superior school, they are admitted to it" (10: 131). Many nursery-school teachers today who are forced to transfer children to separate infant schools, on the very day they become five, would welcome Owen's system of promotion.

While Owen kept children from two to six years of age under one roof, Britain did not follow his example. Traditionally, her nursery schools have admitted children from two to five years of age. More recently, however, a few experimental nursery-infant schools have been set up where children can remain in the same school from their second to their seventh birthday.

FREE PLAY

Owen's school program was amazingly up to date. He appeared to have a clear grasp of the role of free, unstructured play in the education of young children. Usually the children played freely out of doors, under the supervision of a young woman; sometimes they played inside. Professor Griscom spoke of this in recalling his visit to the school. He said: "One apartment of the school afforded a novel and pleasing spectacle. It consisted of a great number of children, from one to three or four years of age. They are assembled in a large room, under the care of a judicious female, who allows them to amuse themselves with various selected toys, and occasionally collects the oldest into a class, and teaches them their letters" (11: 143).

REST PERIOD

At a time when it was generally accepted in educational circles that children were alike, Owen was aware of individual differences and made provision for them. In his school no child was forced to take a midday rest. The children were free to sleep or to stay awake and play. Before World War II it was quite common for British teachers to insist that all children should sleep in the afternoon. Uniformity of procedure was expected. It was only after knowledge of individual differences in basic metabolic rates reached teachers in the thirties and the forties that relaxation of rigid routines came.

In New Lanark routines were flexible. Timetables were not strictly followed because Owen was not a great believer in straight instruction. He encouraged teachers to let children have first-hand experiences and to give their pupils the opportunity to understand situations rather than merely memorize facts. To let memory usurp the place of reasoning and observation was mere folly to Owen. Consequently, he advocated informal rather than formal methods of teaching. For example, nature study lessons were used for field studies during which the children themselves collected nature specimens. While Dewey was criticizing rote learning and advocating the use of concrete material in the second decade of this century, Owen was making war on mere bookish learning in the second decade of the last. Even so, the notion that "the curriculum should be thought of in terms of activity and experience rather than of knowledge to be acquired and facts to be stored" came to many as a revolutionary concept when it appeared in an official publication in 1931 (12: 75).

VISITING SEAMAN

According to Owen, children should have interesting encounters. They should meet enthusiasm and reality in adults. For this reason he invited informed people to share their experiences with the children in his school. Once he persuaded an admiral who had sailed around the world to come and tell the children about his travels. A century later when Kilpatrick and others recommended this method to teachers as sound educational policy it was considered to be *avant garde*.

Long before object lessons came into vogue, Owen was advocating the use of visual aids. A visitor to his school reported that he used a magic lantern and large pictures painted by the best artists he could procure (13). Owen stressed the importance of appealing to more senses than one and of making sight as well as hearing the servants of education. When children were not outside making direct observations, he wanted them taught inside by the use of maps, charts, colored blocks, and other visual material.

Let us turn now from the success story to the failings of Owen's school. By today's standards the school would be deficient in many respects. To us, the play material, books, art and craft materials, music, and physical education would all be inadequate. Perhaps the major criticism that could be leveled against the school now would be that, although Owen was not unaware of discovery methods, his Institution was largely concerned with teaching rather than with helping children learn. In this respect his school did not differ from most of those founded a hundred and fifty years ago.

REFLECTIONS

What perhaps is a little surprising at first sight is that Owen's school did not long survive. Why, one may ask, did this institution, which was regarded by many distinguished visitors as one of the philanthropic marvels of its day, not continue and grow? Why did those who followed Owen not develop his educational practices? Why did his other ventures such as New Harmony and Queenswood fail? Could it be that, while in theory the things Owen suggested were admirable, the philosophy on which they were based was inadequate?

Owen, right in his diagnosis that the world would not be transformed unless individuals changed, was wrong in thinking that selfishness could be permanently eradicated by education and environment alone. Right in his view that human nature could change, Owen was wrong in thinking that human nature was perfectible without God's help. Right in trying to focus the attention of responsible citizens on the need to develop man's character and his ability to co-operate with others, he was wrong in thinking that "character is universally formed for, and not by, the individual" (1: 10).

It was only in his eighties that Robert Owen turned toward the spiritual world. If he had taken that step sixty years sooner, he could have discovered that God was able to change human nature without a change in environment; that God was able to cure the selfishness in man which created and perpetuated the social divisions and injustices that he failed to eradicate. If he had known from experience that God can produce a change in the character of men and if he had been able to pass this secret on to others, he could have radically altered the course of history; for he already had at least three characteristics of a great man—world goals to shape his living and the single-mindedness and the spirit of sacrifice to pursue them.

A SCHOOL TO REMEMBER

Perhaps the school in New Lanark was one of the most successful experiments of this well-meaning reformer. There his natural unselfishness and his humanity flowered as he struggled to provide for children a schooling that was spontaneous, stimulating, and undoubtedly enjoyable. There perhaps we should best remember him, for there, in spite of all his mistakes, he succeeded in founding Britain's first nursery-infant school.

REFERENCES

1. R. OWEN. *A New View of Society*. London: Dent, 1927.
2. R. OWEN. *Life of Robert Owen*. Volume 1. London: Wilson, 1857.

3. R. R. Rusk. *A History of Infant Education.* London: University of London Press, 1933.

4. Nursery School Association. *Planning the New Nursery Schools.* London: University of London Press, 1947.

5. Nursery School Association. *Infant School Playgrounds.* London: Nursery School Association, 1964.

6. G. A. N. Lowndes. *Margaret McMillan.* London: Museum Press, 1960.

7. R. Owen. *The Life of Robert Owen by Himself.* London: Bell, 1920.

8. E. Bradburn. "Friendliness in Schools," *12, Educational Review* (February, 1960), 112–24.

9. J. Murphy. Robert Owen in Liverpool. *Transactions of the Historic Society of Lancashire and Cheshire.* Volume 112, Appendix A, 1960.

10. R. Owen. Minutes of Evidence Taken before the Select Committee Appointed To Inquire into the Education of the Lower Orders of the Metropolis. Quoted in R. R. Rusk, *op. cit.,* p. 131.

11. J. Griscom. *A Year in Europe.* Volume II, p. 385 (New York: Collins and Company, 1823). Quoted in F. Podmore, *Robert Owen.* Volume 1. p. 143 (London: Hutchinson, 1906).

12. Ministry of Education Consultative Committee. *The Primary School,* London: Her Majesty's Stationery Office, 1931.

13. G. J. Holyoak. *The Times.* November 13, 1877.

11

THE BEHAVIOR ANALYSIS
CLASSROOM

DON BUSHELL, JR.

INTRODUCTION

Behavior Analysis is a new strategy for education. During the past five years, it has grown from a handful of experimental settings to hundreds of elementary classrooms throughout the nation. Successful Behavior Analysis classrooms have begun to transform the learning experiences of thousands of children. In the rural south, the industrial northeast, the urban midwest, and on Indian reserva-

The Behavior Analysis Classroom. U.S. Department of Health, Education and Welfare. Reprinted with permission of author.

tions in the west and southwest, children are learning more, with greater enjoyment and confidence than has been possible in the past.

Behavior Analysis combines familiar educational techniques in a unique way to provide a new kind of learning opportunity for young children. The program includes aspects of team teaching, nongraded classrooms, programmed instruction, individualized teaching, and token reinforcement systems. The result is an education system which—

> *accelerates the learning and achievement of the children, and unites professional educators, para-professionals, and parents in the teaching process.*

There is no mystery connected with this new system. The basic principles of human learning have been understood for some time. Behavior Analysis has taken these principles out of the laboratory classroom and put them to work in schools.

As an instructional system, Behavior Analysis follows a standard but flexible pattern. The first step, whether the child is being taught social or academic skills, is to *define an instructional objective*. The goals of teaching a child to say "Good morning" when he enters the classroom, or to put materials away when he is finished with them, are just as legitimate as instructional objectives in reading and mathematics. The second step in Behavior Analysis is to *determine how much the child already knows* about what you are trying to teach. The skills which children bring into the classroom vary so much that it is not realistic to begin everyone in the same lesson. A special Entry Behavior Inventory and diagnostic tests help a teacher decide where each individual child needs to begin working in the sequence leading to several instructional objectives in academic areas. At higher levels of achievement, these diagnostic tests are imbedded in the materials to insure that each child is mastering each instructional objective before being moved on to the next part of the sequence.

With an established instructional objective and knowledge of a child's current skill in relation to that objective, the steps between can be taught more easily if the child is well motivated to learn.

MOTIVATION: THE TOKEN ECONOMY

Behavior Analysis assumes that "motivation" does not just happen—*it is taught.* It is the result of carefully executed procedures which provide the incentives needed to guarantee that a child will begin and carry through on learning tasks. There are many potential incentives present in every classroom. The smiles and praise of a teacher, the chance to participate in recess and games with classmates, stories, attractive materials, and the chance to select a particular favorite activity can all be good incentives if properly used.

When activities the children prefer are available as a direct consequence of a particular behavior, they are valuable incentives, or reinforcers, which can generate and sustain motivation and progress. If these same activities are available automatically, regardless of what the child may do, they have very little incentive value. The timing of the consequence and its clear relationship to a particular behavior make a crucial difference. When praise *immediately* follows a child's behavior, it will usually reinforce, or strengthen, that behavior. If it comes too soon or too late it will have little or no effect—*timing is the key.*

Because many reinforcing events are hard to deliver with the necessary immediacy, Behavior Analysis classrooms use a Token Exchange System to sustain a high level of motivation. As each child in the class works at various learning tasks, he is given tokens for his progress and improvement. Later, after he has accumulated several tokens in this way, he has the opportunity to exchange them for events and activities which are important to him. These back-up activities give meaning and value to the tokens. As long as the back-ups are exciting and enjoyable, the tokens will support the child's motivation to learn and to succeed.

Tokens, in addition to being properly timed, must be delivered frequently to be most effective. When a child is faced with a new and difficult task, tokens are given often for small amounts of progress. At a later stage, as the child's skill improves, fewer tokens are needed to support progress. Consequently, the way a child earns tokens is constantly changing. At first, tokens and praise will follow a child's first attempt at holding a pencil correctly. Later, as skill increases, the tokens and praise will follow the writing of a complete sentence.

THE CLASSROOM STAFF AND THE PARENT PROGRAM

The requirement of frequent attention and reinforcement for each individual child is difficult, if not impossible, for one teacher who must deal with an entire class of thirty or more children. To provide the necessary amount of individual attention, Behavior Analysis classrooms are staffed by four adults. The lead teacher heads the team and generally takes special responsibility for reading instruction. The full-time aide usually takes special responsibility for the small math groups and two parent aides concentrate on hand-writing and spelling lessons and individual tutoring. This kind of team arrangement insures that every child receives the personal attention and reinforcement needed for him to learn at his maximum rate.

A program of parent participation is one of the key factors in the success of the Behavior Analysis approach. With proper training, the parents have become valued instructors in the classroom. Without them it would not be possible for the lead teacher and aide to enjoy the advantages of small group teaching. Parents who have worked in the classroom are also extending the benefits of the program into the home situation. With an understanding of classroom process and the principles of positive reinforcement, the parents are able to join professional teachers as partners in the education of the community's children.

Parents are employed in the classroom in a series of positions which provide improved career opportunities. During the first year, a parent serves for six to eight weeks in the classroom as a trainee. This relatively short work period enables a large number of parents to have direct contact with the program. At the next level, some parents who have been trainees are employed as aides for an entire semester. Finally, some of those who have been semester aides are employed to fill full-time positions as teacher aides. The result of this sequence is a new kind of unity between school and community, a new set of opportunities for parents, and a new potential for truly individualized classroom instruction.

THE CURRICULUM

To take advantage of these new opportunities, Behavior Analysis classrooms select curriculum materials that:

1. describe the behavior the child will be capable of at the end of the sequence,
2. require frequent responding by the child,
3. contain clear criteria for a "correct" response,
4. allow for individual rates of progress, and
5. provide for periodic testing of achievement gains.

The combination of (a) materials which meet these requirements, (b) multiple teachers, and (c) a token exchange system creates a new kind of educational setting where children learn more rapidly —and enjoy it. Following an initial emphasis on the development of social and classroom skills, the core subjects of reading, mathematics, and handwriting are stressed in Behavior Analysis classes. Instruction in these areas begins during the child's first year in the program (Head Start or Kindergarten). There is no longer any doubt that children of four and five are willing and able to learn these subjects when they are presented in small group and individual situations, supported by effective reinforcement.

THE DAILY SCHEDULE

The daily schedule of a Behavior Analysis classroom can be described in three parts:

1. planning
2. formal instruction
3. special activities, or back-ups

Twenty-five to thirty children at different performance levels and four adults make a complex organization which must be carefully managed if it is to be successful. To insure a smooth operation that is always ready to meet the changing needs of the children, a period is set aside each day for staff planning. Directed by the lead teacher, these sessions allow the classroom team to discuss specific strategies to be used with particular children, new or problematic sections of the curriculum, revisions in classroom routine, and back-up activities.

The specific lesson plan for any given day is *always determined by the progress of the children.* In general, however, the three core subjects are all taught during each instructional period. By providing at least three periods during the day, each child receives instruction in every subject.

Every instructional period is planned in conjunction with the back-up activity which will follow. At the beginning of a year there is frequent alternation between instruction (earning periods) and special back-ups (exchange periods). Ten to fifteen minutes of instruction, followed by twenty to twenty-five minutes of exchange activity, followed by another fifteen minutes of instruction, etc., is a common pattern. As the children become more skillful, the amount of study time increases, and the end of the year may find a schedule which provides for forty-five to fifty minutes of study for each ten to fifteen minutes of special activity. At the second or third grade level it is not unusual for twenty minutes of *contingent* special activity to support an entire morning's work.

DISCIPLINE

When appropriate behavior has the immediate consequence of providing greater access to activities and events of value to the child, low motivation and other factors which contribute to behavior problems are usually eliminated.

Behavior Analysis uses positive reinforcement to build improved student behavior and seeks to eliminate all coercive or negative control procedures. Verbal or physical coercion or threats are not used, but the absence of these techniques should *not* be confused with permissiveness. Misbehavior cannot be tolerated in a classroom for it may accidentally meet with reinforcement that will strengthen (teach) it.

Rather than nagging, scolding, or threatening punishment for inattention, the Behavior Analysis teacher first provides heavy reinforcement to another child who *is* attending to the assignment. Then, when the inattentive child starts to work, he is immediately praised by the teacher. The general strategy is to *ignore inappropriate behavior while providing heavy and frequent reinforcement for desirable behavior.*

Behavior which is potentially damaging or dangerous cannot be ignored. The procedure used in such circumstances is technically known as "Time-Out." Time-Out is accomplished without emotion, lectures, or scolding, but is consistently the *immediate* consequence of dangerous behavior. The child is immediately told what rule he has broken and then seated in a chair away from the other children. He remains there with a kitchen timer set for three minutes. As soon as the bell rings, the child returns to the group to be rewarded for his appropriate behaviors. His penalty is that for three minutes there has been no opportunity to engage in behavior that results in token reinforcement.

These are only two examples of procedures which correct unacceptable classroom behavior without the unwanted side effects which are part of harsh, coercive punishment.

PROGRAM AND STAFF DEVELOPMENT

The full development of a Behavior Analysis program usually occurs in *three* phases. Initially, substantial support is provided by the University of Kansas. During this phase, the local school district provides an organizational base with a Program Coordinator and a Parent Coordinator. The Program Coordinator is responsible for making the many elements of the project mesh together in a coherent program, and the Parent Coordinator introduces the program to the community and recruits parents to work in the classrooms. For the first year or two, advisors from the University of Kansas provide necessary training in the procedures and techniques of the program. Workshops at Regional Training Centers, District Workshops, and an inservice course in the Principles of Behavior Analysis are among the procedures used to supplement and support program implementation.

During the second phase of the program, local leadership reduces the district's need for strong support from the University of Kansas. As the project grows in size, local Staff Training Coordinators assume more and more of the training and support responsibility. Staff Training Coordinators and Parent Training Coordinators are the local experts in the methods and procedures of Behavior Analysis; and they are skilled in teaching this to other teachers, aides, and parents. People who fill these positions are generally drawn from the group of Behavior Analysis teachers and parents who have had classroom experience in the program. The third phase of the program generally begins as the first group of children complete the third grade. By this time, local training staff, experienced teachers, aides, and parents are able to continue the program and extend its benefits to children in other parts of the school system. From this point on, only periodic consulting by the University of Kansas is needed to maintain the vitality and progress of the program.

BEHAVIOR ANALYSIS IN HEAD START

The basic ingredients and strategies of Behavior Analysis are as relevant in Head Start as in elementary classrooms. Four co-operating adults use carefully timed and frequent reinforcement to accelerate the children's progress toward clearly stated instructional objectives.

The curriculum used in Head Start is designed to teach the skills needed to succeed in the elementary grades whether the child continues in a Behavior Analysis program or not. By the end of the year, Behavior Analysis Head Start children work in prereading, mathematics, and hand-writing groups, although a variety of pre-academic behaviors are emphasized during the first half of the year.

Positive and systematic reinforcement is used to teach the entire constellation of behaviors which make up the social role of the student. From the beginning of the year, teachers reinforce a child immediately and enthusiastically for following simple directions in all situations where instructions are used. Children who say "Good morning" to their teacher, who raise their hands when appropriate, who can distinguish between the time to talk and the time to listen, who can stay with an assigned task and who respond appropriately to the praise and compliments of the teachers, have an advantage in mastering the school situation. These skills can be clearly analyzed and effectively taught as a background to more formal academic lessons.

The unfortunate assumption that Head Start children are not "ready" for formal instruction is no longer true. When lessons are correctly presented and responses result in *positive reinforcement,* the Head Start child quickly learns the excitement and enjoyment of reading and mathematics.

EVALUATION

Continuing evaluation of student progress is the guide to program development. During the opening year of a project, this evaluation is provided by the University of Kansas. Gradually, *all* evaluation procedures are taken over by the lead teacher in each classroom or by Staff Training Coordinators.

Straightforward procedures allow a teacher to adjust the allocation of her instructional periods to meet the changing needs of the students, and Individual Progress Records chart the advances of every child in the class. Easily kept, these records provide continuing feedback which the teacher can use to assess the appropriateness of her classroom organization, to modify her procedures, and to adjust quickly to the needs of any child whose progress is lagging.

Video tapes of small group lessons, coupled with clear definitions of appropriate and inappropriate teaching behaviors, allow each teacher to alter her techniques so as to maximize the progress of every child. Special training is given to Staff Training Coordinators to help them give personal coaching to teachers as they view their own video tapes. In addition to the large array of internal evaluation and feedback procedures, the usual range of achievement tests and class records permit each project to be clearly *accountable to the community* which it serves.

REFERENCES

Introductory Books

BECKER, W. C., THOMAS, D. R. and CARNINE, D. *Reducing Behavior Problems: An Operant Conditioning Guide for Teachers.* Urbana, Illinois: ERIC, 1969.

Behavior Analysis Sponsors, *A Token Manual for Behavior Analysis Classrooms.* Department of Human Development, University of Kansas, Lawrence, Kansas, 1970.

BIJOU, S. W. and BAER, D. M. *Child Development Vol. 1, A Systematic and Empirical Theory.* New York: Appleton-Century-Crofts, 1961.

HALL, R. V. *Improving Teaching Skills, Unit Eight: Classroom Discipline.* Chicago: Science Research Associates, Inc., 1969.

MADSEN, C. H., JR. and MADSEN, C. K. *Teaching/Discipline: Behavioral*

Principles Toward a Positive Approach. Boston: Allyn and Bacon, Inc., 1970.

PATTERSON, G. R. and GULLION, M. E. *Living with Children: New Methods for Parents and Teachers.* Champaign, Illinois, Research Press, 1968.

Intermediate Books

AYLLON, T. and AZRIN, N. *The Token Earning: A Motivational System for Therapy and Rehabilitation.* New York: Appleton-Century-Crofts, 1968.

BIJOU, S. W. and BAER, D. M. *Child Development: Readings in Experimental Analysis.* New York: Appleton-Century-Crofts, 1967.

REESE, E. P. *Introduction to Psychology: A Self-Selection Textbook. The Analysis of Human Operant Behavior.* Dubuque, Iowa. Wm. C. Brown Co. Publishers, 1966.

SKINNER, B. F. *Science and Human Behavior.* New York: The Free Press, 1953.

ULRICH, R., STACHNIK, T., and MABRY, J. (Eds). *Control of Human Behavior.* Glenview, Illinois: Scott, Foresman, 1966.

Advanced Books

BURGESS, R. and BUSHELL, D., JR. *Behavioral Sociology.* New York: Columbia University Press, 1969.

MILLENSON, J. R. *Principles of Behavior Analysis.* New York: Macmillan Company, 1967.

REYNOLDS, G. S. *A Primer of Operant Conditioning.* Glenview, Illinois: Scott, Foresman, 1968.

THARP, R. G. and WETZEL, R. J. *Behavior Modification in the Natural Environment.* New York: Academic Press, 1969.

ULLMANN, L. and KRASNER, L. *Case Studies in Behavior Modification.* New York: Holt, Rinehart and Winston, 1965.

Introductory Articles

BARRISH, H. H., SAUNDERS, M. and WOLF, M. M. Good behavior game: Effects of individual contingencies for group consequences on disruptive behavior in a classroom. *Journal of Applied Behavior Analysis*, 1969, *2*, 119–124.

CLARK, M., LACHOWITZ, J., and WOLF, M. M. A pilot basic education program for school dropouts incorporating a token reinforcement system. *Behavior Research and Therapy*, 1968, *6*, 183–188.

HART, B. M., ALLEN, K. E., BUELL, J. S., HARRIS, F. R. and WOLF, M. M. Effects of social reinforcement on operant crying. *Journal of Experimental Child Psychology*, 1964, *1*, 145–153.

MANDELKER, A. V., BRIGHAM, T. A., and BUSHELL, D., JR. The effects of token procedures on a teacher's social contacts with her students. *Journal of Applied Behavior Analysis*, 1970, *3*.

STAATS, A. W. and BUTTERFIELD, W. H. Treatment of non-reading in a culturally deprived juvenile delinquent: An application of reinforcement principles. *Child Development*, 1965, *36*, 925–942.

WARD, M. and BAKER, B. Reinforcement therapy in the classroom. *Journal of Applied Behavior Analysis*, 1968, *1*, 323–328.

WHITLOCK, C. and BUSHELL, D., JR. Some effects of "back-up" reinforcers on reading behavior. *Journal of Experimental Child Psychology*, 1967, *5*, 50–57.

Intermediate Articles

BUSHELL, D., JR., WROBEL, P. A. and MICHAELIS, M. L. Applying "group" contingencies to the classroom study behavior of preschool children. *Journal of Applied Behavior Analysis*, 1968, *1*, 55–62.

HARRIS, F. R., WOLF, M. M. and BAER, D. M. Effects of adult social reinforcement on child behavior. *Young Children*, 1964, *55*, 35–41.

JACOBSON, J., BUSHELL, D., JR., and RISLEY, T. Switching requirements in a head start classroom. *Journal of Applied Behavior Analysis*, 1969, *2*, 43–47.

LOVITT, T. C., GUPPY, T. E. and BLATTNER, J. E. The use of a free-time contingency with fourth graders to increase spelling accuracy. *Behavior Research and Therapy*, 1969, *7*, 151–156.

MCKENZIE, H., CLARK, M., WOLF, M., KOTHERA, R. and BENSON, C. Behavior modification of children with learning disabilities using grades as token reinforcers. *Exceptional Children*, 1968, *34*, 745–752.

WOLF, M., GILES, D. and HALL, R. V. Experiments with token reinforcement in a remedial classroom. *Behavior Research and Therapy*, 1968, *6*, 51–64.

Advanced Articles

HAWKINS, R., PETERSON, R., SCHWEID, E. and BIJOU, S. Behavior therapy in the home: Amelioration of problem parent-child relations with the parent in a therapeutic role. *Journal of Experimental Child Psychology*, 1966, *4*, 99–107.

PHILLIPS, E. L. Achievement place: Token reinforcement procedures in a home-style rehabilitation setting for "pre-delinquent" boys. *Journal of Applied Behavior Analysis*, 1968, *1*, 213–223.

REYNOLDS, N. and RISLEY, T. The role of social and material reinforcers in increasing talking of a disadvantaged preschool child. *Journal of Applied Behavior Analysis*, 1968, *1*, 253–262.

SURRATT, P., ULRICH, R. and HAWKINS, R. An elementary student as a behavioral engineer. *Journal of Applied Behavior Analysis*, 1969, *2*, 85–92.

12

OBSERVATIONS ON THE USE OF DIRECT INSTRUCTION WITH YOUNG DISADVANTAGED CHILDREN

CARL BEREITER AND SIEGFRIED ENGELMANN

Many experimental projects in early education of disadvantaged children are concerned with the *what* of compensatory education, the content; typically, however, these projects do not depart from the low-pressure, activity-centered methods of the traditional nursery school and kindergarten. The methods are often accepted as the part of the project that is "given." The writers believe that the *how* of educating disadvantaged children is as important as the *what* and that to fail in developing more effective teaching methods is

Journal of School Psychology. Spring 1966. Reprinted by permission.

perhaps to fail completely in equalizing the educational attainment of children from differing cultural backgrounds.

One of the major obstacles to experimentation with new teaching methods for preschool children is the widespread belief that any very demanding or rigorous teaching methods would be harmful to young children. The writers, in their work with preschool children, have made extensive use of teaching methods which, according to popular beliefs about early childhood education, should not have worked at all or should have encouraged extreme anxiety, dread of school, or robot-like conformity. These dire results did not emerge, however; in fact, the overall effect of the teaching methods on the children seems to have been beneficial.

This paper will describe the teaching methods employed and report observations and data on the feasibility, educational effectiveness, and apparent effects of these methods on children's attitudes, motivation, and personal adjustment. It is hoped that these observations will encourage other educators to experiment more freely in a search for improved methods of teaching young disadvantaged children and to question those popular beliefs that have served to restrain experimentation in the past.

METHODS

The writers' preschool program for disadvantaged children is built around three daily 20-minute sessions of intensive direct instruction—one devoted to language learning, one to arithmetic, and one to reading. The distinctive characteristics of the instructional method are:

1. Fast pace. During a twenty-minute period as many as 500 responses may be required of each child. Usually five or more different kinds of tasks are presented during a single period.

2. Reduced task-irrelevant behavior. The teacher controls the session relying only incidentally on spontaneous exchanges

to dictate the direction of instruction. Efforts of both teacher and children are focused on the tasks being studied.

3. Strong emphasis on verbal responses. These are often produced in unison, so that each child's total output can be maximized.

4. Carefully planned small-step instructional units with continual feedback. The teacher is not receptive to irrelevant exchanges but is very sensitive to possible areas of difficulty, possible ambiguities that arise from her presentation. She quickly corrects mistakes. She tries to anticipate and avert them.

5. Heavy work demands. Children are required to pay attention and to work hard. They are rewarded for thinking; half-hearted or careless performance is not tolerated.

Although the classes are conducted in a business-like manner, the atmosphere is usually friendly and pleasant, occasionally lightened by humor or playfulness. The following sketch of a typical language lesson will illustrate how the methods are put into practice. The children are disadvantaged four-year-olds who have been attending preschool for about three months. There are 15 children in the preschool, divided into groups of about five each. While one group is receiving language instruction, the other groups are receiving instruction from other teachers.

The lesson begins with review of a concept that has been studied previously. The children still have some difficulty with it. The teacher draws a circle and a square on the chalkboard, the square partly hidden by the circle. The children, who are seated in a row facing the chalkboard, talk freely among themselves and to the teacher until she has completed the drawing and turns toward them. They then quiet down and attend to the figures on the chalkboard.

TEACHER   Is the circle in front of the square?

CHILDREN   (in unison, rhythmically) Yes, the circle is in front of the square.

TEACHER	How do you know?
SEVERAL CHILDREN	(ad lib) Cause you can't see the whole square . . . Cause it cover it up.
TEACHER	Is the square in front of the circle?
CHILDREN	(ad lib) No . . . In back . . . No, circle in front.
TEACHER	All right, give me the whole statement. Is the square in front of the circle? No, the square is——"
CHILDREN	(in unison) The square is *not* in front of the circle. The square is *in back of* the circle.
TEACHER	(to James, who has stumbled through the last statement) James, where is the square?
JAMES	Back.
TEACHER	That's right. You're getting it. Now try to say the whole thing. The square is *in back of* the circle.

After about four minutes devoted to elaborations of this task, the teacher switches to higher-order class concepts. First comes a quick review of a previously learned—and popular—class concept.

TEACHER	Tell me something that is a weapon.
CHILDREN	(ad lib) A gun . . . A rifle . . . A sword . . . Bow'n arrow . . .
TEACHER	What's the rule? If you use it——"
CHILDREN	(in unison): If you use it to hurt someone, it's a weapon.
TEACHER	Can you use a stick to hurt somebody?
CHILDREN	(ad lib) No . . . Yeah . . . You can hit 'em . . . You can throw it . . . If it a big stick . . .
TEACHER	If you use a stick to hit somebody, then what do you know about it?
CHILDREN	(more or less in unison) It's a weapon.
TEACHER	Tell me something that is *not* a weapon.

The review takes less than two minutes. The teacher then moves immediately into the presentation of a new concept—*part*.

TEACHER   (pointing) This is Tyrone. Now listen. (Holding up Tyrone's hand and speaking slowly and methodically in a way that the children have learned to recognize as a signal that something new is being presented.) This is a *part of* Tyrone. This part of Tyrone is a——

CHILDREN   Hand.

TEACHER   (pointing to Tyrone's nose) And this is a part of Tyrone. This part of Tyrone is a——

CHILDREN   Nose.

Several other parts of Tyrone are introduced in this way and then the teacher alters the presentation to require the children to provide more of the statement.

TEACHER   (pointing to Tyrone's ear) Is this a part of Tyrone?

CHILDREN   Yeah.

TEACHER   Yes, this is a——

CHILDREN   Part of Tyrone.

Progressively the children are led to the point where they are supplying the entire pair of statements. Negative instances are introduced.

TEACHER   (pointing to Marie's nose) Is this a part of Tyrone?

CHILDREN   No, this is not a part of Tyrone.

Consideration is then shifted to parts of a chair and parts of an automobile (using a picture in a picture book). At the end of six minutes the children have achieved a tenuous mastery of the concept but have started to become restless and to make thoughtless errors. The teacher then shifts to a concept that had been introduced the day before—*vehicle*. She will return the next day to further work on the concept, *part*. During the closing minutes of the period, when some of the children are becoming inattentive, the teacher says, "Try real hard to get this, and then we'll have time to do some more jungle animals." This enticement serves to pull the group together for the final exercise on vehicles.

She then opens a picture book to a double-page spread of pictures of jungle animals which the children had become fascinated with during earlier work on the concept, *animal*. The last two minutes of the period are spent in a more informal exchange, with practice in identification, using the statement form, "This animal is a ——," interspersed with casual commentary about the animals depicted. As the children leave the room, the teacher shakes the hand of each one and gives him a personal word of commendation, encouragement, or exhortation. "Marie, I want you to talk more. Talk, talk, talk."

FEASIBILITY

A natural question to ask is whether children of four to six years of age can be brought to behave in such a highly disciplined and purposeful manner. Approximately 150 disadvantaged children in this age range have taken part in programs that included regular instruction of the kind indicated above. Teachers generally have reported no difficulties at all in getting children to participate enthusiastically in the intensive instruction sessions. No long breaking-in period is required. The pace and pattern are usually established the first day of school. The writers know of only one case where a teacher purportedly tried to establish such a teaching program and failed. The teacher was also unsuccessful in managing a traditional activity-type program with the children. The writers visited the class during its sixth week (when it was in a sorry state of chaos); they were nevertheless able to involve the children immediately in a lively and well-controlled instructional session, which suggested that the source of the difficulty was the teacher rather than the children or the method.

The same direct instructional method has been tried successfully with four-year-olds from more privileged homes. If anything, lower-class children seem to adapt to direct instruction somewhat more readily than middle-class children. Middle-class children are more likely to come to the preschool with preconceptions of what it should be like—a place to play—and are more likely to have become accustomed to a casual and somewhat haphazard kind of relationship with adults in "teaching" situations. By contrast, the disadvantaged child usually enters preschool with no preconceptions and no previous experience with such teaching situations.

As in any preschool, there are likely to be occasional shy, rebellious, or hyperactive children who have trouble adjusting to the school routine. The very clearly defined and consistent behavioral rules of the direct instruction sessions, however, tend to minimize such problems and to speed up adjustment. The short attention span that is sometimes attributed to disadvantaged children has presented no problem. For the first week or two of instruction, intensive teaching sessions are limited to 15 minutes rather than 20 and, as illustrated in the sample lesson, it has been found desirable to change tasks every five minutes or less.

EDUCATIONAL EFFECTIVENESS

The only group of children who have received direct instruction over a long enough period to permit objective assessment of educational gains is the original pilot case, which consisted of 15 four-year-old children, all Negroes, from a very low income area. The children were identified by public school teachers as coming from particularly deprived homes in which there were older siblings who were having school problems. According to scores on the Illinois Test of Psycholinguistic Abilities, the children selected were a year and a half below average in language abilities at the time they entered school. By the end of seven months their scores had risen to approximately normal—a gain of two years. In the same period of time their mean IQ on the Stanford-Binet rose from the low 90's to slightly over 100. By the end of nine months (shortly before they entered kindergarten), they scored at the second grade level on arithmetic and at the first grade level in reading on the Wide-Range Achievement Test. At this writing, after 14 months, all of the remaining 14 children are well into first grade reading work, are doing arithmetic at the upper primary level, and are progressing success-fully in a science program that teaches concepts ordinarily reserved for the upper elementary grades.

It is not possible to separate the effects of teaching method from the effects of the curriculum, which also involved radical de-partures from tradition. However, it is important to recognize that the language, arithmetic, and reading curricula used in this experi-ment—as well as any other carefully organized and sequenced cur-riculum—could not be implemented with the indirect teaching methods generally employed in early childhood education. Some method would have to be used which ensured closer control over the children's attention and over relevant responses.

ATTITUDINAL EFFECTS OF DIRECT INSTRUCTION

The major worry that teachers express about the use of more intensive or directive teaching methods with young children is that it may somehow harm the children or warp their development. Some of the worries merely reflect an unrealistic perspective. For instance, concern that direct instruction will deprive a child of needed time for play and interaction with his peers and "rob him of his youth" seems quite unrealistic if one is considering devoting only one hour a day to such instruction. The harm, if any, that might result from direct instruction would have to arise from what *does* happen during direct teaching and not from what the child misses as a result of devoting an hour a day to it. The folk-lore of education suggests a number of potential ill-effects, which we shall consider in the light of our experience.

Excessive Stress and Anxiety

The mounting pressures on school children to compete and achieve are a just cause for concern. We have tried to minimize competition and emphasis on error avoidance, placing the emphasis instead on hard work, attention, and improvement. Exertion in itself—as shown by children at a playground or swimming pool—does not seem to be either harmful or unnatural. After a morning of spaced sessions of intense "mental" exertion, the children show many of the same characteristics as children who have spent the same length of time in intense physical play. They are tired but relaxed and cheerful.

Among the children whom we have observed most closely there have not been more than the usual number of anxiety symptoms. When an occasional child has shown signs of mounting disturbance in school, he was almost invariably attempting a task for which he was inadequately prepared; the disturbance generally abated as soon as the learning problem was taken care of, usually by some modification in the instructional program that proved to be of benefit to the other children as well.

If anything, the stable and work-oriented atmosphere of the school seems to have made it an island of security. The home lives of many of the children have been chaotic and filled with violence. During the early months of the school the behavior of the children clearly reflected the ebb and flow of crises in the home neighborhood. As time went on, however, their school behavior became more and more equable and independent of outside influences. Recently close relatives of three of the children in one class were involved in a sensational killing; yet, hardly a ripple of the turmoil invaded the classroom.

Dislike for School and Learning

Starting children too young in academic work has often been blamed for school failures and the development of a chronic dislike for school. The writers fully acknowledge the dangers in presenting young children tasks for which they lack the prerequisite learning, and for this reason would urge that direct teaching not be attempted without a carefully worked out curriculum that starts with the abilities the children already have, building up from that point in a way that insures that the children can handle each new task that is presented.

However, our experience does not suggest, that early exposure to academic instruction *per se* develops negative attitudes toward schooling. What it does, rather, is build up attitudes toward school work that should provide a basis for better adjustment to school in later years. Direct instruction is not as much fun as some other kinds of nursery school activities, but we do not know of any responsible early childhood educators who use "maximizing fun" as a major criterion for designing a curriculum. Most children seem to enjoy direct instruction most of the time, so long as it is enabling them to make steady progress; but what is more important, they learn that it is worthwhile and that it will bring them benefits even when it is not great fun. Thus they develop a more mature kind of motivation toward learning that can sustain them through the inevitable ups and downs of school experience.

Lack of Spontaneity, Independence, and Creativity

Although the kind of instruction we have used is highly controlled and makes a great deal of use of repetition and patterned responses, the children have shown a general increase rather than decrease in the spontaneity with which they approach new tasks. Like many groups of disadvantaged children, the ones in the pilot experiment were initially rather stolid and self-effacing, lacking in curiosity and intellectual assertiveness. Over the months they have become bold, inquisitive, and argumentative, confident of their intellectual strengths.

The curriculum we have used includes a number of divergent thinking tasks—from thinking of things that are not weapons, inventing new verses for songs, devising possible uses for an unfamiliar object such as a tea strainer. The children approach these tasks with considerable alacrity. Training in divergent thinking does not occupy a major place in the program, but this is a curricular decision and is not dictated by the teaching method. From what little is known about methods of fostering creative thinking, it would seem that direct instruction in divergent thinking tasks should be a better means of promoting creative abilities than the conventional unstructured nursery school activities, which may provide a child with opportunities to think creatively but seldom challenge him to do so, or teach him much about how to do it.

As the preceding conclusions suggest, we have found direct instruction to be a thoroughly feasible and highly effective way of teaching needed academic skills to young disadvantaged children. Even though the teaching procedures are more rigorous than those found in many elementary schools, we have found the side effects to be beneficial rather than harmful. From the point of view of overall personality development, perhaps the most important side-effect has been the children's development of a self-conscious pride and confidence in their own ability to learn and think. Indirect teaching, even if it is effective, tends to produce learning of which the children are only vaguely aware. They learn but do not know that they have learned, don't realize that they have accomplished something significant. Through direct instruction, on the other hand, children are fully aware of what they have learned and aware that they have learned it through their own effort, concentration, and intelligence. They come to think of themselves as being good at learning and thinking. They acquire the well-rounded and realistic self-confidence that one usually finds only in bright children from the most favorable home backgrounds, the kind of self-confidence that enables a child to excel rather than merely to adjust.

13

A SKILL DEVELOPMENT CURRICULUM FOR 3-, 4-, AND 5-YEAR-OLD DISADVANTAGED CHILDREN

Demonstration and Research Center
for Early Education
George Peabody College for Teachers

JANET C. CAMP

The instructional program of the DARCEE [Demonstration and Research Center for Early Education] Training Centers of George Peabody College for Teachers is research-oriented. Its primary purpose is to implement research objectives on a minute-to-minute, day-to-day, month-to-month, and year-to-year basis through a curriculum sequentially organized to realize the goals of the research design. The major research goal is to develop in the preschool-

ERIC document PS003123. Reprinted by permission of author and Demonstration and Research Center for Early Education.

age disadvantaged child the aptitudes and the attitudes which past research has shown to be correlated with academic achievement. Our responsibility has been to develop a comprehensive developmental curriculum to foster socialization for competence—development of the cognitive skills for environmental mastery and the sustaining motivations necessary for continued growth.

This paper will focus on the theoretical basis for the skill development program and will present the curriculum model as it exists after three years of development and refinement. The instructional program will be discussed in terms of the skill development objectives of the curriculum and the role which content plays in the implementation of the goals.

I. SKILL DEVELOPMENT PROGRAM

Initial work with young disadvantaged children in our first Early Training Center revealed evidence to support previous research findings that, as a group, these children exhibit skill deficits in all areas of informational processing—those skills necessary to perceive and discriminate environmental stimuli, to order this information in a conceptual framework, and to express the results of this structuring process. These are the skills necessary for cognitive growth and the development of intellectual competency. There is research evidence that these organizing and structuring skills are learned. As the child learns to impose order and structure upon his environment, he is able to process information more economically and efficiently. Unfortunately, the home environment of these children is strikingly lacking in structure and organization, both temporally and spacially. Our goal was to develop an instructional program which could help the disadvantaged child develop the skills to impose order and structure upon the environmental chaos in which he finds himself.

After the skill deficits of these children were determined, a curriculum framework was designed based on an informational processing model. Using as a guide the basic stages in the processing of information, the skill development objectives were organized in three categories of processing skills—Sensory Skills, Abstracting and Mediating Skills, and Response Skills. Each of these three skill groups is subdivided into skill objectives which, through continuous refinement, have been translated into sequences of specific behavioral expectations. The skill development program will be outlined by exploring each one of the three skill divisions and their component parts.

Sensory Skills

The first division of skills, Sensory Skills, can be labeled "Input" skills. These are the processes which must operate in order to receive and decode environmental stimuli through the senses. The skill development program was carefully constructed to consider all of the conceptual dimensions used by the major sense modalities— visual, auditory, tactile-kinesthetic, taste-olfactory—in the ordering process. Such conceptual areas as color, shape, size, volume, time, texture, temperature are a few of the relatively invariant dimensions for the organization of environmental stimuli. These areas were then task-analyzed according to the sensory processes needed to assimilate information.

The most basic sensory process is what we call the Orienting or Attentional skill. This is a basic learning skill whereby a child learns to focus attention on the relevant stimuli in his environment. For example, in dealing with the visual modality, our concern is that the child develops an awareness of color, size, shape, position, number, etc., as consistent conceptual dimensions by which he can order the visual stimuli he receives. In the initial stages of the classroom program, we attempt to develop the Orienting skill by carefully controlling stimuli in order to make salient those which are relevant.

A second sensory process is the Discriminatory skill—the ability to perceive likenesses and differences between stimuli received by the four sensory modalities. A more complex process is involved with the Relational skill where a child must deal with interrelated stimuli which occur simultaneously. An example of this skill in the visual modality is the child's ability to work a puzzle by perceiving the relationships among the parts and constructing the whole. The fourth sensory process is the Sequential skill by which the child learns to perceive a repeating pattern of stimuli which occur in a certain spacial or temporal order.

The development of each one of these four sensory skills, for each of the sensory modalities, is programmed over time through a carefully developed sequence of behavioral expectations which require increasingly finer and more precise discrimination, with stimuli which become more complex and abstract. For example, the Discriminatory skill in the visual modality begins at a gross level with the perception of likenesses and differences of whole concrete objects (as with two cups and a spoon) and then moves to discriminations among similar objects on the basis of likeness and difference in parts, color, size, shape, number, or position. As this skill is gradually refined, the child is able to discriminate fine differences among small, detailed, abstract configurations and symbols such as designs, words, numerals, and letters.

Abstracting and Mediating Skills

The second division of informational processing skills, Abstracting and Mediating Skills, is concerned with what could be termed "Organization" processes. This area includes skills which are critical in the assimilation of stimuli into a logical and orderly cognitive framework to facilitate retrieval of information and to foster transfer of learning. We have designated these areas as Basic Concept Development, Association, Classification, Sequencing, and Critical Thinking. As the child learns to focus attention on relevant stimuli in his environment and develops the ability to discriminate among stimuli perceived through the four sensory modalities, basic concepts begin to develop based on the invariant conceptual dimensions used in the sensory ordering process.

The area of Basic Concept Development includes such concepts as color, shape, size, number, position, volume, texture, weight, temperature, motion, speed, taste, time, age, affect. Through Association processes, the child builds connections between objects, events, and concepts which are spacially, temporally, or functionally related. He learns to associate labels with every object, action, sound, and concept he encounters. He learns to associate basic concepts to develop higher-level concepts. For example, concepts of color, shape, size, number, texture, motion, etc., are used as "building blocks" to form the concept of a particular animal.

We work on the assumption that the more sophisticated Classification skills develop through the process of association. During planned activities, the child is directed to associate or group certain objects or concepts which all share a particular characteristic to form a class of objects or concepts defined by the common characteristic. The child learns to classify deductively by sorting concepts with a common characteristic into their appropriate categories which are identified by the teacher. He then learns to classify inductively, by abstracting a shared characteristic of given objects or concepts and formulating the class defined by the common characteristic. Activities are sequenced to increase the amount of conceptual differentiation demanded of the child and to move the child from the classification of objects or concepts using concrete or representational materials to the classification of objects or concepts using verbal labels only.

Sequencing skills are the tools used by the child to arrange experiences in a logical spacial or temporal order. These are the mediating skills utilized by the child in ordering motor and verbal responses when dramatizing the action patterns of stories or events; when executing a series of verbal directions; when verbalizing the serial order of numbers, days of the week, seasons of the year; and when verbalizing the sequence of episodes of familiar stories and events or activities which the child has experienced. Eventually the child utilizes this skill at a very abstract and complex level as he learns to develop his own stories exhibiting a sequence of events in a logical order. In activities of this type, the child is also using many complex Critical Thinking processes which are emphasized in the program when working with stories and problem situations. These are the very complex and abstract skills of drawing relationships, making inferences, analyzing problems, synthesizing ideas, hypothesizing, evaluating, drawing analogies, and analyzing absurdities. With the Abstracting and Mediating Skills, as with Sensory Skills, the curriculum is organized to develop increasingly more sophisticated schemata for organizing information to encourage the continuous segmentation and differentiation of the child's cognitive field.

Response Skills

The third division of informational processing skills, Response Skills, can be called "Output" skills. These are the processes required to express, through both motor and verbal responses, the resultant product of the decoding and organizational processes. The curriculum for this process area is designed to develop the verbal and small motor coordination skills essential for self-expression and the effective communication of thought processes. The objectives for the Motor Response Skills are concerned primarily with the development of eye-hand coordination since these particular children tend to be extremely well coordinated in tasks involving gross motor skills. Again, as with Sensory Skills, classroom activities are sequenced throughout the program to refine coordination from the relatively gross control required in manipulating objects, modeling with clay, painting on large surfaces, drawing, stringing beads, and cutting to the fine control required in tracing, following dots, coloring in small areas, and printing.

The objectives in the sub-division of Verbal Response Skills are concerned with both quantity and quality of verbalization. The learning milieu of the classroom is organized to stimulate individual expression. Each child spends approximately two-thirds of his time in a small group situation with four other children and a teacher. Individual expression is constantly reinforced with verbal praise, with physical gestures of approval, and, initially, with a concrete reward. Many activities are planned and many instructional devices are utilized to augment the quantity of verbalization. Conversation of child with teacher and child with child is encouraged particularly in small groups during the snack and lunch periods.

Quality in verbalization is developed through the use of very carefully programmed reinforcement schedules to realize continuous improvements in articulation and in sentence structure. The child is reinforced for closer and closer approximations of complete sentence structure in encoding declarative (affirmative and negative) and interrogative statements. Lessons are planned whereby the child can develop the ability to use present, past, and future tense forms in actual situations. Certain sentence patterns are reinforced because they demonstrate evidence of complex thinking operations: negative statements used in classification activities to indicate objects or concepts which do not belong to a designated class; comparative statements used to describe the relationship between two objects exhibiting comparative forms of polar concepts of size, texture, weight, etc., "if-then" statements used to state deductions when certain qualifying conditions are given; statements with "or" used to imply choice. Succinctness of expression is developed by encouraging the child to reduce redundancy in consecutive sentences through consolidation of adjectives, verbs, and nouns using the coordinating conjunction "and".

Use of "standard" grammatical forms and sentence patterns (a reflection of environment and thought process) is secondary in importance to the ability to use many variant forms employed in both the child's environment and a school-type situation. The child is encouraged to decode and encode grammatical and structural alternative forms, a skill without which comprehension handicaps and communication impediments could develop with individuals from differing environments in a later school-learning situation.

II. CONTENT

As previously stated, the focus of the curriculum is not on the learning of specific information but is on the development of skills needed to process information more effectively. The basic conceptual skills are assumed to be relatively invariant while content changes over time. Much more important than changing content is the ability to recognize a set of three or five; to understand the position concepts before, behind, or through; and to discriminate rough from smooth or hot from cold. Content plays the role of the vehicle for the development of skills. Although the content is subsidiary in importance to skill development, it must be carefully selected and organized to ensure maximal opportunities for the development of the informational processing skills.

A unit approach for ordering content was adopted on the assumption that learning experiences organized around a central theme would encourage more meaningful learning for the child. In addition, this organizational plan would aid the teacher in presenting the learning situations in an order of increasing complexity and abstraction, following the sequencing directions for skill development. In the implementation of the unit approach, both the activities within a unit and the units themselves are sequenced to augment the continuing growth of more abstract and complex skills. Units chosen for the initial stages of the classroom program are those which provide opportunities for the development of Sensory Skills and basic concepts in very concrete situations. Subsequent units utilize these basic learning skills and concepts to build higher-level concepts and to develop skills in organizing and expressing experiences.

By using an interrelated unit approach, each successive unit utilizes concepts and skills in each of the preceding units and develops them to a higher-level of sophistication. For example, the first unit used is about the child himself. The content is exciting to the child and obviously offers the most concrete and real situations for learning. The concepts and skills developed here are transferred to and repeatedly utilized in a sequence of units on family and home, neighborhood, and city. With this interrelated unit approach, skills in experiencing, in organizing experiences, and in expressing experiences become increasingly more refined and complex. The child is steadily carried from proximal to distal situations in space orientation, encouraging him to move from reliance on perceptual media into the use of conceptual and language media for learning.

Similarly a sequence of units on animals moves the child from the concrete, proximal environment to the abstract, distal environment beginning with pets, followed by farm animals, small wood animals, and finally large wild animals. This series of units provides maximum opportunities for developing Association and Classification skills using both basic concepts and more complex concepts as the building blocks for class formation. A series of units on the four seasons provides opportunities to develop Sensory Skills and concepts basic to seasonal change and to review and expand them over a period of one full year. This series is particularly effective in developing Association skills and in encouraging the drawing of relationships between seasons as their sequential order is recognized.

Although the units which have been implemented appear very similar to those of most preschools, our curriculum approach is far different. The content itself is not the primary focus; the main thrust is on the aptitude development. The DARCEE instructional program, therefore, makes a pronounced departure from the traditional nursery school program. It is a structured program in which every moment has a designed instructional purpose in terms of an established objective.

The rationale for a structured instructional program which is sequentially programmed and conscientiously implemented is formulated on the basis of previous research projects with disadvantaged children. Studies have consistently indicated that culturally deprived children do not come to school with the experiential background of middle-class children, and, therefore, are placed immediately at a disadvantage. Achievement grades and intelligence scores of these children indicate a pattern of accelerating decline over the school years. In addition, learning studies have shown that deprived children do not learn incidentally but do benefit from direct instruction. We cannot assume that in the framework of a traditional program these skills for achievement would develop. This view would be a romanticism which we cannot afford. Our program is designed to meet the particular needs of our children. Rather than accommodating our objectives to match their particular learning deficits, we have established a high goal: to take their very skill weaknesses and

Diagram of DARCEE Curriculum Model   June 1969

I. Sensory Skills
Orienting and Attentional

Visual
Auditory
Tactile-Kinesthetic
Taste-Olfactory
Discriminatory
Visual
Auditory
Tactile-Kinesthetic
Taste-Olfactory
Relational
Visual
Auditory
Sequential
Visual
Auditory

II. Abstracting and Mediating Skills

Basic Concept Development

color	pitch	speed
shape	length	taste
size	volume (aud.)	flavor & odors
number	texture	time
position	weight	age
volume	temperature	affect
	motion	

Association
1. Objects with objects—functionally, spacially, temporally
2. Labels with objects, sounds, actions, concepts
3. Labels with labels

Classification
1. Deductive classification
2. Inductive classification

Sequencing
1. Motor—sequencing series of actions, directions, events
2. Verbal—sequencing a series of concepts, events

Critical Thinking
1. Drawing relationships
2. Making inferences
3. Making predictions
4. Analyzing problem-situations
5. Synthesizing ideas
6. Hypothesizing
7. Evaluating
8. Drawing analogies
9. Analyzing absurdities

III. Response Skills

A. Verbal
   Fluency
   Articulation
   Syntax
      a. Single-word level—identification of objects, actions, sounds, concepts
      b. Phrase level
      c. Complete sentence level
         simple declaratives
         interrogatives
         negatives
         "and" statements
         "or" statements
         "if-then" statements
         "I don't know" statements
         complex sentence—adverbial clauses

B. Motor
   Small-Motor Coordination (eye-hand coordination)

pasting	cutting
modeling	lacing & weaving
painting	tracing
coloring	solving mazes
stringing	following dots
drawing	printing

   Orientation
      left-to-right progression
      top-to-bottom progression
      front-to-back progression

develop them into competencies for coping with the environment.

It would be naive to assume, however, that preschool intervention would be a panacea for all the problems which are characteristic of these children. Indeed, results of early intervention projects have shown that gains are not necessarily sustained as the subjects move through the public schools. There is a crying need for a total system change in our school programs in order to assimilate these groups of very different children. Both attitudes and curricula must be altered if these children are to retain and augment the competencies which programmed early intervention can develop.

14

OVERVIEW OF RESPONSIVE MODEL PROGRAM

GLEN NIMNICHT

ORIENTATION

The Problem

Our program for Head Start and Follow Through is based on the assumption that the public schools are failing large numbers of children because they are not responding to children as individuals with different cultural backgrounds. The schools are currently designed to serve students who are reasonably quiet and submissive, and who hold the same values as the teachers. Either they are white, middle-class children or they emulate white, middle-class adults; the schools nurture these children and aid their intellectual development. Our program is based on the idea that if culturally different

ERIC document PS004024. Reprinted by permission of author.

children are to thrive either they must be helped to operate in a system designed for others, or the system itself must be changed to serve all children equally.

The Approach

The central idea of our Responsive Model program is that a school environment should be designed to respond to the learner. The activities within the environment are autotelic; that is, they are self-rewarding and do not depend upon rewards or punishments unrelated to the activity.

This learning environment satisfies the following conditions:

a. It permits the learner to explore freely;

b. It informs the learner immediately about the consequences of his actions;

c. It is self-pacing, with events occurring at a rate determined by the learner;

d. It permits the learner to make full use of his capacity for discovering relations of various kinds; and,

e. Its structure is such that the learner is likely to make a series of interconnected discoveries about the physical, cultural, or social world.

The program is not based on any single theory of learning since there appears to be no single theory that adequately accounts for all the ways children learn. The program does, however, draw from many different theories. Much of the program is based on the assumption that there is a relationship between maturation and learning, although this relationship between maturation and the learning of specific skills or concepts is not altogether clear.

Although the program is based more heavily on the work of developmental theorists, we also find some of the ideas of operant conditioning useful. For instance, to define objectives in clear behavioral terms is sometimes useful, but we do not believe that every objective can be defined in behavior which can be immediately observed. We think in terms of reinforcement of learning and feedback to the learner. We use intrinsic reinforcers in autotelic activities instead of extrinsic reinforcers. We believe that a wide variety of autotelic activities are necessary, since no one activity is rewarding to all children. This is consistent with the behaviorists' notion that a varied reward system is necessary to reinforce learning.

While we develop learning sequences, we do not assume that every child must follow that sequence. In many instances we do not claim to know how the learning of a particular behavior contributes to the future learning ability or achievement of a child. This has sometimes been described as a "sandpile theory of learning"; that is, we know that it takes a tremendous number of grains of sand to support more sand. But we are not at all certain which grain of sand is necessary to support the next one. And, as the analogy implies, we are not certain that any particular grain is necessary—others could be substituted and still support the sandpile.

The program is suitable not only for low income or culturally different children, but for all children.

The Objectives

The major objectives of the program are to help children develop a healthy self-concept as it relates to learning in the school and in the home; and to develop their intellectual ability, specifically, the ability to solve problems. In order to do this the child must develop his senses and perceptions, since the senses are the source of data for the thought process; his language ability, because language is a tool of the thought process; and his concept formation ability, because he needs to be able to deal with abstractions and to classify information to organize thought.

A child has a healthy self-concept in relationship to learning and school, if:

a. He likes himself and his people;
b. He believes that what he thinks, says, and does makes a difference;

    c. He believes that he can be successful in school;

    d. He believes that he can solve a variety of problems;

    e. He has a realistic estimate of his own abilities and limitations; and,

    f. He expresses feelings of pleasure and enjoyment.

After being in the program two or three years, most children should be able to:

    a. Recognize, complete, extend, and discover patterns in one direction;

    b. Recognize, complete, extend, and discover patterns in two directions (matrix games);

    c. Recognize, extend, and discover rules from examples (inductive thinking);

    d. Persevere, concentrate and succeed on problems involving the breaking of "set";

    e. Adapt to games involving rule changes;

    f. Eliminate what is known to determine what is unknown;

    g. Use feedback productively to modify actions;

    h. Solve verbal and math puzzles;

    i. Seek a solution to one-person problems without assistance;

    j. Recognize that a problem cannot be solved with information at hand;

    k. Anticipate the probable response of the other player in interactional games;

    l. Anticipate the probable response of others to alternative actions of the individual in some social situation; and,

    m. Cope with the emotions of other individuals.

The other important objective is that the child have a knowledge and understanding of his cultural background. We will not only have to develop more materials to obtain this objective but develop different criterion for measuring the success of children from different backgrounds.

POPULATION

The program has been used with low-income children, mainly black, Mexican-American, other Spanish-speaking children, and American Indian, as well as some white middle-class children. As of September 1970, there will also be Chinese children in the program.

We are currently serving 3948 children in Head Start and 5722 children in Follow Through. The Head Start children are predominantly 3 to 5 years old, and Follow Through children are in grades as follows: K–1 374; first grade 1704; second grade 1301; third grade 169; not known 1165. Forty percent of the Head Start programs last year (1969–70) were in rural areas, and 60 percent in urban areas, while Follow Through had 1700 children in rural programs and 4000 in urban programs.

Throughout the country, the Head Start program involved 39 percent black children, 27 percent white children, 28 percent Mexican-American children, 1 percent Oriental children, 2 percent Indian children, and 2 percent from all other ethnic groups.

The Responsive program is based on the assumption that parents must be involved if the program is to be successful. This means that a representative group of parents must approve of the program before it is introduced in a community, and parents have the right to review that decision after they have an opportunity to observe it in action.

It is designed to encourage parents to participate as paid assistants or volunteers, or attend meetings. The intention is to encourage parents to participate without requiring participation. In addition to approving programs, parents in some of the communities are currently involved in the decision-making process by helping to select both program advisers, teachers and teacher assistants.

In June 1970, we started developing a training program for parents and parent coordinators to help parents improve their effectiveness in the decision-making process.

CURRICULUM/PROGRAM DESCRIPTION

The curriculum focuses on the process of helping children learn how to learn rather than on specific subject matter content. There is enough material written in careful detail to provide a comprehensive program for children ages 3, 4, and 5, and the materials are currently being extended for children through age 9.

These materials are organized in a parallel and sequential development using materials and equipment that are usually found in a classroom or are easily available locally. Some special materials have been developed which will be generally available by January 1971. The arrangement at present is that the core materials for the program which have little or no cultural bias are provided by the Laboratory and any culturally relevant materials used are provided by the local program. The Laboratory is developing ethnic materials for use in the Responsive program and the first materials for Black children and Mexican-American children will be ready in September 1970.

The typical program classroom situation in Head Start and Follow Through kindergartens is as follows:

As the children enter the room they are free to choose from a variety of activities such as painting, working puzzles, playing with manipulative toys, looking at books, listening to records or tapes, using the Language Master, and building with blocks. They can stay with an activity as long as they like or they can move on to something else whenever and as often as they like. As the day progresses, small groups will play games, which are learning episodes, with the teacher or assistants, and others will ask to be read to. During the day, the teacher and assistants are engaged in reading to the children, playing games with them and responding to the spontaneous activities to build the experience that precedes instruction in some skill or concept. The teacher and assistants respond to the children rather than having the children respond to them. Adult-initiated conversation is limited, but child-initiated conversation is encouraged.

About 15 or 20 minutes a day are devoted to large group activities such as singing, listening to a story, show and tell, or participating in a planned lesson. A child does not have to take part in group activities if he does not want to, but he cannot continue in any activity that disturbs the group.

Once each day in kindergarten and first grade classes with learning booths, a booth attendant will ask a child if he would like to play with the typewriter. If the child says "yes", the attendant takes him to a booth equipped with an electric typewriter. The child begins by simply playing with the typewriter and the attendant tells him what he is doing. Whatever keys he strikes—*X, A, Y, comma, space,* or *return*—the attendant names them. The child moves from this first free exploration phase through matching and discrimination to production of his own words and stories. At each phase we stress his discovery of the rules of the new phase (game).

In the first and second grade programs being developed, the same general procedures will be followed; but the activities will change and there will be more small group activities and perhaps two or more large group activities a day. The children will still have large blocks of time for individual activities. There probably will not be a block corner and dress-up area, but there will be more educational games and toys related to math and science. There may be small reading or arithmetic groups or reading and math may be taught on an individual basis. The first and second grade children should still be free to choose their own activities and to opt out of large or small group work.

The Head Start program is currently organized on a half day basis in groups of 15 to 20 children with one teacher and one assistant. The Follow Through program is a five- or six-hour program for groups of 25 children with one teacher and one assistant plus volunteers.

In addition to the Head Start and Follow Through programs, we are developing and testing a Parent/Child program designed to help parents to:

a. Help their child develop a healthy self-image;
b. Aid their child's intellectual development, using toys and

games designed to teach specific skills, concepts, or problem-solving abilities; and

c. Participate in the decision-making process that effects the education of their children.

The parents meet one time a week for ten weeks. Each time they learn some general principle of child growth and development, see a demonstration of how to use a toy or game with their children, practice its use, and then take it home. After ten weeks they can continue to use the Educational Toy Library as long as they like.

We believe that any program that is designed to serve children from low-income homes and different cultural and ethnic groups must be flexible. The program emphasizes flexibility in various ways:

a. In the procedures for responding to individual children;
b. In the range and difficulty levels of the materials used;
c. Current materials have little or no cultural bias, but local groups can add culturally relevant materials, some of which will be developed by the Laboratory; and,
d. The parents can make choices; for example, they can choose to have English taught as a second language or have a bilingual program or use some other language.

DELIVERY

The Inservice Training program is designed around training *local* Program Advisers who train ten teachers and ten assistants. The Laboratory provides training materials for the teachers and assistants and training guides for the Program Advisers.

The training of Program Advisers begins in the summer with a two-week, in-depth orientation to the model and the Program Advisers return for three additional one-week workshop/seminars over the rest of the year.

The training for the teachers is organized into three twelve-week cycles to cover one year. Each cycle has eight training units designed to help a teacher improve specific skills and learn general concepts.

The Laboratory provides the following materials:

1. Text: Introduction to the New Nursery School and Pamphlets #1 to #6 by Nimnicht, McAfee and Meier, published by General Learning Corporation, 1969;
2. Teachers' Notebook, Training Units, Program Advisers' Supplement, and Four Resource Packets;
3. Brochure: "The Responsive Head Start Program," script and black and white slide set;
4. Films: "Introduction to the New Nursery School," 27 minutes, color; and "Intellectual Development at the New Nursery School," 18 minutes, color (available free from Modern Talking Pictures, Washington, Chicago and San Francisco offices);
5. Films: sixteen learning episodes demonstrated by a model teacher (about five minutes each);
6. Film: "Free Exploration in a Responsive Environment (in preparation); and,
7. Sound/Slide Sets Describing Selected Learning Episodes.

The cost of operating the Head Start program is about the same as any other program with one teacher and assistant for fifteen to twenty children. The initial cost of training includes the salary and expenses of the Program Adviser, about $25 per teacher for training materials, and the cost of six weeks of training for the Program Adviser each year for two years.

EVALUATION

The final evaluation of the program will be based upon how well it meets the objectives stated [pages 201–3]. In the meantime, the various components of the program are being systematically evaluated. The Laboratory uses a systematic development process with four major steps: selection of approach and designing prototype; preliminary testing with a limited sample; performance testing with a larger sample but under careful supervision of the Laboratory; and, operational testing under normal field conditions with limited involvement of the Laboratory. At any point the process can be recycled if the desired results are not obtained.

The development and testing of the model program for children and the training program for teachers and assistants are parallel developments. The first concern in evaluating the program is to determine how effective the training program is in producing the desired changes in teacher behavior. The primary techniques that are being used are periodic classroom observations by trained observers and audio and video recordings of classroom behavior of teachers.

After the teacher's performance is satisfactory, the second concern is to determine the effects upon the children. Does the changed teacher behavior significantly affect the growth of children toward the objectives of the program?

We have collected baseline data for evaluation of the children by using standardized tests of intelligence and achievement, but we do not consider these tests as adequate measures of the program so we are developing a responsive achievement test to assess the children's achievement in intellectual development. The emphasis will obviously be on a child's problem-solving ability. We are currently devising situational tests and observational techniques to assess a nine- or ten-year-old child's behavior on the thirteen indicators of a positive self-image stated [pages 201–2]. In the meantime, we are relying upon observations to make some estimate of a child's self-concept at earlier ages.

The Laboratory does not anticipate having a final evaluation of the first phase of the total program for at least four or five years, but in the developmental process there are enough check points to ensure against a complete failure. One thing seems to be certain. If the program does not meet our expectations, the alternatives are to revise the program until it does or replace it with a better model—we cannot return to current practices.

15

A SKETCH OF THE PIAGET-DERIVED PRESCHOOL CURRICULUM DEVELOPED BY THE YPSILANTI EARLY EDUCATION PROGRAM

CONSTANCE KAMII

When an early childhood educator reads Piaget's theory, he is likely to be convinced that in view of these insights we must change the way we teach young children. While this need for change is obvi-

Reprinted from *History and Theory of Early Childhood Education*. Edited by Samuel J. Braun and Esther Edwards. Worthington, Ohio: Charles A. Jones Publishing Company, 1972. Abridged and reprinted with permission of the author and publisher.

The Ypsilanti Early Education Program was in operation in 1967–70 with funds under Title III, ESEA, No. 67–042490. One of the objectives of this program was to develop a preschool curriculum based on Piaget's theory for socioeconomically disadvantaged 4-year-old children. I am grateful to M. Denis-Prinzhorn of the University of Geneva for critically reading this paper and contributing many ideas.

209

ous to most people who study the theory, how to go about applying it to preschool education is not at all obvious.

When we try to apply Piaget's theory to preschool education, our first tendency is to simplify certain Piagetian tasks and try to help children to go from one stage to the next as quickly as possible. This tendency can be seen in my earlier papers written on the Perry Preschool Project (Kamii & Radin, 1967; Sonquist & Kamii, 1967) and the Ypsilanti Early Education Program (Kamii & Radin, 1970; Sonquist, Kamii, & Derman, 1970).

As I continued to study the pedagogical implications of Piaget's theory, it became increasingly clear that our aim should be not to move the child from one stage to the next in concepts studied by Piaget, but, rather, to enable him to develop his total cognitive framework so that he will be able to apply it to any task including classification, seriation, conservation, arithmetic, and reading. If, in contrast, we teach classification, seriation, number, etc., as separate skills, we end up in effect fertilizing only a few soil samples when our real aim is to fertilize the entire field.

One of the most intriguing and fundamental aspects of Piaget's theory is the fact that when the child has attained a certain level of cognitive development, he becomes able to solve a host of problems that he has never encountered before. Cross-cultural replications of Piaget's research (Bovet, 1971; Dasen, 1970; Elkind, 1961; Greenfield, 1966; Lovell & Ogilvie, 1960) have shown consistently that children all over the world become able to conserve without having been taught to conserve, and become able to seriate without having been taught to seriate.

A difference consistently observed in cross-cultural replications is in rate of development. Generally, children in a more developed culture develop faster than those living in a less developed culture. Within the same culture, children living in the city and more advantaged groups develop faster than those living in the country and in a less advantaged socioeconomic group. Piaget says that the causes of these differences are not known in a precise manner, but the following five factors are necessary for cognitive development (Piaget, 1970a):

1. Biological factors (particularly maturation)
2. Experiences with physical objects
3. Social factors and interindividual coordination
4. Cultural and educational transmission
5. Equilibration.

Piaget's theory thus puts the emphasis on the child's development outside school and laboratory situations where "learning" is studied. It may be useful to base a curriculum on this theory precisely because it examines the mechanisms of cognitive development in a context broader than traditional schools and laboratory situations.

For psychologists and educators who are used to viewing teaching as a series of specific skills to be taught, and broken down into smaller skills when children show difficulties, the idea of a general cognitive framework is hard to accept. However, if we study the research done in Geneva, it becomes equally hard to view cognitive development in any other way except as the development of a total structure. Piaget and his collaborators invent perhaps 30–50 new tasks every year, and with any one of these tasks, we almost invariably find a higher level of solution at ages 7 to 8 than at 4 to 5. Since care is taken to create tasks that children have not been taught to solve before, it is not possible to attribute the correct solution to specific teaching.

The idea of a child's cognitive framework becomes clearer when we try to teach a 4-year-old what we mean by "inflation," "the capital of the U.S.," or "the atmosphere of a place." With older children, verbal explanations quickly produce comprehension. With 4-year-olds, however, not all the language in the world will lead to any degree of understanding. The ability to understand these ideas requires a well structured, rich cognitive framework that takes many years to develop. The word "inflation," for example, can be understood only if the child has a cognitive framework which integrates notions of number, seriation, time, and a system of exchange in which there is a common unit. The "capital of the U.S." can likewise be understood only if the child has a cognitive framework capable of integrating class inclusion, the organization of space, and the political organization of people. Not all the attempts in the world at teaching specific skills (such as how to say by heart the verbal definition of "capital" and "the United States," how to read "t-h-e c-a-p-i-t-a-l o-f t-h-e U-n-i-t-e-d S-t-a-t-e-s," and how to say the names of other capitals such as France-Paris and England-London) will result in the development of the cognitive framework, or "readiness," that enables the child to learn what a capital is.

The causal relationships explaining precisely what environmental factors enhance the development of the child's cognitive framework are unfortunately not yet known. However, the five factors mentioned earlier, plus other ideas which will be elaborated later in this paper (e.g., the distinction Piaget makes between physical and logico-mathematical knowledge, his constructivism, and insistence on the increasing mobility and structure of thought processes) do serve to build a preschool curriculum that attempts to develop children's general cognitive framework, or "readiness" for a wide range of school subjects (e.g., reading, writing, arithmetic, science, social studies, and music).

•   •   •

I have gone to some length to insist on the development of the child's cognitive framework as a whole because the following objectives of the curriculum give the impression of being separate areas to work on separately. Although the objectives are listed in outline form, the teacher needs to remember at all times that intelligence functions as an integrated whole, and develops as an integrated whole. This point will be elaborated further in the second part of the paper on teaching methods.

I. OBJECTIVES

A. Socioemotional Objectives

According to Piaget (1954), there are no cognitive mechanisms that are without affective elements, and there is no affective state that has no cognitive element. The relationship between cognition and affectivity for him is that the latter provides the energy that makes intelligence function.

The more intelligence is used, the more it develops. Therefore, according to Piaget, affectivity can accelerate, retard, or block cognitive development as can be seen in the student who gets excited or discouraged in class. The following socioemotional objectives are thus important not only in themselves but also as essential elements for the child's cognitive development.

1. *In relation to peers*
   a. Ability to respect the feelings and rights of other children (decentering and moral development)
   b. Ability to listen to others and exchange opinions (decentering, which leads to the coordination of different points of view)

2. *In relation to adults*
   a. Ability to listen to adults, cooperate with them, and use them as a source of friendship, guidance, and information.
   b. Ability to control one's own behavior rather than being controlled by adults. By learning to make plans and decisions, carrying them out, and evaluating their own activities, children learn to control their own behavior.
   c. Ability to cope with situations as they come up. By learning to assess situations and making appropriate decisions on their own, children develop independence rather than the passivity of waiting to be told what to do. For example, if someone spills juice, the appropriate action is to bring a wet sponge.

3. *In relation to learning*
   a. Being active. Intelligence develops by being used. As long as children have the initiative to keep doing *something*, each activity is likely to lead to a new challenge. Therefore, we want children to be busily doing things with initiative, enthusiasm, and excitement.

b. Being curious. Curiosity is more focused than the above objective. Examples are (1) exploring things to figure out how they are made and how they work, (2) experimenting with cause-effect and means-end relationships, and (3) asking questions.

c. Being confident. We want children to have the self-confidence that they *can* figure things out on their own (rather than depending on the teacher to provide the answer). Even when their answer is "wrong" from the standpoint of adult logic, we want children to speak their mind with confidence and conviction, rather than scrutinizing the teacher's face for feedback as to whether or not one is saying "the" right thing.

d. Having the habit of divergent thinking. We want children not to look for the one "correct" answer the adult wants, but to come up with many different ways of doing the same thing. Even in simple activities like make-believe, which is described later, and physical activities like going down the slide, we want children to do the same thing in many different ways (e.g., coming down with one hand on the head, on the stomach, or lying down).

If children are excited, curious, resourceful, confident about their ability to figure things out, and eager to exchange opinions with other children and adults, they are bound to go on learning, particularly when they are out of the classroom and throughout the rest of their lives. Therefore, socioemotional development may well give more educational mileage in the long run than the learning of specific skills and behaviors or even intellectual operations. Within the context of the above socioemotional objectives, we conceptualize the following cognitive objectives.

B. Cognitive Objectives

Generally speaking, we stay within the preoperational period and would like to see behaviors which Piaget describes as characterizing stage II. (See Kamii, 1971, for further details.) Our goals, however, are not to produce stage-II *behavior* as such but to develop the cognitive *processes* which might manifest themselves in stage-II behavior and eventually lead to concrete and formal operations.

Although cognitive processes develop as part of a total framework, it is useful to conceptualize our educational objectives in terms of the different areas Piaget delineated as having different modes of structuring. He delineated two major areas of knowledge, i.e., physical knowledge and logico-mathematical knowledge. Sinclair adds a third area, social knowledge. The fourth area, spatio-temporal notions, lie halfway between physical and logico-mathematical knowledge (because time and space are observable like physical knowledge, but are also like logico-mathematical knowledge in that they have to be constructed by the child and introduced into external reality). Finally, the child needs to become able to represent all four types of knowledge both to think about things that are absent and to exchange ideas with other people. These five objectives are elaborated below.

1.   Physical knowledge

Physical knowledge in this context refers to observable properties of objects and physical phenomena such as what happens when we let go of a marble on an incline. The way the child finds out about these properties and phenomena is by acting on objects and observing and systematizing the objects' reactions. Dropping, folding, stretching, squeezing, and tapping are examples of actions the child can attempt on almost any object in his environment to find out how it reacts. Physical knowledge is thus structured from feedback from objects. We see the following two objectives in this area.

  a. Developing the child's repertoire of actions he can perform on objects to find out how they react. For example, the child finds out about the properties of a large ballbearing by picking it up, rolling it, bringing it close to his face and looking at the reflection of his face, etc. If this repertoire is well developed, the child will know the properties of the objects around him and how to go about finding out the physical nature of new, unfamiliar objects.

b. Developing an attitude of curiosity and anticipation of what will happen, and the habit of figuring out means to achieve desired ends. For example, 4-year-old children make an exciting game out of predicting that a ballbearing will sink in water, as they enjoy the suspense before empirically verifying this prediction. They also enjoy being asked how they could make the ballbearing stay on top of the water.

Two remarks are in order. First, preschool children can observe visible mechanical changes that result from their own direct actions (e.g., breaking objects, bouncing them, and rolling them). However, an invisible change such as the transformation of water into steam is too difficult. Second, it is wise with preschool children to stay within the realm of predictions and not insist on explanations.

2. *Logico-mathematical knowledge*

While physical knowledge is structured from feedback from objects, logico-mathematical knowledge is structured from the child's own coordinated actions and the results of these actions. By "coordinated actions" Piaget means coordination in a logical sense and not in a motoric sense. By "the results of these actions" he means results in a logical sense and not in a physical sense (i.e., feedback from objects). For example, when the child brings two, three, or four objects together, the result is a group of objects. When he makes two groups of objects by one-to-one correspondence between the action of the two hands, the result is two groups that are numerically equivalent.

In physical knowledge, the specific properties of each object are all important, since the child finds out about and systematizes the reactions of each object. In logico-mathematical knowledge, on the other hand, what is important is not the properties of each object but the *relationship* between and among objects. The properties of objects exist *in* objects, but the relationship among them does not. They are constructed by the child and introduced by *him,* and not by external reality.

Piaget delineates three areas of logico-mathematical knowledge: Classification, seriation, and number. In classification, the relationships the child introduces are those of similarities and differences (leading to the logic of classes involving the coordination of extensive and intensive properties of groups of objects). In seriation, the relationship is that of relative differences. In number, the child makes groups of objects and compares the number of objects in two or more groups. The objectives we conceptualize for the preschool curriculum are listed below.

a. In classification

(1) Developing the child's ability to find similarities and differences among objects, and to *group* them according to their similarity and *separate* them according to their differences.

(2) Developing the child's mobility of thought, so that he will become able to see many different ways of grouping the same group of objects.

b. In seriation

Developing the child's ability to compare differences among objects along some dimension, and to order them according to their relative differences. (In classification, the child only separates objects that are different. In seriation, he orders them according to their relative differences.) For example, we would like children to group a dog, a horse, a mouse, and a deer together because of their similarity (pre-classification), and to arrange them according to their relative sizes (pre-seriation).

c. In number

(1) Developing the child's logical structure that is necessary to make judgements of equivalence, "more," and "less."

(2) Developing the child's mobility of thought so that conservation will become possible as a byproduct. (Conservation should come as a result of the child's mobility of thought, and not as a result of direct teaching.)

3. *The structuring of space and time*

As stated earlier, space and time lie halfway between physical and logico-mathematical knowledge. Space and time are like physical knowledge in that they are observable in external reality. However, they are like logico-mathematical knowledge in that the space and time that are involved in spatio-temporal *reasoning* have to be constructed and structured by the child himself. (See Piaget, 1970b, and Piaget & Inhelder, 1967, for an elaboration of this statement.) The objectives of the preschool curriculum are listed below.

a. Space

(1) Developing topological structures toward Euclidean structures on the representational level. (See Piaget & Inhelder, 1967, Ch. 2, for an explanation of topological and Euclidean space.)

(2) Increasing the child's mobility of thought on the representational level (e.g., linear ordering, arranging and rearranging blocks to copy a model, and predicting an object's trajectory).

b. Time

Enabling the child to structure time into sequences (intervals come later).

4.   *Social knowledge*

Social knowledge refers to social conventions which are structured from feedback from people.[1] Examples are that tables are not to stand on, that water is not to be spilled all over the floor even in waterplay at school, and that we engage in certain rituals on birthdays and traditional holidays.

5.   *Representation*

a. On the level of symbols[2]

Developing children's ability to represent things and ideas in imitation and sociodramatic play, onomatopoeia (e.g., making the sound of a horn while pretending to drive a car), make-believe (making an object stand for something

---

[1] The distinction among physical, logico-mathematical, and social knowledge is based on different modes of structuring knowledge, rather than different sources of knowledge. Social knowledge is thus not to be confused with moral development.

[2] Symbols, in Piaget's terminology, are individual in nature and bear a resemblance to the object being represented. Signs, on the other hand, do not resemble the object and make up a system which serves social communication (e.g., language, the Morse code, and algebraic signs).

else, such as making a block stand for a car), and making other symbolic representations with a pencil, paint, clay, blocks, pipecleaners, sticks, etc.

b. On the level of signs (See Footnote 2)
   Developing the child's ability to represent things and communicate ideas through arbitrary signs (e.g., traffic signs) and language. We try to develop language as a tool for precise communication and exchange of opinions. While we believe that language is an important tool and stimulator of cognitive development, we do not believe that language is the source or cause of logico-mathematical operations.

II. TEACHING METHODS

The preceding objectives give to the teacher a framework for conceptualizing and diagnosing different aspects of cognitive development as part of an organized whole. Our general procedure is for the teacher to set up a situation, sometimes proposing an activity, and see how the children react. With the above objectives in mind, she tries to use almost any situation that seems particularly suited to activate certain aspects of intelligence. Three activities will be described below as examples that focus on particular aspects of cognitive development (i.e., predicting what will sink and what will float, the pendulum, and make-believe). Two activities will then be discussed as examples of traditional nursery-school situations that can be used within a Piagetian framework (i.e., block building and sociodramatic play). Finally, juice time will be discussed to show that every situation in daily living can be used for educational purposes. Some principles of teaching will be given at the end of the paper.

A. Situations

1. Predicting what will sink and what will float
   This activity focuses on *classification* and *physical knowledge*. For each group of two or three children, the teacher prepares

a pail of water and an array of objects (e.g., a sponge, blocks of various sizes, a fork, a stone, a rubber band, paper clips of various sizes, an old sock, a crayon, a cup, and a small glass bottle). The game is to divide the objects into the two groups of "things that will float" and "things that will sink." After making this dichotomy, the children verify their predictions by putting the objects in the water, discussing all along what they think will happen and what they found out.

2. *The pendulum*

The teacher makes a large pendulum by putting a weight at the end of a long string suspended from the ceiling and almost touching the floor. After allowing a sufficient amount of time for the children to play freely to find out how the pendulum works, she introduces a game of knocking down a rubber doll which is placed standing on the floor. The rule of the game is to hold the weight at a particular spot and let go of it, rather than giving it a push. The children take turns to place the doll at different spots.

This is primarily a *physical knowledge* activity because the doll responds to the child's action by falling to the ground or not falling. However, the activity cannot take place without *spatial reasoning* and the comparison of distances and angles (*preseriation*). When the child lets go of the weight, the weight follows a predictable trajectory in space. As shown below, if he

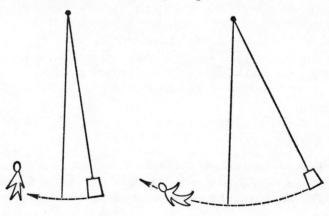

holds the weight at a wide angle from its original position at rest, it will travel farther.

Serial correspondence of angles must also be made on a horizontal plane. If the weight travels as shown below, the child

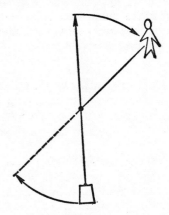

has to correct his prediction. To the extent that he can systematize all the ways in which he missed the target, the child is more successful on subsequent trials.

3.   *Make-believe*

The teacher gives a cylindrical block to each one of the 5 or 6 children sitting around the table. She asks them to think of all the things they can make the block be, and asks them to raise their hand when they have an idea they want to show to the group. The ideas that came out in one of our sessions were "a whistle," "corn on the cob," "pop," "a hotdog," "a comb," "a cigar," "lipstick," "a rolling pin," and "a pirates (meaning a telescope)."

This activity can be varied by using other blocks of different shapes and sizes, paper cutouts, and clay.

The activity focuses on *representation,* and the child has to decenter from one point of view to another as he tries to see something different in the same object. The most noteworthy characteristic of this activity is *divergent thinking.* Within the limits imposed by the task, the children have to come up with many different ideas.

When a child comes up with an idea that has already come up, *time* and *classification* both come into play. *New information* can come in when a child has ideas such as "pirates (meaning a telescope)." A great deal of social interaction takes place as children imitate each other's actions and evaluate whether or not they can see what others claim to be symbolizing.

4.   *Block building*

The first level of play in block building seems to involve *physical knowledge* and *spatial reasoning*. Typically, the child tries to make a taller and taller tower until it topples. He then repeats the same action over and over, sooner or later with variations.

Block building develops into *representation*. Rather than simply experimenting with the spatial arrangements of blocks, the child begins to represent objects and ideas, such as a road, a gas station, and a house. These representations of individual objects can be elaborated into the spatial organization of several objects (the beginning of map making) or the organization of a sequence of activities (going to buy gas, having an accident at the intersection, and ending up going to the hospital).

As they use many short blocks or a few long ones to build a road (or the wall of a house), children compare different sizes (the beginning of *seriation*). At clean-up time, they put away the long blocks on one shelf, the cylindrical ones, curved ones, and hollow ones on other shelves, each with subgroups (the beginning of *classification*).

The pride and excitement children show in their creation are well known. Divergent thinking is enhanced as they represent many different things with the same blocks. For many children, block building is a comfortable situation in which social relationships develop both with peers and with adults.

5.   *Sociodramatic play*

We see sociodramatic play mainly as a reading-readiness activity that strengthens the *symbolic process*. The mechanistic skills of reading (e.g., perceptual discrimination) enable the child to know what sounds the letters stand for. What enables him to derive meaning from written and spoken language is the symbolic process.

In other symbolic activities, the child has to express his ideas indirectly with paint, clay, and blocks. In sociodramatic play, on the other hand, he externalizes his ideas directly with his body. (The child is thus both the symbol and the symbolizer.) Paint and clay do not permit the representation of a sequence of events (e.g., "going shopping" and "having a birthday party"), but sociodramatic play allows symbolization to go beyond static representation. It also has the advantage of involving the use of language.

In a simple situation like pretending to have coffee with friends, children represent their knowledge of reality in all areas of the cognitive framework. For example, they represent their *physical knowledge* by heating the coffee, pouring it, spilling it, stirring it, and burning oneself with it. They represent the idea of pouring more coffee than cream, or giving a lot of cream and sugar to some people, and less or none to other people (*pre-seriation*). They construct elementary *number concepts* as they get just enough cups, saucers, napkins, and spoons for everybody. They represent the *temporal sequence* of making coffee, getting the cups and saucers out, pouring coffee, drinking it, and then cleaning up. They learn to serve the guests first (*social knowledge*). Sometimes, they invite people by phoning them beforehand. In this situation, some children's temporal sequence has been observed to consist of accepting an invitation first before being invited, or dialing first before picking up the receiver!

Children constantly decenter[3] in sociodramatic play to play the part of somebody else in interaction with other roles. As they decenter and externalize their knowledge, they relive, digest, and integrate their previous observations.

---

[3] "Decentering" refers to seeing things from points of view other than one's own. In sociodramatic play, for example, the child has to decenter from his own point of view in order to relate to a baby from a mother's point of view.

6. *Juice time*

Juice time is first of all for drinking juice and for having conversations. When a child says, "I had a tummy ache last night. I ate too much," for example, the teacher can expand the remark into a discussion of stomach aches, illness, health, etc. She can also use juice time in the following ways to activate certain aspects of the cognitive framework:

a. The construction of elementary number concepts

   (1) The teacher can ask a child to take out just enough cups, placemats, or cookies for everybody who is at a particular table (or in school today).

   (2) She can give 3 counting blocks to each child to "buy" what he wants. Since each item costs a block, each child can buy 2 cookies and one cup of juice, or one cookie and 2 cups of juice, or any other combination of 3 items.

b. The comparison of quantities (leading to seriation)

   (1) A helper can go around asking each child if he wants the same amount of juice as another child, or more or less juice.

   (2) Another helper can ask each child how much peanut butter he wants on his cracker (a lot, a little bit, or none at all).

c. Classification

   (1) When everybody has finished, the teacher can ask one helper to collect "all the cups and empty cans" and another helper to collect "everything that we don't throw out."

   (2) The teacher can ask, "What do you see on the table that rolls (can be eaten, broken, poured, folded, torn, etc.)?"

d. Physical knowledge

   (1) The teacher can ask whether or not the juice can on the table is empty, and how we can find out (and how else we can find out).

   (2) She can ask where the juice will go "if I spill this much juice right here on the table."

e. The structuring of space

   (1) When juice is spilled by accident, after cleaning up the mess, the teacher can ask where the juice ran, and where it is likely to run if we spilled some again.

   (2) The teacher can ask the children to break their cookies and see whether or not the pieces can be reassembled into the original shape.

f. The structuring of time

   Juice time lends itself to reviewing what the children did earlier in the day and exchange opinions about what happened (e.g., "Would you like to tell us what you built with the blocks today?"). It is also a good time to plan the activities for the rest of the day (e.g., "What do we do next?" "What would you like to do then?" "What do we have to get ready to make Play Doh?").

B. Principles of Teaching

As stated earlier, in our general approach the teacher sets up a situation, sometimes proposing a specific activity, and watches how children react before deciding what to pick up on to extend the child's thinking. This diagnostic interpretation of the child's reaction is one of the most crucial points in the teaching process, where Piaget's exploratory method [4] must be applied skillfully. The teacher's ability to figure out what goes on in the child's head at each moment makes the difference between elaborating *his* way of thinking and disrupting it. Piaget's theoretical framework enables

---

[4] In a standardized test situation, the examiner asks one question after another by following precisely and literally the directions given in a manual. In a Piagetian interview, in contrast, the examiner has a theory behind what he wants to find out, and formulates one question after another depending on what the child said before. In the conservation of liquid task, for example, if the child says that the tall, thin container has more water than the original wide container because the level of water is higher in the former, the examiner can pose a variety of questions, e.g., "But this one is narrow. Doesn't that make a difference?" or "Do you remember how we poured the Kool-Aid out of the bottle?" This flexible way of interviewing children is called the "exploratory method." (Piaget used to call it the "clinical method.")

her to make this diagnostic interpretation of how the child is thinking.

In the classification of "things that will sink" and "things that will float," for example, the teacher needs to give to the children enough time to explore each object before suggesting that they make a dichotomy. Children need to examine each object by assimilating it to their previous knowledge (i.e., schemes) and accommodating to its particular aspects before they can think in terms of whether it will sink or float. When the object contradicts his anticipation, the child often does many things to make it conform to his anticipation (e.g., holding a block down at the bottom of the pail for a while, and repeating this action several times when the object returns to the surface). The teacher in this situation can pick up on the child's line of reasoning by saying, "Can you think of another way to make it stay down?" She can also turn to other children and ask if *they* can think of a way to make the block stay down.

In block building, if the child has been experimenting with the stability of a tower by rebuilding it each time it topples, the teacher might suggest that he build another tower next to it and lead him to compare the two towers in various ways. She might also suggest trying to build a small tower that will topple, or she might try to involve other children in the activity. When the child is concentrating on physical and spatial reasoning, one thing she might do well to avoid is the sudden imposition of a totally different line of reasoning. For example, suddenly shifting into representation by saying "Let's pretend it's the church tower across the street" is probably the wrong thing to do.

In sociodramatic play, the teacher needs to know the events in the child's real life before trying to elaborate his play. For example, she can try to elaborate the play by saying "Let's plan a birthday party" or "Can you call a taxi for me?" only if she knows these activities to be familiar to the child. Since the child cannot represent knowledge that he does not have, any imposition of foreign ideas is likely to interfere with his thinking.

The role of the teacher thus grows out of Piaget's interactionism. The teacher does not shape a response, nor transmit or program the input of knowledge (the empiricist approach). She does not go to the other extreme either of passively watching children play while waiting for "readiness" to unfold (a maturationist approach).[5] She structures the environment for children to activate and apply their schemes (i.e., the cognitive structures through which external stimuli are understood). She then intervenes unobtrusively by applying Piaget's exploratory method so that the children will test out their ideas against objects and other people, and build new schemes by differentiation and integration of previously constructed schemes. A curriculum based on this interactionism can, therefore, never be presented in a cookbook fashion. It goes without saying that the six situations described above can easily turn into teaching that is completely contrary to Piaget's theory.

Many important aspects of the curriculum have been left out of this paper, such as how we approach language development, how we try to achieve our socioemotional objectives, and how we adapt some Piagetian tasks from time to time in the classroom. We believe these tasks are very useful, provided they do not become the central part of a Piagetian curriculum, and the focus is on the process of reasoning rather than on the answer the child gives. In the limited space available in this article, I overemphasized the use of rather common activities to insist that the way to develop the preoperational child's general cognitive framework is not by having him go through all the stages on Piagetian tasks.

How to help disadvantaged children develop this cognitive framework is not obvious, and I do not claim to know how to accomplish this task. Nevertheless, I tried above to sketch some recent ideas based on the implications of Piaget's theory as I understand it today. We are, after all, still far from being able to isolate the environmental variables that make a difference to the long-term cognitive development of preschool children.

---

[5] See Kohlberg (1968) for a clarification of the empiricist, maturationist, and interactionist views of "learning."

REFERENCES

BOVET, M. Etude interculturelle des processus de raisonnement—notions de quantités physiques et relations spatio-temporels chez des enfants et des adultes non-scolarisés. Unpublished doctoral dissertation, University of Geneva, 1971.

DASEN, P. *Cognitive development in aborigines of central Australia.* Unpublished doctoral dissertation, Australian National University, Canberra, 1970.

ELKIND, D. Children's discovery of the conservation of mass, weight, and volume: Piaget replication study II. *Journal of Genetic Psychology,* 1961, *98,* 219–227.

GREENFIELD, P. *On culture and conservation.* In Bruner, J., Olver, R. R., Greenfield, P., et al. *Studies in cognitive growth.* New York: Wiley, 1966.

INHELDER, B., & PIAGET, J. *The early growth of logic in the child.* New York: Harper & Row, 1964.

KAMII, C. Evaluation of learning in preschool education: Socio-emotional, perceptual-motor, and cognitive development. In B. S. Bloom, J. T. Hastings, & G. Madaus (Eds.), *Handbook of formative and summative evaluation of student learning.* New York: McGraw-Hill, 1971.

KAMII, C., & RADIN, N. A framework for a preschool curriculum based on some Piagetian concepts. *Journal of Creative Behavior,* 1967, *1,* 314–324.

KAMII, C., & RADIN, N. A framework for a preschool curriculum based on some Piagetian concepts. In Athey, I. J., & Rubadeau, D. O. (Eds.) *Educational implications of Piaget's theory.* Waltham, Mass.: Ginn-Blaisdell, 1970.

KOHLBERG, L. Early education: A cognitive-developmental view. *Child Development,* 1968, *39,* 1013–1062.

LOVELL, K., & OGILVIE, E. A study of the concept of conservation of substance in the junior school child. *British Journal of Educational Psychology,* 1960, *30,* 109–118.

PIAGET, J. Les relations entre l'intelligence et l'affectivité dans le développement de l'enfant. *Bulletin de Psychologie,* 1954, *7,* 143–150.

PIAGET, J. *Play, dreams, and imitation in childhood.* New York: Norton, 1962.

PIAGET, J. *The child's conception of number.* New York: Norton, 1965.

PIAGET, J. *Psychologie et Epistémologie.* Paris: Denoël, 1970a.

PIAGET, J. *The child's conception of time.* London: Routledge & Kegan Paul, 1970b.

PIAGET, J., & INHELDER, B. *The child's conception of space.* New York: Norton, 1967.

SONQUIST, H., & KAMII, C. Applying some Piagetian concepts in the classroom for the disadvantaged. *Young Children,* 1967, *22,* 231–245.

SONQUIST, H., KAMII, C., & DERMAN, L. A Piaget-derived preschool curriculum. In Athey, I. J., & Rubadeau, D. O. (Eds.) *Educational implications of Piaget's theory.* Waltham, Mass.: Ginn-Blaisdell, 1970.

16

THE TUCSON
EARLY EDUCATION MODEL

MARIE M. HUGHES, RALPH J. WETZEL,
AND RONALD W. HENDERSON

I. DESCRIPTION

History

The Tucson Early Education Model (TEEM) began in 1965 as a three-year cooperative project on the intellectual development of young Mexican-American children conducted by the University of Arizona, represented by Dr. Marie M. Hughes, and Tucson District No. 1, represented by Mrs. Jewell Taylor. There were several factors which led to the development of this project. First, the school

Revised November 8, 1971. Reprinted by permission of authors.

superintendent's committee on dropouts reported that Mexican-Americans as a group had the highest rate in Tucson for leaving school before the twelfth grade. Second, test results in reading and social studies indicated that the discrepancy between the achievement of young Mexican-American children and their Anglo-American counterparts increased as they progressed through school: Mexican-Americans were nearer the norm of their Anglo-American counterparts as first and second graders than they were in the middle grades. At the sixth grade they were, as a group, one and one-half to three years below the test norms.

In general, the data on the Mexican-American child's progress in schools in the Southwest were similar to those data for certain other groups of children; namely children of minority groups and the rural poor, from families of unskilled parents living close to a subsistence level.

The new educational program as it evolved was successively implemented in grades one through three in eight public schools in the metropolitan Tucson area. The continued elaboration and evaluation of this Model became the focus of the Arizona Center for Early Childhood Education at the University of Arizona in 1967.

Rationale

Participation in the technical, social and economic life of contemporary America requires particular skills and abilities. These skills and abilities are frequently missing in the behavioral repertoires of individuals whose backgrounds fail to provide an adequate foundation for such learning. The content and procedures of this program are, therefore, based on the definition and specification of the following.

1. The skills and attitudes necessary to function in our technical and changing society.
2. The behavioral characteristics which children bring to the educational situation.
3. The nature of the learning process.

The program procedures suggested by these considerations differ significantly from conventional curricula and modes of instruction for young children. If the requisite skills are to be developed, new program objectives and priorities must be established.

Major Objectives

The major objectives of the Tucson Early Education Model can be classified into four categories:

1. LANGUAGE COMPETENCE. Language competence is one of the major technical skills of the culture to which the child must adapt. Critical information is transmitted principally in verbal form. This requires an acquaintance with a variety of linguistic labels, concepts, language forms, and an awareness of the function of language.

2. INTELLECTUAL BASE. The intellectual base is a collection of skills assumed to be necessary in the process of learning. These skills are as yet only partially recognized and defined and are usually not formally taught. Yet their importance in every learning process is becoming increasingly recognized. Some of the intellectual base skills involve the organization of stimuli in the environment. For example, ordering events along certain dimensions such as size, color, and form, sequencing events according to time. Some intellectual base skills are more complex behaviors which are difficult to define: to be able to attend, to recall significant events, to be able to organize one's behavior toward specific goals, to evaluate alternatives, and to choose, to plan and to develop expectations, to be able to discriminate significant and important behaviors in others and to imitate.

3. MOTIVATIONAL BASE. By motivational base we mean a collection of attitudes and behavioral characteristics related to productive social involvement. These include positive attitudes toward school and toward the learning process, an appreciation for learning and a willingness to persist at learning tasks, an expectation of success and a willingness to change.

4. SOCIETAL ARTS AND SKILLS. Our culture is characterized by

a wide range of arts and skills which constitute social interaction, information transmission, and scientific advance. Here we classify reading, writing, and mathematical skills as well as the social skills of cooperation, planning and democratic process. Although certain arts and skills have traditionally constituted the primary focus of school curricula, in the Tucson Early Education Model they are only a portion of the total program.

Organization

There are three major components of the Tucson Early Education Model: instruction, psychological services, and parent involvement.

1. INSTRUCTION. The purpose of the instructional program is to structure about the child a learning environment designed to promote the development of the behaviors defined by the four TEEM goal areas. Several aspects of the instructional program process and organization have been delineated. The process variables include:

A. *Individualization.* If we believe that the children differ when they come into the educational environment; if we believe that children bring to the school different sets of attitudes and different sets of skills; if we finally believe that children must begin from where they are in order to be brought into the educational process, then it is clear that teachers must individualize their teaching procedures. It is a characteristic of the organization of the Tucson Early Education Model that frequent opportunities are provided in the classroom for one-to-one adult-child interaction; for observation and recognition of individual differences in skill and interest. A variety of behavioral options are constantly available to the child, providing opportunities to develop individual skills at individual rates.

B. *Imitation.* Although imitation is widely recognized as a significant process by which the young child acquires behavior, it is seldom formally incorporated into classroom practice. In this program, frequent opportunities are provided for the modelling of behaviors that facilitate the continual development of skills and abilities valued and useful in a scientific and technically-based society. The attention of children is directed toward the important and significant behaviors of others and they are encouraged and reinforced for imitating. The variation in behaviors in settings which the program provides encourages a wide range of skills. Imitation is a particularly important process in the acquisition of language. Adults consciously and continuously work to model elaborated and extended examples of the child's own communications. The verbal forms of information-seeking, *e.g.*, question-asking and "thinking out loud," are modelled in demonstration and in adult-child interaction.

C. *Gratification.* It is clear that rewarding and gratifying experiences are crucial elements in the learning process. Reinforcement plays an important role in classroom procedures. Classroom adults are trained in the techniques of social reinforcement including praise, attention, affection, and the like. Materials are chosen for their reinforcing value and activities are arranged so that they may naturally result in reinforcing events. Every effort is made to ensure that the child experiences frequent gratification as a result of his behavior and skill acquisition. It is intended that, through these multiple reinforcing experiences, the child comes to regard learning as a satisfying experience and school as a source of significant and rewarding activities.

D. *Generalization.* It is crucial to the success of an educational program that the skills which it teaches can be extended by the student to a variety of settings, objects, and events. Frequently in traditional programs the curriculum experiences are limited and opportunities to generalize skills restricted. In the Model, few skills are taught abstractly through rote-exercise or drill. A skill is always taught in a functional setting, and almost always in multiple functional settings. Concepts are illustrated by a variety of examples in several contexts, skills are extended across content areas within the classroom, and from the classroom to the natural environment of the child. Frequent field trips, walks, and visits to the children's homes extend the learning environment and increase the array of experiences thus facilitating the generalization of skills and abilities to the child's own environment. He learns that his own neighborhood is a context for observation and learning.

E. *Orchestration.* The various skills which reflect the four principal goals of the program (language, intellectual base, motivational base, and societal arts and skills) are seldom exercised independently of each other. For example, language competence can hardly be displayed independent of content and thought processes within some societal skill. Almost all intellectual activities require some combination of these discrete behaviors. It is a central aspect of TEEM that these skills are not taught separately, one from another. This is a significant departure from the linear quality of traditional programs in which time segments devoted to individual skills follow each other in repetitious fashion. When skills are acquired in real and meaningful settings, it is possible to develop more than one skill simultaneously. A teacher organizing a small group of children in the activity of ice-cream-making, for example, will be teaching new words, the processes of proper order and sequence of events, new concepts, new technical and social skills. In addition, the manner of her interaction with children plus, in this case, the eating of the product will significantly influence the child's attitude toward the activity and the learning experience. The technique of simultaneously attending to and developing a variety of skills in children, of developing language, intellectual, motivational, and societal skills in a single context, is defined as orchestration. In orchestration the teacher provides instruction to the child in the context of an experience which offers the opportunity for interrelating his skills with respect to a variety of goals.

Organization variables in the instruction component of TEEM include:

A. *Room arrangement.* The physical environment of the room is organized into behavioral settings. It is arranged to facilitate interaction between the child and his environment, between the child and his peers, and between the child and adults in the classroom. Interest centers include materials which provide open-ended experiences, making it possible for children differing in their levels of development to acquire skills through their interaction with the materials. Tables are arranged to facilitate small-group instruction and to make it possible for children to work independently in small groups. Classroom groupings are kept heterogeneous, as a means of increasing opportunities for children to learn from peer models.

B. *Interaction.* In the Tucson Early Education Model, most structured lessons are carried out with small groups in which the teacher, or her aide, work with about five children at a time. This makes it possible for the teacher to respond to each individual child, utilize his current skills, and build upon and extend this base. In traditional classrooms, in which a great deal of instructional time is taken up by total group activity, it is easy for a child to "tune-out." In small group activities, on the other hand, the teacher can attend to each child every day, reinforce his participation, and help him toward the skills designated as program objectives. In a sense, this mode of organization provides a way of artificially reducing the child-to-adult ratio.

C. *Behavioral options.* The organization and atmosphere of the TEEM classroom provides the child with a variety of behavioral options. At least one period during the program day is open to self-selection activities in which the child has responsibility for the organization of his own activities around available materials and space. During more structured activities, children are encouraged to verbalize, to handle materials, to participate in demonstrations, and to engage themselves actively in the learning process. The guiding principle is that in order to learn, the child must have the opportunity to engage in a variety of behaviors. It is the teacher's responsibility to encourage selectively those aspects of his repertoire which are congruent with educational aims. Unless he is permitted to act, the child cannot learn.

D. *Adaptation to local populations.* The major objectives of the instructional program specify the development of skills and attitudes necessary to function in a technical and changing society. It is recognized, however, that in coping with their own environments, children develop other skills and attitudes which are quite functional and appropriate in their own homes and neighborhoods. Traditional programs, consisting of prescribed curriculum materials, usually ignore or attempt to eliminate these elements of the child's behavioral repertoire. Teachers trained in the use of the Tucson Early Education Model learn to use the experiential backgrounds of pupils to further instructional objectives. The child's home and neighborhood are viewed as instructional resources, thus avoiding the discontinuity of cultural values which often confronts minority group children who are presented with a stereotyped middle-class curriculum.

E. *Planning.* Within the open-ended context of this organization, lessons and experiences for the children are given definite structure and direction by the careful planning of the staff. The distribution of children in centers, the presentation and withdrawal of materials, the extension of learning experiences into selected aspects of the natural environment, all require careful planning for optimum utilization of time and resources.

2. PSYCHOLOGICAL SERVICES.[1] The TEEM psychological services component focuses on learning and adjustment problems identified by teachers and other personnel associated with the Model's instructional component. The word "problems" as used here does not have the negative connotation of inherent inadequacies or inabilities. It refers, rather, to situations which may be modified to enable a child to achieve desired goal behaviors. Too often in education the label "problem" is dissociated from its ordinary concomitant—solution—and masks an apathetic maintenance of the status quo. Implicit in TEEM's concept of problems is the need for formulating and implementing helpful strategies, to move the child from a present level of performance to a desired one. This re-

---

[1] For further explication of the psychological services approach used by TEEM, the reader is referred to John R. Bergan, Dal R. Curry, Elaine Nicholson, Sara Currin, Karen Haberman, Richard W. Brown, and Margaret Ronstadt, *Tucson Early Education Psychological Services Program* (Tucson, Arizona: Arizona Center for Early Childhood Education, University of Arizona, September 1, 1971) and John R. Bergan, "A Systems Approach to Psychological Services," *Psychology in the Schools,* Vol. VI, No. 4, 1970.

definition of the role of the school psychologist has important implications: No longer is the psychologist merely a psychometrician-diagnostician, who stops with the labeling or identification of a problem. He is a facilitator of change, working with those in the child's environment to remedy undesirable situations, and improve acceptable situations, in an effort to maximize desirable outcomes of school experience. Traditionally, it is the so-called deviant behaviors which have been the province of school psychologists. The TEEM psychological services component has expanded this role to permit use of psychological staff services to facilitate the further development of existing intellectual skills, leadership skills, social skills, or creativity in children.

The consultation process is central to TEEM psychological services. It is through consultation that the techniques of psychology are made available to educational change agents for the solving of educational problems. Consultation is neither teaching nor management: the psychologist does not tell the change agent how to solve a problem. It is the agent—whether teacher, parent, or paraprofessional—who is responsible for defining the problem, planning a solution to it, and in most cases implementing whatever intervention is undertaken.

A major advantage of this shift in responsibility is the greater likelihood that the educational problem will be handled in a manner relevant to the on-going educational program of which the child is a part. Such relevancy might not be present were the psychologist to deal with the child directly. A second advantage is that the change agent is more likely to design a program which he can implement readily, and there is thus a greater probability of following through on the problem.

The consultation process is conceived in four stages: problem identification, problem analysis, intervention, and evaluation. These have been described as follows (Bergan and Curry, 1970).

A. *Problem identification.* Problem identification has two purposes: to obtain a definition of the problem in behavioral terms, and to establish recording procedures for measuring the incidence of the problem behavior. These purposes are accomplished in an interview between the psychologist and the change agent.

B. *Problem analysis.* The purposes of problem analysis are: to identify those variables which might be controlling behavior chosen for modification, to define goal behaviors, and to establish a plan to enable the child to achieve goal behaviors. Problem analysis also requires an interview between the psychologist and the change agent.

C. *Intervention.* The purposes of intervention are to implement the modification plan and to measure child behavior during modification.

D. *Evaluation.* In the evaluation interview, data collected prior to and during intervention are assessed to determine whether or not intervention has been effective. If the goal established in problem analysis has been achieved, services may terminate. Sometimes, however, the change agent may identify other behaviors for modification. In such cases, the interview shifts from evaluation to problem identification. If the goal has not been attained, further problem analysis is undertaken and a new intervention plan devised.

The psychological services component of TEEM was added after instructional component implementation had begun. During the 1969–70 academic year it was piloted in three school systems in the Follow Through Project. Evaluation of the data from these communities on consultation cases opened and successfully terminated showed the program to be well-received. Accordingly, it was extended in the following year, and is being offered to still more communities in the 1971–72 school year.

3. PARENT INVOLVEMENT. It is the intent of the TEEM parent involvement component to emphasize the complementary roles of school and home as loci of intellectual development. Specifically, the parent involvement program aims to modify the natural environment in ways that support and supplement classroom instruction. The design of the parent involvement (PI) program is guided by two conceptual frameworks. The first of these is a model (Figure 1)

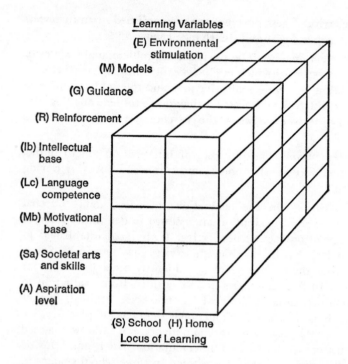

FIGURE 1.   Interrelationships among learning variables, objectives, and environments.

which defines educational objectives in terms of learning objectives (the four goal areas mentioned earlier); process variables; and the two learning environments of school and home. As an example, PI personnel may generate a range of activities which the family (H) could provide with a minimum of resources to introduce environmental stimulation (E) designed to foster skills in the intellectual base (Ib) category. This would be represented by cell Ib·E·H of Figure 1.

The second framework orders activities in terms of the amount of involvement they require of parents. As Henderson has pointed out,[2] "Target families in Follow Through programs are often those who have been most alienated from the schools through a long history of aversive experiences . . ." Although most parents have no contact with the school, a few of them are vocal and actively involved in organizations such as the Policy Advisory Committee (PAC). Accordingly, the PI program must accommodate parents at many points on the involvement continuum, and at the same time provide continuity of effort.

A. *Positive communication.* At one end of the continuum is the goal of establishing positive contact with parents. The first objective here is to reduce parental feelings of alienation from the school by initiating frequent, always positive, communications to the home concerning the child's progress in school. Many parents have learned to expect only negative communications from the school, and this expectation must be changed before further progress can be made.

A second objective is to begin to acquaint parents with the instructions program. This is particularly important for any program dedicated as TEEM is to objectives beyond those of traditional education.

B. *Parental reinforcement.* At the second stage, there is an effort to elicit from parents responses that reinforce the child's school-related behaviors. For example, a parent may be asked to question a child concerning one of his school products which has been sent home, thereby providing reinforcement through parental attention. This example is taken from the motivational base—reinforcement—in the home cell of the model presented in Figure 1.

C. *Guided observation.* The third stage includes a variety of opportunities for parents to participate in guided observation of classroom activities. Observation is best preceded by an orientation,

---

[2] Ronald W. Henderson, "Research and Consultation in the Natural Environment," *Psychology in the Schools,* Vol. VII, No. 4, 1970. Readers are referred to this paper, on which the present discussion is based, for a more detailed treatment of TEEM Parent Involvement.

to focus attention on particular activities and procedures in the classroom. For example, early observation might focus on the use of positive reinforcement by classroom adults. Discussions following observation can further clarify the teacher or aide's reinforcement of approximations to a desired behavior, and identify a variety of reinforcers used to accomplish this. Later, attention may be focused on the use of the reading environment, and follow-up discussion can indicate the importance of modeling as a means of influencing children to use reading materials. This example builds upon the relationship between the cells for motivational base—models—home and motivational base—models—school.

D. *Guided participation.* The next stage is guided participation in the classroom. Following opportunities to learn classroom procedures through observation, parents are invited to serve as volunteers in the classroom using their own special skills and experience with the TEEM framework.

E. *Transfer to home environment.* In the fifth stage, the goal is to promote transfer of principles which parents have observed and applied in the classrooms, to application in the home environment. Small groups of parents, working with parent involvement coordinators and psychological services personnel might discuss their classroom experiences, and suggest ways in which the home may support and supplement the activities of the instructional program.

F. *Providing for parent interests.* In the final stage, there is provision for a number of alternatives, to allow for the different interests of parents. Some may wish to learn behavioral recording techniques and other skills useful for classroom aides or psychological services aides. They may follow their specialized interests by working as volunteers in either of these program components. In some communities it will be possible to help them become involved in training programs for new careers. Other parents may wish to gain added skills in working with other parents in their neighborhoods and may assume paraprofessional positions in the PI program. Still others may wish to have a more direct influence on educational policy, and should be provided with knowledge of the administrative structure of the schools and of political pressures which influence educational policy. The alternatives suggested here are intended merely to illustrate the possibilities, because the intent of the program is that by this point parents will be sufficiently aware of a number of alternatives that may help to develop those alternatives identified by the parent group itself.

The parent involvement component is being implemented in six communities during the 1971–72 academic year.

II. DELIVERY

Implementation of the Tucson Model, as described above, depends for its realization on a system of training and support services. This is the TEEM delivery system. In developing the TEEM delivery system, it was assumed that programs which provide continued input, demonstration, and evaluation are vital to the maintenance and continued development of the new skills and attitudes basic to improvement of educational practices. It was also assumed that this continued input should take place for the most part in the settings in which the new skills will be exercised.

The delivery system relies on the "multiplier effect" (see Figure 2) to make a minimum of training time and effort produce maximum impact on children in the participating Follow Through communities. As indicated in Figure 2, the system of educational services has three components at the community level: (1) classroom instructional staff: teacher aides, teachers, and program assistants; (2) parent liaison personnel, who work to organize, develop, and implement significant parent activity in TEEM; and (3) school psychologists and their aides, who serve as consultants to instructional personnel and parents concerning learning and adjustment in children.

Instructional, parent involvement, and psychological services field representatives from the Arizona Center and their community counterparts (program assistants, parent coordinators, and psycholo-

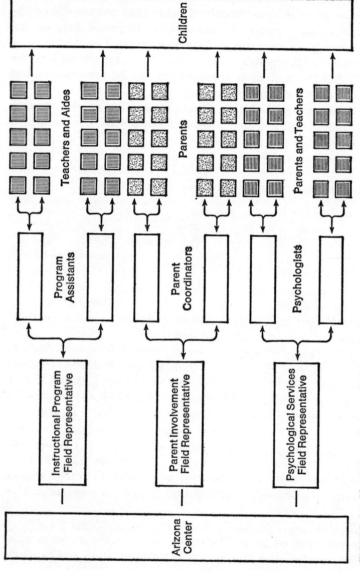

FIGURE 2. The Arizona System of Educational Services

244

gists) play key roles in the delivery system. They provide the vehicle for information transmission among system components and the means for implementing the multiplier effect.

Field representatives operate from the Arizona Center for Early Childhood Education, traveling into the field to offer support and guidance to training implementation personnel. Pertinent research findings, tested and demonstrated on a limited scale within program classrooms at Ochoa Elementary School, are communicated to program assistants, parent coordinators and school psychologists in the communities by the field staff. Questions from the field that generate testable hypotheses for research or that indicate a need for further development and explication of the Model, are communicated back to the Center by the field representatives, thus completing the vital cycle of communication within the program. In this manner the delivery system insures a constant flow of communication concerning research, development, and implementation among classroom personnel, researchers, and training personnel.

III. EVALUATION

In order to determine the success of present implementation efforts, and to give direction to future program development, evaluation becomes an essential part of any innovative program. TEEM evaluation efforts are carried out on three levels.[3] Table 1 gives a summary of these efforts.

Level I: The Local Community

Many communities routinely incorporate Follow Through classes into a larger system-wide testing program, and administer to

---

[3] The following material has been adopted from Robert K. Renfrow, *Current Evaluation Model: 1971* (Tucson, Arizona: Arizona Center for Early Childhood Education, University of Arizona, January 26, 1971). Readers are referred to this paper for a more detailed discussion of the subject.

TABLE 1. Current Summary of Outcome Research Activities—TEEM Model

	Agency	Focus	Techniques
Level I	Local Community	Pupils	B
Level II	University of Arizona—TEEM Research Staff	Pupils	C
		Teachers	E,B
		Aides	E,B
		Parents	D,G
Level III	Stanford Research Institute	Pupils	A,B,C,F,G
		Teachers	F
		Parents	C,D
		Institutions	A,G

A-Case study   B-Standardized tests   C-Situational tasks   D-Interviews
E-Attitude inventory   F-Classroom observaion   G-Demographic inventory

TEEM pupils a battery of standardized tests of school achievement. A few communities have conducted extensive longitudinal studies of TEEM children (notably Wichita, Kansas) or (like Vincennes, Indiana) attempted the use of measures of the affective domain. Such community-geared information is fed back into the classrooms, and used in making local decisions on program.

Level II: Center-Based Activities

In the past, most efforts in this area have been the work of the research component of the Arizona Center. This group has conducted research into such program-related matters as the use of modeling in concept acquisition, facilitation of question-asking behavior, and use of reinforcement in the classroom. Information gained from these studies was integrated into the teacher training program.

In 1970–71, the Center staff was expanded to permit a greater emphasis on evaluation efforts. In that year, an evaluation program was begun which offered services to TEEM communities in the areas of research design, statistical analysis, and report preparation.

In addition, the Center is developing an evaluation model which will complement current standardized achievement tests with measures better suited to the population of Follow Through and the objectives of the Tucson Model. The new evaluation program is based on the concept of "criterion-referenced" performance. That is, a set of objectives is developed for performance in TEEM classrooms, taking into account TEEM activities and the types of materials used, and evaluation focuses on how well these objectives are met. One aim of the Center in relation to this approach is to develop daily recording procedures to provide the teacher with immediate feedback on classroom performance.

Level III: National Evaluation Efforts

The National Follow Through evaluation effort has been contracted by the U.S. Office of Education to the Stanford Research Institute. SRI has the task of assessing all Follow Through programs in the areas of cognitive development (school achievement), noncognitive development (attitudes and motivation), and community impact (parent participation).

To meet this need, SRI has developed the Joint Fellow Program, in which each sponsor has a staff member shared jointly with SRI. This staff member interprets his program's goals to SRI, and assists in task development to insure that his program is being adequately assessed in the overall data collection design. For example, TEEM evaluation staff members are conducting research on the development of a measure called Activity Preference Task. APT will permit assessment of the relative "press" different aspects of the classroom environment have for a child. It will also make it possible to assess the relative preference of children for school as compared to other parts of their daily environment. Such information should prove valuable in evaluating school attitudes of children in the different Follow Through models.

Results of the SRI project will be recorded in an extensive report due for completion in 1973. An interim report was made available in Spring 1971.

17

GOALS AND METHODS IN A PRESCHOOL PROGRAM FOR DISADVANTAGED CHILDREN

BARBARA BIBER

Today there are many different kinds of programs for "disadvantaged" preschool children—children who come from families so burdened with poverty that they have been unable to provide the basic early essentials for normal intellectual development.[1] While not all children from poverty-stricken families are so deprived, a great many of them are and their deprivation shows up in develop-

Children, January–February 1970. Reprinted by permission of the author.

---

[1] Sylvia Krown, Preschool programs for disadvantaged children. *Children*, November–December 1968.

mental deficits. Different ways of assessing these deficits account for differences in programs—in the goals they set, in the materials they use, and in their definitions of success.

In describing here some of the methods employed at the Early Childhood Center of the Bank Street College of Education in New York City and the rationale behind them, I must necessarily narrow my focus to concentrate on the direct work with children. I want to point out, however, that the center, which was developed under the leadership of Elizabeth Gilkeson, chairman of the college's children's programs, proceeds on the theory that to work with children alone is to invite failure and frustration. It therefore operates as a multi-purpose facility with a multidisciplinary professional staff working with auxiliary personnel to serve not only the children in the pre-school program but also their parents and other members of their families through the provision of health services, an afterschool program, and a program of community relations. In concentrating on the direct work with the children, I will inevitably be giving an in-complete, oversimplified picture.

Behind the center's work is the belief that programs for disad-vantaged children should be geared to the same developmental goals set for all children. However, experience has shown that the meth-ods for reaching these goals have to be adapted to the children's de-velopmental deficits. These deficits show up as two main types:

1.   *Deficiencies in verbal-conceptual functioning:*
       Paucity of names for everyday objects; restricted use of qualify-ing terms; incorrect pronunciation and grammatical usage; im-maturity of thought processes that go beyond concrete, imme-diate experience and depend on language for expression; poor discrimination; a paucity of information.

2.   *Deficiencies in how to connect with the world of things and people:*
       Difficulty in listening, attending, focusing, and sustaining in-terest or contact; a motoric, staccato, disordered release of en-ergy; difficulty in fitting into a situation that is ordered with respect to time and space; immature ways of dealing with im-

pulses and feelings such as anger, frustration, and denial; expectation that the adult will be distant, denying, punishing; vagueness of self-concept; and so forth.

From our viewpoint at the center, these deficits are regarded as the behavioral manifestations of fundamental faults in the developmental process, and we try to work at what we consider to be the roots of these problems. In doing so, our primary goals are: (1) to advance the child's ability to use language functionally and to be able to systematize experience through mastery of conceptual-cognitive processes; and (2) simultaneously to help him develop a solid sense of self and an internalized code of behavior, to build ego-strength in terms of becoming an effective, nonpredatory person, capable of acting autonomously—making choices, taking initiative, setting his own course for problem-solving.

These goals give us a dual mandate: To choose methods for fulfilling the first goal that support and never violate the second goal; and to choose methods for fulfilling the second goal that make the first goal potentially more realizable.

Helping a child with language and thinking requires an understanding of what is behind his inadequacy. At the Early Childhood Center we see a child's impoverished speech, restricted information, and primitive cognitive processes as derived from multiple causes: (1) the absence of models of spoken language that is correct in structure and elaborate in shadings of meaning; (2) an environment in which communication has been limited to the minimum essentials, resulting in a lack of experience in conveying meaning, observation, and feeling and in having one's meaning understood and received with interest and concern; (3) little experience in exploring the physical world in an atmosphere that encourages trying out what can be done with things; and (4) lack of "as if" experience —playing "make believe" or reproducing reality in one's own terms with dolls, blocks, or trains—the basic symbolic experience of childhood that seems to be a prerequisite for subsequent symbolizing with abstract forms.

THE PROGRAM

The center's program, therefore, is designed to initiate the children into many different kinds of experiences: Experiences that, on the sensory level, sensitize them to seeing, feeling, tasting, hearing, and discriminating elements of the environment; experiences that, on the motor level, widen their knowledge of the physical world through their own activity in it—strenuous activity such as climbing, stacking, riding, and steering, and also manipulative activity such as filling pails with pebbles or cutting with scissors; and experiences that, on a symbolic level, develop their representational functioning through painting, building with blocks, dressing up, playing at cooking supper, or pretending that it is moving day.

While providing opportunities for such experiences, the teacher seizes every opportunity for direct interchange with the children, even if only an exchange of facial expressions or gestures when there are no words to share. In doing so the teacher is trying to set up a path of communication, meaning, and feeling that will be translated into verbal form as the child gradually masters the use of language. The goal is to strengthen the capabilities that are the child's underpinnings for learning language, the most important means of human communication, and the symbol system without which higher order cognitive processes—thinking, reasoning, generalizing—cannot be attained.

For the disadvantaged child, the usual developmental sequence cannot be followed. The shift from predominantly perceptive-motor experience to the symbolic stage of verbalization cannot take its natural course. The sequence must be telescoped. At our center the educative process works simultaneously at what would ordinarily be successive stages of development. There is no waiting for so-called unfolding or undefined "readiness." But there is no skipping of the experiences that are needed as solid underpinning for more advanced development.

Thus our approach owes much to the theory of developmental psychologists such as Piaget, Bruner, and others—a theory which has also influenced other programs, for example, those of Sigel [2] and Weikart.[3] According to this orientation, the goal to be accomplished in the preschool years as the basis for competence in language and thinking can be briefly described as having five aspects:

1. To develop the capacity to deal with abstract symbols—words and numbers—by providing the necessary foundation through varied opportunities to know the physical world and human reality through direct, active experience and through communication in symbolic, albeit nonverbal, ways.

2. To develop thinking power by stimulating grouping processes and by encouraging the child to see similarities and differences in the perceived attributes of objects, in functions, in roles played by people, and in the feelings people have.

3. To stimulate ordering processes by encouraging the child to compare sizes, amounts, differences in degree, and the condition of opposites.

4. To establish the basic framework for orientation in space and time.

5. To bring to awareness the variety of transformations through which change takes place over time, through growth or decay or through direct making and doing in the object world.

By what methods are these goals for advancing language and thinking to be reached? Of first importance is the setup of the school as a learning environment—the kinds of materials presented, the clarity of functional areas, the implicit teaching of "things-in-position" so that the child will learn where to find what he needs, the accent on regularity in a timed world by repeated reference to the

---

[2] Irving E. Sigel, Child development and social science education: Part I through Part IV. Social Science Education Consortium, Purdue University, Lafayette, Ind. 1966. (Now at University of Colorado, Boulder.)

[3] David P. Weikart (ed.), Preschool intervention: a preliminary report of the Perry Preschool Project. Campus Publishers, Ann Arbor, Mich. 1967.

sequence of activities, including the child's coming and going, and the availability of enough adults for each child to have individual contacts with an adult in the center and to be known well by at least one member of the center's staff.

SOME TECHNIQUES

One of the center's highly regarded methods for achieving its developmental goals is to teach the use of language and to advance thinking processes in the context of the child's own activities and play. A few of the specific techniques developed by the teachers for doing this are illustrated here. The examples have been provided by Jane Catchen and Theodora Sklover of the center's staff.

Organization of the classroom so that sorting, according to some dimension, is a built-in part of the daily activities.

Separate shelves are provided for blocks of different shapes. Blocks of the same shape belong on the same shelf. Putting the blocks away involves repeated practice in sorting by sameness of shape. Each shelf is marked with a symbol in the form of the shape of the block. Similarly, other objects also have their own "homes" with like objects.

Jennifer has been playing in grownup clothing and is now putting things away. She moves methodically from place to place—putting the high-heeled shoes on a shelf with other shoes, the long skirt in a box with other clothing. The teacher comments that Jennifer is putting everything with other things just like it.

Jennifer's activities involve the following cognitive operations: sorting and classifying objects and orientating self and objects in space. The teacher translates Jennifer's experience to a more abstract level and introduces an idea of commonness that is not dependent on perceptual likeness.

Translation of the activities into verbal statements; accenting words with tone and gestures.

Teacher to the children who are climbing on the jungle gym: "You're climbing **up**, you're climbing **down**." Going up to the play area on the roof of the center's building: "We are walking **up**—let's look **up**; let's walk with our hands **up**; let's jump with our hands **down**."

At a later stage, going to the roof becomes more than an up-down learning experience. The teacher calls attention to what the children pass on their way—a radiator, another door, and so forth. She asks, "Is this the door to the roof, or is **this** the door to the roof?" The teacher is stimulating the children to analyze the passing perceptual stimuli and to weigh the relevance of what they see to their ultimate destination. Thus they are learning both to discriminate perceptually and to think in terms of a pathway to a goal.

The teacher establishes the custom of having the children call out the names of the objects on the roof as they see them in approaching the play area. One day she introduces a variation: "Let's go a different way this time," choosing alternative paths around the equipment. This stimulates the children to appreciate the sameness of objects seen from different perspectives.

Work on formal aspects of language usage as part of ongoing communication with the children, while keeping in mind the importance of not violating the child's efforts at communicating in nonverbal ways and of maintaining her role as an adult who cares about meeting the child's wishes.

Teacher to the child: "What do you want?" The child points to an object on the shelf. Teacher: "You want the red truck. Say: 'I want the red truck.' " The child refuses. After one repetition, the teacher says: "You can say it next time." She gives the child the truck.

Encouraging problem-solving by putting into question form the things children are confused about, stimulating them to ask questions themselves, and guiding them to sources of information.

While reading a story about firemen, the teacher recalls the children's confusion about the many different roles people carry. She asks: "Is a fireman a daddy?" The children answer, "No." The teacher is clearing the way for the children to learn from each other; she knows that one child's father is indeed a fireman and this child will contribute the answer that will enlighten the others.

Further reading of the same story leads to other questions: What do firemen do? How does water get into the truck? Where do they get it? The teacher encourages the children to guess and tells them they can check their answers with the firemen. Later she takes them to the firehouse, where they ask their questions.

The teacher asks the children if they know any place on the street where they can get wet. They describe the fire hydrants, which in some streets of New York are opened on hot days for children's water play. The realization that the firemen come to the same place they do to get water thrills them. The teacher supplies the word "hydrant," and takes the children out walking to spot the hydrants in their neighborhood.

This experience stimulates dramatic play—building fire engines with large blocks. For these children, dramatic play often needs priming and, at first, they prefer to use themselves rather than miniature figures as the actors.

Introduction of written symbols in a way that is functional to the children's activities.

In each of the rooms the paintings done by the children are displayed with a large clear name label attached to each. In the room for 4-year-olds each child is asked to turn over the card with his name as he comes into the room.

A little girl asks to visit in another room. The teacher writes a note in her presence, tells her she can go "tomorrow," giving her the name of the day, and posts the note on the blackboard. When the child forgets the next day, the teacher reminds her, repeats the name of the day, and arranges for the visit.

PRESTRUCTURED EXPERIENCES

Another method for advancing verbal-conceptual skill is the more familiar use of planned lessons and readymade materials for teaching specific aspects of such skill. Materials for providing prestructured experiences—such as form boards, Lotto games, matrix games, the electric typewriter—are abundantly available today, since innovation has been prolific in this area. Planned lessons are part of every trained teacher's repertoire and are today more highly developed and systematized than they once were. Nimnicht's "learning episodes" are, perhaps, the most elaborate.[4]

Such readymade materials and prepared lessons—except those that are strictly programed or automated—are very much in use in

---

[4] G. Nimnicht, Oralie McAfee, J. Meier, Inservice education for Head Start teachers and aides: training unit IX. The Far West Laboratory for Educational Research and Development, Berkeley, Calif. 1969. (Mimeographed.)

the center. They are valuable in separating the mental maneuvers involved in dealing with concepts of similarity and difference between pure shapes and forms from the analogous thinking processes that take place in the context of complex life situations. They serve the functions of rehearsal and consolidation. By requiring the child to deal with abstract symbols, they prepare him for the later task of processing the symbols of a printed page. They also provide the child with the gratification of succeeding at a clearcut task.

The teachers at the center preplan sessions aimed at promoting the learning of specific concepts—color, size, shape, and the like. In such sessions any given concept appears over and over again in a wide variety of contexts. For example, the color orange is first brought to the children's attention through showing them an orange (the fruit) itself. Then the children play a game to spot the color elsewhere in the room—on some of the children's clothing or on a pumpkin the teacher has brought in. Easels are set up and the children are given only yellow and red paint; they delight in finding that orange comes through when one color is put over the other. The children are given orange transparencies to look through.

In addition to supplying varied contexts involving a common phenomenon, the teacher tries to lift the level of fun and pleasure and to introduce dramatic, unexpected turns. Thus, she helps the children focus their attention on the activity in which she is engaging them.

The center's teachers alternate between teaching directly, with the use of planned learning episodes or readymade materials, and indirectly eliciting learning through bringing the relationships that are implicit in their activities to the children's awareness. Often they use both methods to help the children go through the same conceptual process—for example, dealing with the important question of how things can be the same in one way and different in others.

In one group the children were bothered by differences in two books about the story of Mary and her little lamb. The teacher cued into their annoyance and used it to further their growth. She called attention to the different houses each of them built with blocks. She showed them a grapefruit and a lemon (both yellow fruits but one much bigger than the other) and cut them open so that the children could see the difference in the seeds. Then she brought out the materials that require the child to work with the concept of similarity and difference on an abstract level, asking them to find the triangles, regardless of differences in size, among an assortment of other shapes.

BUILDING MOTIVATION

Thus far I have alluded only to the question of motivation in the methods we use to advance the children's verbal-conceptual skill. At the center we do not use rewards like food or stereotype forms of praise through words or gestures, nor do we use punishment. Instead, we build motivation through other means: One is by relying on the intrinsic pleasure and satisfaction of learning and becoming skillful and knowledgeable; another is by grounding learning in the real experience of living; another is by building a special kind of relationship between the children and all those who stand in the teaching role.

The question of motivation carries us back to the second area of developmental deficits observed in the disadvantaged child at school; his poor ways of connecting with things and people. Such deficits show up in the extremes of withdrawal and inhibition exhibited by some children and in the tempestuous, unfocused behavior of others; in a transient relation to objects; in a lack of sustained interest or attention; in an absence of modes of coping with impulses of destruction or feelings of anger and fear; in an inability to fit into an ordered environment; in perception of adults as restricting, denying, or punishing. In short, the disadvantaged child, being uncertain about himself and who he is, feels that he is at the mercy of unpredictable adults whom he cannot trust to be on his side.

Behind this shaky position in life are several possible causes. For some children, it can be attributed to the lack of an active, meaningful connection with people in their earliest years, to their having missed the experience of being listened to, played with, noticed, and understood as individuals. For other children, it goes back to even more debilitating conditions: Inconstant and traumatic relationships; uncertain care and protection; threats and punishment that are often only randomly related to their behavior; punitive suppression of their assertive or exploratory drives; exposure to frightening, often violent, behavior on the part of adults.

At the center we proceed on the premise that these deficits— the fears, the inhibitions, the uncontrolled impulses, the distrust of people—can be ameliorated gradually through the development of a particular kind of relationship with a teacher, a relationship that offers wholehearted support while it controls and channels behavior. Here the teacher's choice of method is tied not only to the goal of establishing the emotional equilibrium needed as the basis for learning, but also to the goal of developing an autonomous, self-initiating human being.

The question of how to achieve these goals requires as much analysis and experimentation as the search for methods of developing verbal-conceptual skill. I would like to stress four points:

1. As her fundamental task, the teacher makes every effort to understand the child's wishes and needs; she "takes responsibility to recognize the bases of his strivings and to help him harness them to a learning task which he is able to recognize as consistent with his desires and goals." [5]

Remembering the child's deficit in important relationships with people and his sense of distrust toward those who have power over him, the teacher invests energy and imagination in finding ways of making contact with him and building up an image for him of an adult as a giving, supporting, caring person. She not only expresses pleasure in the child's accomplishments, but shows as much affection as the child can accept, often doing so through physical contact— touching, soothing, taking the child on her lap. She listens hard for

---

[5] Elizabeth Gilkeson, Notes on a viewpoint about learning with special reference to Follow Through. Presented at Follow Through meetings, Kansas City, Mo., February 21–28, 1968.

the meaning the child is trying to convey with his poor speech and protects his early efforts at communication by giving his message back to him in correct form while sparing him the negative impact of correcting his usage.

2. The teacher activates the theme of giving to the children; she does not rely on them to be able to take on their own initiative the opportunities laid before them. She introduces them to the use of equipment, demonstrates as much as tells, joins them in exploring the toys and other things around them, and starts them off in using the housekeeping corner as a way of sifting and rehearsing their experiences. The teacher fulfills the basic giving function of her role as a teacher by leading the child to greater use of his powers to do, to make, to speak, to think. She does this in much the same way that she works for verbal-conceptual development while making the school environment a known, understood, manageable world for children.

3. The teacher manages the task of socialization—helping the child to control unacceptable behavior—by redirecting his drive to alternative channels. When she stops children from fighting, she says, "You could fix it with words," thereby offering them an alternative in the idiom of childhood. When a child is disrupting other children's play by throwing a ball wildly in their midst, she leads him to a place where it is all right to throw a ball. When she stops a child from dashing out of the room, she asks him where he is going and why he needs to go there. Her intention is not to elicit answers —she knows his running comes from an inner drive or turmoil and has no direction—but to initiate an exchange of communication that may help him begin to integrate purpose into his actions to replace his aimless release of energy.

Helping a disadvantaged child learn to get along with others requires constant repetition of such techniques until the child can internalize control and establish purpose for himself. It is important that during the process the child is experiencing a new kind of control: the authority of a closely involved, caring adult, the same person who also respects his wishes and offers him opportunities for free choice. Thus a foundation is being laid for a relationship through which trust might replace distrust.

4. The teacher engages the children in analysis of the component parts of situations in which she must exercise control of their impulses. Thus she helps the children perceive specifically what is happening. From the viewpoint of cognitive development, this is another experience in differentiation; from the viewpoint of socialization, it is a means toward maintaining rational rather than arbitrary control.

Sometimes this happens when the teacher is trying to explain the children to each other. For example, three children are impatiently waiting for a turn on the much-prized tricycles. The teacher articulates the children's feeling for them: "It is hard for John to wait; it is hard for Susie to wait." Thus the cognitive task of finding the common elements among differences is being exercised in the sphere of human feeling.

In another instance, the teacher tells an impulsive child who is set to rush into the elevator ahead of the others that he can be first to go in when he has learned how to manage the buttons so that he can push the one that will make the elevator go to the right floor. The teacher is channeling the child's drive to the task of discriminating between the symbols on the buttons, thus giving him an opportunity to focus on a goal and master his own actions within the limits of permissible behavior.

It is especially important for disadvantaged children to become perceptive in the sphere of feelings and human relations and to differentiate between people in terms of what to expect from whom. The knowledge they gain in the human-social sphere is at least as crucial for remedying the deficits of their early years as is the mastery they acquire in processing information about the physical world.

The following incident illustrates how learning can take place within a relationship of mutuality between teacher and child. A teacher found a little boy cuddled in a cubbyhole with head on hand. "I s'eeping," he announced. She acknowledged the game and then said, "Say *sl*eeping." No reply. She shaped her lips; she made the sound "*sl.*" No reply. She said, "You can say it another time." Several hours later when the same child was boarding the bus to go home in the afternoon, he turned to her grinning and said, "*sl*eeping." He had learned from his teacher while allowing himself the strength of assertion by refusal; and he reciprocated by giving her what she wanted from him.

18

ENGLISH AND AMERICAN PRIMARY SCHOOLS

VINCENT R. ROGERS

Ideas that American educators have been talking about for a long, long time are being put to practice in a large percentage of English primary schools. Education for life, basing instructional activities on the interests and problems of children, integration of subject matter, emphasis on *learning* rather than *teaching* and on *process* rather than *product*, development of independence and responsibility in children, concern for the creative aspects of learning—all of these are standard phrases in the lexicon of American

Phi Delta Kappan, October 1969. Reprinted by permission of Phi Delta Kappa and author.

education. But in England they are more than phrases. They are being brought to life daily in the primary classrooms which I visited during my stay in England as a Fulbright scholar in 1966.

When I made known my desire to get inside some schools, my English friends and advisers guided me initially to Oxfordshire, where I visited the Bampton, Brize-Norton, and Tower Hill primary schools. I have never been quite the same since. Seventy-two schools later I still found myself wondering if what I saw was real, if such schools and teachers do exist. Four cartons of notes taken on 3 x 5 cards give material support to my impression that these schools do indeed exist, and that they are becoming increasingly influential not only in England but in other countries as well.

I must note here that only about 25 percent of England's primary schools fit the model described in the following paragraphs. Perhaps 40 percent can be described as quite traditional, while another third or so are in various stages of transition. Nevertheless, 25 percent is a significant number of schools when one looks at the size of the total educational enterprise in England, and even more significant is the obvious movement toward this new kind of education among schools which cannot as yet be included among the exciting and innovative 25 percent.

What is there that is so unusual about these schools? To begin with, it seems as if the new English primary school is committed to the notion that children should live more fully and more richly *now*, rather than at some ill-defined time in the distant future. Education, then, is not preparation for life; education *is* life, with all of its excitement, challenge and possibilities. This is happening here and now in perhaps 20 to 30 percent of the primary schools in England.

English teachers and headmasters conceive of the curriculum as a series of starting or jumping-off places. An idea, a question, an observation—child's *or* teacher's—acts as a stone thrown into the middle of a quiet pond. The ripples begin, one idea leads to another, and a study is under way. In contrast, American educators seem far more concerned from a curricular point of view with identifying and then covering a series of ideas, concepts, generalizations, or skills that (theoretically) form the backbone of the curriculum in any area. We shall discuss this in greater detail later. However, it seems worth mentioning that there appears to be very little subject matter that is perceived of as "basic" and "essential" in the eyes of the English teacher or headmaster. The curriculum emerges through the mutual interests and explorations of children and their teachers, working together occasionally in large groups, sometimes in small groups and often as individuals.

Another characteristic of the emerging British primary school, and one that is closely related to the preceding point, has to do with the eagerness of teachers to cut across disciplinary lines in their handling of any study that may evolve in their classrooms. Art, music, history, poetry—all are brought to bear on a given problem or topic, and it is often difficult to tell whether children are studying history or geography, art or science. This, of course, tends to give a wholeness to learning that must be lacking in more compartmentalized curricula, and it helps support and build the image of the school as a place where lifelike questions are investigated as opposed to questions that are narrowly academic.

A fourth observation is that the English teacher is concerned with *learning* as opposed to teaching. Rarely will one find such a teacher standing in front of the room teaching a "class" lesson. Rather, the teacher is largely a stagesetter, a stimulator, who encourages and guides but who does *not* direct. It is often difficult to find the teacher when one first walks into a typical classroom, since she is likely to be working with a child here and a child there, moving around the room and among the children.

Having said all of this, a fifth conclusion is inescapable: The English teacher accepts the significance of *process* over *product* in the education of the child. There seems little doubt that English teachers are greatly concerned with *how* a child learns, the kinds of questions he asks and the ways in which he goes about resolving them. Over the long haul, English teachers believe these learning "strategies" will prove to be infinitely more valuable than the subject matter.

Similarly, English teachers seem greatly concerned about the development of independence and responsibility in children—often to a far greater extent than American teachers. In the best of English primary schools, a degree of individual freedom, flexibility and responsibility exists in a way that is virtually unknown in most American elementary schools. Teachers do not hang over their children, supervise them in every conceivable activity, watch them on the playground, in the halls, in the buses and in the washrooms. All of this is done, of course, in a calculated way, recognizing that such qualities as independence and reliability need to be "practiced" as well as spoken about.

Finally, one might say that the teachers in the kinds of schools I visited seem to care deeply, perhaps passionately, about *children*. Children are to be taken seriously, not laughed at or ridiculed in the staff room. Children are to be watched; children are to be listened to; children are to learn from; children are the essential ingredient in the teaching-learning process; children make one's job exciting, challenging and truly professional. This point cannot possibly be exaggerated. It is, in fact, the day-to-day practical implementation of the intellectual rationale for a very real revolution in education.

As one reads about these exciting developments in English schools, one cannot help but wonder why such ideas have never really caught on here on the scale they have in England. There is, of course, much talk about creativity, the needs of children and the importance of the student taking responsibility for his own learning. Indeed, bits and pieces of the educational processes described in the preceding pages do exist all over America. It is, rather, the complete expression of, and commitment to, a set of educational ideals that seems to be missing in this country.

Let us examine some possible reasons for American reluctance to move in similar directions. One must say at the beginning of such an analysis that a number of American teachers, writers and teachers-turned-writers are passionately involved in a movement to bring a looser, more relevant, more child-centered and experience-based kind of education to American children. One thinks immediately of Jonathan Kozol, Herbert Kohl, James Herndon, and John Holt as examples of the turned-on, deeply concerned teacher who, on the basis of his experiences in classrooms, has something to say about American education. In addition, journalists like Joseph Featherstone and Charles Silberman are also joining the crusade, and even as influential a group as the Educational Development Center in Cambridge, Mass. (the base for Jerome Bruner's curricular operations) has recently hired an Englishman or two to help plan the center's various projects.

Because of the pressures brought to bear by this new breed of educational critic, changes are being made in some public schools, and a few private schools have been founded here and there that are more completely faithful to the educational point of view described in this article. Nevertheless, and in all fairness, it must be said that these disparate efforts are hardly an organized, well-directed and advancing movement.

Perhaps one reason for American failure to move more rapidly in this direction can be traced to the curricular and methodological impact of the launching of the Russian Sputnik in 1957. The event was perceived as an educational humiliation, and the curricular developments that followed it during the next decade all gave a push to a kind of education that was vastly different from the movement that was already under way in England.

It is no news to American or English educators that the search for "structure," for "basic concepts and generalizations" in mathematics, science, social studies, literature and other fields, has dominated curricular activity in the U.S. during the years following Sputnik. This has led, quite logically, to an emphasis upon separate subjects rather than upon the integration or wholeness of the curriculum; it has led to further support for a traditional educational disease which we will call "the covering syndrome," i.e., one *must* deal with certain "basic" ideas, topics, or problems, or else one is clearly derelict in one's duty; therefore, one must avoid those diversions, those side-tracking situations that often lead to relevant and exciting learning, even though they *do* interfere with "coverage."

In an attempt to be as faithful as possible to what we perceive of as the "work-ways" or methods of the various disciplines, American educators have spent a great deal of time and energy in organizing the new curricula so that children will not merely memorize and repeat concepts and generalizations as they memorized and repeated the much despised "facts" of the old. Therefore we talk a great deal about inquiry and discovery approaches to learning. However, a careful examination of the materials and methods that comprise many of the new curriculum projects and packages reveals (with some exceptions) that the kinds of questions raised, the problems studied, the discoveries or generalizations arrived at are rarely the children's. We try valiantly; we smile, entreat and cajole. Some of the kids are caught up in it some of the time—perhaps an unusually challenging topic catches their fancy or perhaps an unusually dynamic teacher draws them out through the force of his personality. More often than not, however, we end up with something Vincent Glennon has described as "sneaky telling." We know where we're going; we know what the questions should be, what the "big ideas" are, and the conclusions one should come away with, if the teacher's manual is followed.

Perhaps, in the final analysis, this is the best way to teach. Perhaps we cannot afford the luxury of exploring children's questions in whichever direction they may take us. Certainly there is little evidence which demonstrates empirically that the less-structured, more child-centered English teacher is producing a "better product" than is the tighter, more discipline-centered American teacher. At the moment, the best evidence I can offer is simply watching children at work and at play over extended periods of time in schools. If their reactions, their activity, their art, music and poetry, their attitudes toward teachers and toward school are valid criteria, then we have a great deal to learn from the English.

Perhaps another reason for our reluctance to move in the same direction as the English is our comparative affluence, which enables us to develop and pay for mechanical panaceas, with whatever educational hardware happens to catch our fancy. In both countries "to individualize" is thought of as a good thing. Increasing numbers of conferences and workshops are devoted to this theme in America, yet American teachers seem not to have learned

the lesson that is grasped so well by many English primary teachers:
One individualizes, as Philip Jackson[1] put it, by

> . . . injecting humor into a lesson when a student seems to need it,
> and quickly becoming serious when he is ready to settle down to
> work; it means thinking of examples that are uniquely relevant to
> the student's previous experience and offering them at just the right
> time; it means feeling concerned over whether or not a student is
> progressing, and communicating that concern in a way that will be
> helpful; it means offering appropriate praise . . . because the stu-
> dent's performance is deserving of human admiration; it means in
> short, responding *as* an individual *to* an individual.

This conception is much, much more than allowing for differences in speed when moving through some particular "program";
it is more than telling us automatically, if politely, that "you are
wrong, please turn to page 15 for another explanation."

In other words, one individualizes by watching and listening to
children. Mechanical aids are useful, but there is no substitute for
the conception of individualization expressed so ably by Jackson
in the preceding paragraph. Many American teachers have been
seduced by the promise of technology; their less affluent English
counterparts know that individualization will come to their children
only if they make a concerted effort to bring it about under classroom conditions that are not likely to change radically soon. So
they collect, construct, beg, borrow and, I suspect, steal materials of
all kinds to provide the kind of learning environment they know
is good—and they often do so for classes of 40 children or more.
Most English teachers are willing to agree with Mort Sahl that "the
future lies ahead." They are not banking on an educational prom-
ised land that may lie just around the corner. They are addressing
themselves to solving the individualization problem in terms of their
own intelligence and energy—now.

A third invidious comparison one is forced to make with

---

[1] P. W. Jackson, *The Teacher and the Machine: Observations on the Impact of Educational Technology.* (Mimeographed, University of Chicago, 1966.)

American elementary schools when he visits an English primary school is in the area of aesthetics. Aesthetics—art, music, movement —is in a dismal state in American schools as compared with their English counterparts. Even for our very young children, many schools have music and art teachers who conduct 20-minute, weekly lessons that become *the* art or music program. Aesthetic activities generally take a back seat to the more academic components of the curriculum.

Perhaps this is a problem inherent in American culture rather than a school problem. These things are considered effete; they are not valued in the same way that reading and mathematics are. It would be rare, indeed, to see an American teacher seriously encourage children to use their bodies as a mode of expression. It would be even more rare to find the teacher herself joining the children and participating in the creation of a dance pattern. (Perhaps a new generation of teachers, reared on the less inhibited use of their bodies that has developed with the universal acceptance of "rock," will see possibilities in movement that their predecessors did not.)

In my judgment, aesthetics plays an infinitely more important role in the education of English children than in that of American children, and the hesitancy of American teachers to utilize these means of reaching children is a major difference between primary education in England and in the U.S.

Another curious factor that gets in the way of American movement toward a more free and less-structured school may lie in our dichotomous treatment of kindergarten and primary children. In England, children are treated as individuals from the moment they enter school at the age of five until they leave the primary school. Teachers of "reception classes" (five-year-olds) move children into reading, for example, if the child seems ready to read. Similarly, a *six*-year-old child in an English primary school is not pushed, hounded and bullied, ready or not, into reading when he reaches that magical age. In other words, we have created a very unreal and unwise division between what learning ought to be for five-year-olds and what it ought to be for sixes. One might call this the kindergarten-primary grade dilemma. We usually find a far greater degree of freedom, child-centeredness, looseness, or lack of structure in our kindergartens than we find at any other level in the elementary school. Many American children begin their education enjoying learning, being happy in school, and contented with themselves. For many of these children, however, first grade becomes a cruel awakening. No more time now for learning as fun; now we must "work"; now we must put away dress-up clothes, blocks and spur-of-the-moment curricular explorations.

In a good English primary school, this dichotomy does not exist. A child comes to school initially to learn, and to learn at his own pace. This point of view is carried continuously through the primary years.

Finally, we might mention one other factor that may play a role in discouraging the adoption on a large scale of the sort of primary school we have been describing in these pages. I refer to the relative freedom that English teachers and headmasters have to develop the kinds of educational programs that they, as professionals, deem right—with minimum concern for outside pressure groups. Conversely, American teachers and principals are subject to tremendous pressures from the community, and no state-supported school can casually ignore them. This means that some changes will be easier to bring about than others; that what the lay public conceives of as "good" education may be adopted in the schools more readily than other changes. At this point, the American public seems to see "good" education as a hard-driving, highly competitive academic race, and educational innovations fitting that image stand a better chance of acceptance than do other innovations.

In England, which has traditionally had an exceedingly competitive education system, the movement toward drastic change in the education of young children originated and was carried out largely by professionals and often *against* the wishes of parents. This is not to say that English teachers and headmasters can do as they please. It does mean, however, that they are more independent of, and more protected from, outside pressures of all kinds than American educators. Vulnerability to public pressures probably causes American school people to be reluctant to adopt a child-centered approach to teaching.

Having examined and compared English and American primary school programs, I turn now to criticism. This will be difficult, since I have not attempted to hide my considerable admiration for what I see happening in the modern English primary school. Nevertheless, what seems good can no doubt become better, and perhaps some of the following questions may serve to further that purpose.

The first point is really not a criticism of classroom practices at all. Rather, it is a plea for some form of systematic evaluation of the achievements of the schools described in these pages. Those of us fortunate enough to have visited good English primary schools recognize almost intuitively that what we are seeing is mostly right, mostly effective, mostly sound. On the other hand, many educators have a way of asking questions that cannot be adequately answered by referring to one's personal observations. How, in fact, do children in such schools perform on various objective measures when compared to children who have had quite a different sort of school experience? Obviously, academic achievement is not the basic goal of such schools, but since it is not, what effects do these schools have on children's attitudes toward school teachers and peers? How does this experience affect their approach to learning, the problem solving strategies they adopt, their persistence, their curiosity?

A more direct criticism is exemplified, perhaps, by a description of an afternoon spent in what was, in many ways, a fascinating primary school in rural Leicestershire. During the entire afternoon the children were free to carry out projects that were of interest to them. There was a great deal of arts and crafts activity—carpentry, weaving, block printing, etc. The children were obviously well-behaved, busy, and interested in their work. Yet I couldn't help but feel that this happy, involved group of children were somehow existing in the middle of what we all know to be a terribly complex, rapidly changing world—divorced from its reality, protected from its problems and uninvolved in its conflicts and dilemmas.

Somehow, the "real" world that children explore in such schools is often a rather limited version of reality. It is a real world of fields, streams, trees, rocks, stones, flowers, birds, and insects if it is a country school. If it is a city school, it is a real world of traffic patterns, nearby shops, local museums and libraries, parks and gardens. The "real world" is often conceived of as that world which is nearby, and more precisely, that world which can be seen, felt, smelled, touched, or listened to.

One might suggest, then, that there are, after all, limits to how far one can go with personal, concrete experience as *the* essential teaching technique. Children can study only a small part of the world by direct observation and experience, and one must question the hours that are spent in making, building and physically "doing" that could, conceivably, be used in other ways as well. One wonders, for example, if in studying the wool industry the process of making wool does not get treated all out of proportion to some of the related economic, social and political problems that might be implied in such a study—granting, of course, that much of this "activity" would be intellectual rather than physical, vicarious more than direct.

If one largely limits the objects of one's study to those found only in the local environment, it is difficult to see how the school can play a significant role in helping children understand the broader world in which they live. Conflict exists about Rhodesia and about the immigrants who have recently settled in sections of English cities such as Wolverhampton and Bradford. Those problems are important to all English people. The fact that they do not lend themselves to direct or "concrete" experience does not render them any the less important.

The real world of social conflict exists, and no school, no teacher, no syllabus will ever completely isolate children from it. Yet the schools' responsibility would seem to include some attempts at increasing children's awareness of the inadequacies and inequalities that exist in both their local and their wider environments. Failing this, children will, of course, muddle through, picking up ideas and attitudes wherever they find them and becoming more and more aware (perhaps through harsh personal experience) of the conflict that exists between the school world and the world of social reality.

Similarly, one might question the degree of curricular egalitarianism that exists in the emerging British primary school. Obviously, only the simplest of societies can hope to teach its children "all they need to know." Therefore, it has become increasingly important to ask, what knowledge is of the most worth to *our* society at this particular moment in time? Which ideas will help the nonspecialist citizen to understand the world in which he lives? Which ideas are fundamental enough to have transfer value? Which ideas will help one to better understand a unique phenomenon that has not been formally studied before?

My English colleagues will immediately argue that only the *child* can know what knowledge, what information, what understanding, is important and necessary to him. Identifying significant ideas seems to smack of pre-digested academic luncheons that have little relevance to children's interests or needs. I would also agree. I would indeed argue further that this appears to be the major weakness in many of the American curriculum projects which were developed during the Brunerian revolution of the sixties.

However, this does not negate the argument that there *are* some things worth knowing, that some ideas help to order and explain our lives and the lives of others while other ideas do not. It seems to me that the great weakness one observes in both English and American schools is the lack of knowledge about and understanding of such ideas among *teachers.*

It would be foolish indeed to suggest that a discipline like anthropology has developed no ideas that are really worth teaching to children, no concepts that help order, classify, and explain the social world in which we find ourselves. The real value, the ultimate utility of such ideas, however, lies *not* in the creation of pre-packaged "teacher-proof" curricula; rather, it is the classroom teacher who must grasp them and utilize them at the appropriate moment. In other words, "structure" belongs in the minds of teachers.

One might mention other arguments, other "weaknesses"; these, however, seem to me to be among the most fruitful to discuss and perhaps are among the questions most likely to be raised by American educators.

19

REACHING THE YOUNG
CHILD THROUGH PARENT
EDUCATION

IRA J. GORDON

What does it take to be a good mother? The answer depends on what the mother wants her child to be like when he grows up.

All parents dream for their children. Some imagine their son as President of the United States and their daughter as First Lady. Others wish their children to be happy, regardless of outward success. Most parents desire their children to be able to achieve more than they themselves were able to accomplish. Some parents simply

Childhood Education, February 1970. Reprinted by permission of the author and the Association for Childhood Education International, 3615 Wisconsin Avenue, N.W., Washington, D.C. Copyright © 1970 by the Association.

hope their children will survive to reach adulthood in order to make their way in the world. But in today's world the wish does not necessarily lead to the act.

The gap between desire and ability to implement it in helping the child may be very large indeed. A crowded home, a low income, a lack of formal education may all inhibit the ability of the parent and may actually lower his level of aspiration for his child. Some difficulties lie within the parents themselves. Many of these difficulties have been imposed originally from without but now are carried on and perpetuated.

Some parents lack any notion that they are or should be teachers of their very young children. Some lack the ability to teach a child. They do not understand what behaviors on their part help a child to learn and what things they do prevent or inhibit learning. They may lack knowledge of what kinds of conditions and experiences seem to open the world for the development of the child and what other conditions close it down. Their own verbal facility may be so limited that they do not communicate with the young child. They may have a belief that after all each person is a victim of chance, fate and circumstance and that there is little an individual can do to affect what might happen to the child.

Parents who seem endowed with many material possessions may also fail to provide specific opportunities that might enable their young child to develop to match their aspiration. The warm adult-child interaction a young child needs may be absent in the busy professional home as well as in a center city tenement. A young child needs direct, specific verbal instruction, which also may be absent regardless of social setting. A young child needs the love and affection of mature adults. The parents' own needs and concerns may prevent them from furnishing what one would think is so natural.

If it is true that the beginnings of intellectual as well as emotional development take place in the first few years of life and if language learning depends so much upon the family's intellectual and emotional climate, how can we help supply these cognitive and affective characteristics in homes in which they are deficient?

One attempt to answer this question is the Parent Education Program of the Institute for Development of Human Resources of the University of Florida.[1]

Our basic assumptions were:

> the more limited the mother's background, the more difficult it is for her to provide intellectual stimulation for the child
>
> children learn from their surroundings; a home that lacks intellectual materials not only fails to encourage intellectual behavior but teaches that such materials are not important
>
> the child's structure of language is originally set by the linguistic pattern of the home
>
> language is learned early and influences the development of thought
>
> the lower-class mother often does not see herself as a teacher of her child and lacks effective motivational and instructional techniques.

We developed the Parent Education Program accordingly to try to provide the mother not only with particular activities to teach her very young child, beginning at three months of age, but also to provide these activities in such a way that (1) her self-esteem would grow; (2) her belief that she might be a victim of chance and fate would change to a belief that she could affect what happened to her child; (3) she would value the kinds of materials that might enable her child to reach the aspirations she was setting for him; and (4) she would be exposed to language and language materials that might enable her to provide the child with an increased verbal facility.

We feel that the best teacher of the parent is someone with a background similar to hers, who has been specifically trained in interview techniques and with a set of materials (based largely upon

---

[1] This program has been partially supported since September 1966 by the Fund for the Advancement of Education; the Children's Bureau; the National Institute for Mental Health; and, in its Follow-Through Program, the U.S. Office of Education.

Piaget and Basil Bernstein) designed to bring mother and child together in interaction, through play, in ways that would be mutually satisfying and that would enhance the intellectual and personality development of the child.

We believe that the best place to teach the infant is at home; therefore the Parent Education Program for mothers of three-month- to two-year-old children is a home visit program. The parent educator, visiting mothers in their homes once a week, teaches them concrete, specific activities to do with their children as well as why these are important. She also teaches simple toy-making skills so that the mothers themselves can make hand puppets, mobiles, stuffed toys and feel and know that they are contributing. Each task is taught essentially through the demonstration approach, in which the mothers observe the parent educators and then model their behavior on what they see. Tasks include the provision of verbs, adjectives and total sentences (we found early that the mothers' main approaches were nonverbal). Parent educators stress the importance of language and through the task material provide examples of words that could be used.

The program for two- to three-year-olds combines the once-a-week home visit with what we call a "backyard center" setting. Each child spends four hours a week in the home of one of the project mothers, along with four other children. He receives direct individual tutoring for about ten to fifteen minutes in each two-hour session from the parent educator who is his mother's teacher. The rest of the time he spends in play activities with toys that have been selected because they offer cognitive opportunities, he is read to or handles books, and he learns some group games. The mother who lives in the home is employed to assist the parent educator; a graduate assistant serves as a data collector and third adult. Each center is directed by the paraprofessional parent educator. These centers, in which 130 children are involved (November 1969), opened in December 1968.

The third element of the program is the Follow-Through model being implemented in six communities in 1968–69 and eleven in 1969–70. Here the weekly home visit is still the core of the program. The paraprofessional parent educator is again a key person who serves part of the day in the classroom and part of the day as a vistor in the home, linking the two, teaching the mother specific tasks which complement what the child is learning in school. These tasks, prepared locally, follow the same basic rationale used in the development of the infant and toddler tasks, stressing warm mother-child interaction, language development and cognitive challenge.

What have we learned to date? The data on children one year of age reveal they outperform control-youngsters on both the Griffith Mental Development Scale and the specially prepared series materials. The two-year-olds also outperform their controls. The data on their mothers indicate movement on their sense of power. Observations in the backyard or home learning center give indications of language and cognitive gains as well as of enlarged self-confidence. It is too soon to tell about Follow Through in terms of post-data, but unquestionably mothers value this type of program, respond to home visits, increase their participation and involvement in school, and use what they are learning to teach their children.

A brief report by a Florida parent educator expresses the flavor of the impact of the program:

> . . . this mother was so interested that after we started she looked forward every week for my coming in. I do feel very earnestly that this mother is working with her baby. From time to time we would go to the theories about child development and these exercises. This mother would always ask questions about the theories. She let me know she was interested in what she should do about the theories for her baby. When we did the testing on her baby, she was delighted to know that the baby would do as much for the tester as she would do for herself and me. I enjoyed very much working with Mrs. Adams, and I think she enjoyed, too, the improvement of the baby. Mrs. Adams is now working, but she is still interested in how and in what ways she can get me to cooperate with her, so that she may be home on her days off for me to continue work with her baby. So I have arranged to go on her off days even though it might interfere with my schedule. I do hold back this time for them because she is very interesting and I enjoy it very much.

If being a good mother means providing the type of cognitive and affective climate described above, the program demonstrates not only that mothers desire this label but are willing to and can learn to achieve it.